C000225238

Work–Family Balance, Gender and Policy

Work–Family Balance, Gender and Policy

Jane Lewis

Professor of Social Policy, London School of Economics, UK

Edward Elgar

Cheltenham, UK • Northampton, MA, USA

© Jane Lewis 2009

All rights reserved. No part of this publication may be reproduced, stored
in a retrieval system or transmitted in any form or by any means, electronic,
mechanical or photocopying, recording, or otherwise without the prior
permission of the publisher.

Published by
Edward Elgar Publishing Limited
The Lypiatts
15 Lansdown Road
Cheltenham
Glos GL50 2JA
UK

Edward Elgar Publishing, Inc.
William Pratt House
9 Dewey Court
Northampton
Massachusetts 01060
USA

Paperback edition 2010

A catalogue record for this book
is available from the British Library

Library of Congress Control Number: 2008943837

ISBN 978 1 84844 211 5 (cased)
ISBN 978 1 84980 170 6 (paperback)

Printed and bound in Great Britain by
Marston Book Services Limited, Didcot

Contents

List of tables and box   vii
Acknowledgements   viii

1 Introduction   1
     Family change   3
     Welfare state change   6
     Illustrating policy change: the EU level   10
     Gender equality   15
     The book   20

PART I

2 The policymaking context: behaviour and attitudes   25
     with Mary Campbell
     Paid work   26
     Childbearing   43
     The household level   48
     Attitudes and preferences   59
     The implications for policy   67

3 Work–family balance policies: comparisons and issues   71
     Policy logics   72
     Problems of care work for policy   77
     Work and family balance policies   82
     Conclusion   115

4 Patterns of development in work–family balance policies for
   parents in France, Germany, the Netherlands and the UK
   during the 2000s   119
     Co-authored with Trudie Knijn, Claude Martin and Ilona Ostner
     Context   120
     Policy change in France, the UK, Germany and
        the Netherlands   123
     Continuity and change in policy goals and instruments   132

Policy development and gender in relation to attitudes and
   behaviour   135

PART II

5 Policy development in the UK, 1997–2007   141
   Context   142
   Labour's approach to work and family balance policies   149
   Childcare provision   153
   Childcare leaves   167
   Flexible working   174
   Conclusion   187

6 Concluding reflections on gender equality and work–family
   balance policies   191

Bibliography   204
Index   241

Tables and box

TABLES

2.1 Employment rates for men and women and gender
employment gap, 1994, 2000 and 2006   30
2.2 Women's employment levels by education and age   34
2.3 Women's employment rates with and without children, 2003   36
2.4 Working hours (mothers) and parents' long-hours working,
2004–05   38
2.5 Fertility rates, 1980–2005   44
2.6 Household structure according to working hours, 2004–05   50
2.7 Time use of employed men and women, 1998–2003   55
2.8 Attitudes of mothers and fathers on work–care prioritisation,
2004   62
3.1 Formal childcare and hours of education, children 0–12,
2004–05   86
3.2 Childcare use and formal childcare preferences among
mothers of young children in paid work, 2004–05   88
3.3 Costs of childcare to parents, 2004   93
3.4 Various estimates of 'effective' employment-protected
statutory birth-related leaves   100
3.5 'Atypical' working hours: parents with children aged 0–15   111
3.6 Statutory rights to flexible working: Germany,
the Netherlands and the UK   113
5.1 Employment rates and usual hours worked in the UK, 1997
and 2007   144
5.2 Attitudes to women's employment by sex, 1989–2006   148
5.3 Three- and four-year-olds benefiting from some free early
education, 2003 and 2007   158
5.4 Childcare provision, children 0–7, England   160
5.5 Flexible working practices, 2000, 2003 and 2006   182

BOX

5.1 Leaves: glossary of terms   170

Acknowledgements

I am grateful to the Economic and Social Research Council (ESRC)'s Gender Equality Network programme (coordinated by Professor Jackie Scott), which provided the financial support for Mary Campbell who worked as the Research Officer on the project. She co-authored four arti-cles from the project and also provided assistance in drawing up most of the tables.

The work also owes much to the support I have received from continental European colleagues over the years, which has benefited from EU-level financial support, most recently under the Civil Society and New Forms of Governance in Europe Network (CINEFOGO), coordinated by Professor Thomas Boje, Social Quality and the Changing Relationship between Work, Care and Welfare in Europe Coordinated Action (WORKCARE), coordi-nated by Professor Claire Wallace and Reconciling Work and Welfare in Europe Network (RECWOWE), coordinated by Professor Denis Bouget and Dr Bruno Palier programmes, which allowed the co-writing of Chapter 4. Discussions over the years with Professors Jeanne Fagnani, Barbara Hobson, Trudie Knijn, Ute Klammer, Arnlaug Leira, Marie-Thérèse Letablier, Claude Martin, Ann Orloff, Ilona Ostner, Janneke Plantenga and Chiara Saraceno on a wide range of topics touching on the subject of this book have been enormously important.

I am particularly grateful to Trudie Knijn of the University of Utrecht, Claude Martin of CNRS Rennes, and Ilona Ostner of the University of Gottingen for their collaboration in the writing of Chapter 4.

I am also grateful to Dr Carmen Huerta, now Economist/Analyst at the Organisation for Economic Co-operation and Development (OECD), and to Ludovica Gambaro for their help in manipulating the European Social Survey and Labour Force Survey data sets.

Finally, this book has been written since my return to the London School of Economics (LSE), where I am very appreciative of the support and intellectual stimulation I have received from colleagues, especially Howard Glennerster, David Piachaud and Anne West.

1. Introduction

Paid work and care work are fundamental to the lives of adult family members and it has become increasingly difficult and onerous to manage successfully a job alongside care for dependants in the context of rapid and dramatic family and labour market change. Men and women must juggle the competing demands of work and family and many commentators have documented the overspill of stress due to work–family imbalance into both the workplace and, more often, the family. The problems of balancing responsibilities are not the same for both sexes. Women and, during recent decades, mothers in particular, have increased their participation in the labour market greatly, but men have not increased their participation in unpaid household work to a matching degree. The issue underlying work–family balance is that of the gendered divisions of paid and unpaid work, which has also long been a fundamental source of gender inequalities.

Public interest in work and family balance policies has expanded significantly in recent years. From the policymaker's perspective, the issue is the extent to which state intervention in helping family members to balance work and family responsibilities is justified. If a case can be made, there is the further issue as to whether more effort should go into targeting the work or the family side of the equation, and what form policy should take. The provision of childcare, the possibility of taking leave from work to care for dependants, and the development of more flexible working patterns on the job have been the main policy initiatives directly targeted on the problem of work–family balance. In large measure, the focus of Western governments has remained the paid and unpaid work involved in fulfilling work and family responsibilities, even when the terminology used to describe the policy field has shifted to 'work–life balance', signalling the desire both to include those without care responsibilities and to find new ways of managing increasingly diverse workforces.

Policies to address the problem of work and family balance have been and are a rather small part of the welfare state when measured in terms of the public expenditure devoted to them, even though rising policy interest in this field since the late 1990s has been matched in many countries by rising expenditure – nowhere more so than in the UK. It is notable that the broad field of family policy, which may include the provision of a variety of cash benefits and services, has expanded significantly, unlike

many other areas of the welfare state, and has tended to be directed particularly towards the support of working parents (Gauthier, 2002). Many
countries with historically low levels of public expenditure on the family
have increased the amounts they spend (OECD, 2007), and the amount
spent on formal provision for social care (for all dependants, young and
old) has also increased in most Western states since the mid-1990s (Daly,
2002, 2005). On the employment side, considerably more attention has
been paid by Western European governments to the promotion of labour
market participation by all adults via so-called 'activation' policies.

The mix of government initiatives has included the direct provision of
services, but also: the funding of services delivered by a variety of providers
and the provision of cash benefits directly to the consumers of services;
the provision of cash benefits to those taking leave from work to care; and
efforts to regulate conditions at work. Thus, intervention to enable paid
and unpaid work has focused on both the care and employment sides of
the equation and has blurred the boundaries between cash and services.
Some costs in respect of flexible working, as well as to permit employees to
stay at home to care and, more rarely in most countries, in relation to the
provision of care services, have also fallen on employers.

The task of reconciling work and care has long been accepted as a job for
government in most Western and Northern European countries. The term
'reconciliation' comes from continental Western Europe, with 'work–family
balance' and 'work–life balance' as much later additions from the English-
speaking countries. Work and family balance only became an explicit
policy goal in the UK in 1997, with the election of the first New Labour
government. In the English-speaking countries, the problem of combining
paid and unpaid work has long been considered a private matter, and for
the most part still is in the US, whereas in countries such as France or those
of Scandinavia it has long been accepted as a legitimate role for the state.
However, since the late 1990s, at the European Union (EU) level and in
member states, this policy field has increasingly been recognised as having
a significant bearing on some of the new challenges facing modern welfare
states (Pierson, 2001), particularly the achievement of higher employment
rates as a means to economic competitiveness and growth.

Work and family policies are often seen as a solution to a range of other
policy problems as well: particularly as a means of addressing the challenges
of an ageing society by enabling women to work and thereby improving the
dependency ratio, and of countering falling fertility rates, which are the
main cause of population ageing and which are often thought to be exacer-
bated by lack of support for women workers (for example OECD, 2007). In
some places work–family reconciliation has also been seen as the best way
of tackling child poverty (in the UK, by encouraging and enabling mothers

– especially lone mothers – to work), and of promoting children's educational achievement (particularly in the UK and Germany, by promoting high-quality early learning). These policies fit the criterion of 'social investment' (Lister, 2003) – designed to ensure sustainable economic prosperity – which has increasingly been used to justify public expenditure on social issues in the European context since the late 1990s. As the agenda for work and family policies has widened, so has the political interest in them.

However, in the vast majority of EU member states gender equality has been either a secondary goal, or has not been an explicit goal at all. Yet at base, the problem of work–family reconciliation arises from asymmetric gendered behaviour (which may or may not be voluntary): women have increased their hours of paid work to a much greater extent than men have increased their hours of household work, and this holds true for all developed countries (Gershuny, 2000). The problem, therefore, is fundamentally one of gender inequalities. But it is as easy in this analysis as with one centring on employment or demographic change to perceive the issue in terms of problems affecting women alone: women used to do most of the unpaid work of care in families, but now that they have entered the labour market in large numbers there is a looming 'care gap'. The problem thus becomes one of enabling women to work more and to continue to do care work. A more gendered analysis of work and family balance issues at the level of the household also swiftly arrives at the issue of unpaid work, but does not necessarily conclude that the nature of the problem consists of enabling women to carry on doing it. Nevertheless, governments tend to focus their attention on paid work and to address care work only insofar as it impinges on employment goals.

If reconciliation policies are seen as the province of women, they are likely to fail to address the role of men and hence the issue of gender equality. Indeed, in many countries outside Scandinavia, policy in this field has been relentlessly gender-neutral. In most Western European states, and increasingly in some Nordic countries, the recent emphasis has been on the importance of increasing 'parental choice', which obscures both the differential interests and power of men and women in the family. In fact, work and family policies involve consideration of the politics and distribution of time and money between families with and without care responsibilities, and also between men and women.

FAMILY CHANGE

Family change has been large and rapid over the 30 years since the late 1970s. It has multiple dimensions; two of the most important are changes

in family form and the changing contributions that men and women make
to the family.

   On the first of these changes, there is now much greater 'family fluidity',
with people moving in and out of marriage and cohabitation, at least in
Northern and Western Europe, resulting in a growing proportion of lone-
mother families, which inevitably experience particular difficulty in combining paid work and care work. Furthermore, in these new circumstances
the meaning and implications of marriage and family-building change.
For women in particular, marriage may now be perceived more as a risk
than a protection against risk, as was traditionally the case (Lewis, 2005).
Certainly, traditional specialisation by men as breadwinners and women
as carers appears risky in those countries where the divorce rate is high
and stable (Oppenheimer, 1994, 2000). Cohabitation may appear easier
to get out of, but poses a risk of additional instability in some countries –
particularly the UK – especially if the couple have a child.

   On the second of these changes, a married or cohabiting couple who
reach a satisfactory accommodation as joint earners prior to having
children must usually renegotiate their financial and care contributions
to family life once children arrive. This is often achieved by the mother
'scaling back' in some way, often by taking a lower-level job and/or by
working fewer hours (Becker and Moen, 1999), which may cause tensions at the household level and may also result in inequalities as social
provision of all kinds becomes more firmly attached to labour market
participation.

   Indeed, the nature of the contributions that adults make to families has
changed dramatically, and, taken alongside the changes in family form,
have made policy assumptions based on the traditional, two-parent, stable,
male breadwinner/female carer family model difficult to sustain. Dual-
earner families have become the norm in most Western countries, although
the number of hours women work outside the home varies hugely between
countries (Rubery et al., 1999; Lewis et al., 2008; see also Chapter 2).
While female labour participation rates remain lower in Southern Europe,
those women who are in the workforce tend to work full-time. In much of
Western Europe many more women work, but part-time, often in a 'one-
and-a-half earner model' family, extending to a 'one-and-three-quarter
earner model' in the Scandinavian countries. Indeed, Mutari and Figart
(2001) have argued that gender differentiation is increasingly based on
time – with men working full-time and women part-time, so that their paid
work is combined with domestic work. Some form of part-time work for
women has historically been the main way of reconciling work and family
responsibilities in much of Western and Northern Europe, supported in
varying degrees by state policies that, for example, provide a statutory

entitlement to mothers of young children to work fewer hours and/or guarantee pro rata benefit entitlements to those in part-time employment. In the US, women have tended to work full-time and to rely on (the relatively cheaper) market provision of care along with tax allowances for childcare that benefit the better-off in particular.

While fertility rates have fallen, dramatically so in Southern Europe, the volume of informal care has not noticeably lessened. First, there are growing proportions of frail elderly people needing care (indeed, in Southern Europe, particularly in Italy, families provide more care for this group than elsewhere); second, the expectation of more intensive parenting has grown (Bianchi, 2000); and third, despite the growth in the provision of formal institutional care, this is often fragmented between different public and private providers and substitutes imperfectly for informal provision (Lewis, 2006). The time-use data on care work for children show that men have increased their contribution, albeit from a very low base, and that women have also increased their care work slightly, but have reduced the time they spend on housework the more time they spend in the labour market (Bianchi, 2000; Gershuny, 2000). People report feeling more rushed in many countries, notwithstanding the fact that the reported amount of leisure time has not decreased (Folbre and Bittman, 2004). The key to understanding this probably lies in the extent to which the majority of households now have two earners, and that even in countries where a high proportion of women work part-time, their hours have tended to increase. This means that the constant negotiation and juggling of work and family responsibilities is the order of the day (Jacobs and Gerson, 2004).

Trends in the two main dimensions of family change are by no means the same in different EU member states – while fertility is very low in Southern Europe, it is much higher in countries such as France and the UK, although still under the 2.1 children needed for replacement. There is also considerable variation in both the rate of female employment and the number of hours women, especially mothers, work. It is very difficult to establish how far these differing patterns are voluntary and how far they are the product of structural constraints or ideas about what should and should not be done. This is a crucial issue, because if adult family members are merely exercising their preferences for a certain number of children and a particular set of household working arrangements, then, in a liberal democratic state, it is difficult to justify state intervention intended to modify or change them. In this respect, the boundary between public and private life, which has been subject to considerable erosion and change, still holds. However, if people would like more children and wish that it could be made easier to have them, or if mothers would prefer to work more hours and would do so if only childcare were more available, accessible, affordable and of good quality, then there is a clearer case for state intervention. But it is by no means easy to establish what the actual position is. Attitudes towards these central matters of family life – caregiving and doing paid work – vary between countries as well by region, age, ethnicity and gender. They can be contradictory, and are certainly hard to interpret.

Family changes have led to an appreciation of the family as an independent variable by both social policy analysts and policymakers (Esping-Andersen, 1999; Esping-Andersen et al., 2002), something that qualitative sociologists have argued for many years (for example Morgan, 1996). Family change has also changed the nature of risk and thus has the potential to create new demands for social welfare systems. Indeed, it has begun to be argued that family changes result in 'new social risks' (Bonoli, 2005; see also Taylor Gooby, 2004), which fall outside the established insurance-based frameworks for social protection, based as these have been on a stable, married, male breadwinner family, with a fully employed husband/ father and primary carer wife/mother (Supiot, 2001; Lewis, 2001, 2002). The welfare systems based on social insurance for male breadwinners and their dependants that grew up in Western Europe during the twentieth century protected male workers against external risks; something like divorce was explicitly excluded from social insurance cover because it was impossible to exclude the possibility that either a husband or wife was 'to blame' for the event (Lewis, 2001a). In addition, care work was assumed to be the province of the wife and therefore not a primary issue for the state, although historically some countries did more in respect of the care of children, and others for elderly people.

Families have become dependent on two earners and labour markets have become more flexible, with short-term contracts and more precarious employment, particularly for women and particularly in Southern Europe, but also in France where such employment has increased, and among part-time workers in the UK. So leaving the labour market to have a child has become more risky, especially if there is no right to return to the same job and of substantial help with childcare. Policymakers want to promote labour market participation for all adults, male and female, and people may also respond to the new circumstances by wishing to secure their financial position as individuals. However, there is still, in all countries, a gender gap in how far they are able to do so.

WELFARE STATE CHANGE

The major changes in families and labour markets have coincided with a period of welfare state restructuring. The main feature of this has been an effort to shift the emphasis from rights to responsibilities and from so-called 'passive' to 'active' welfare provision, such that claimants on the welfare system are 'encouraged' into work and work is made 'to pay' (Lødemel and Trickey, 2000). In the European context, welfare state change has been largely driven by the aim of promoting employment as a means of ensuring competitiveness and growth (CEC, 2000), and has been justified in terms of widening the tax base and thus also coming to the rescue of the continental European social insurance model (Esping-Andersen et al., 2002).

In the face of common economic and demographic challenges, European welfare states have sought to increase the proportion of adults active in the labour market and to expand the length of working life for men and women (Maier, 2007). Enabling transitions between employment and unemployment, and paid and unpaid work (Schmid, 1998; Gautié and Gazier, 2003) becomes crucial to this endeavour. Work–family policies are increasingly conceptualised in relation to the reform of welfare systems such that they encourage 'flexibility', rather than assuming the existence of 'jobs for life', and protect against a clearly defined range of mostly extra-familial risks. Since the late 1990s, policy at the European level has promoted 'flexicurity', that is, flexible labour markets in a framework of security that is in keeping with the idea of a European Social Model (CEC, 2006). Work–family balance policies are seen as having the double advantage of promoting both flexibility and security. In the Danish case, which epitomises changes in line with flexicurity, there are high employment rates of men and women, low protection against dismissal in the workplace, a high degree of flexible working with the possibility for the mothers of young children to reduce their hours, but also labour market activation policies to promote retraining and re-entry to employment, and highly developed support services such as childcare. Policy attention in respect of work and family balance policies has to date focused on the care of children, rather than dependent elderly people, in large part because the main goal has been to encourage employment among the mothers of dependent children.[1] Thus despite ageing populations, relatively little attention has been paid to the care of elderly people, and even in some of the Scandinavian countries services for this group of the population have been cut. Indeed, the focus in regard to elderly people has also been on 'active ageing', defined as the need to keep people in employment for longer. However, as Jaumotte (2003) has suggested, policies that help women to reconcile work and family responsibilities are more politically acceptable than policies aimed at keeping older people in work for longer.

Thus the work–welfare relationship has been substantially recast (Pierson, 2001; Ferrera et al., 2000). Gilbert (2002) characterised the trends emerging at the turn of the century in terms of a series of shifts: from social support to social inclusion via employment; from measures of 'decom-modification' (that enable people to leave the labour market for due cause) to ways of securing commodification; and from unconditional benefits to benefits that are heavily conditional on work or training. Welfare states were built around the paid work–welfare relationship and the incentive and disincentive effects of social provision on the worker's inclination to search for employment and to support himself and his family. Crucially, for the first time in the history of modern welfare states, the assumptions underpinning this recast work–welfare relationship have in the twenty-first century been increasingly extended to women as well as men (Lewis, 2002). The aim of higher employment rates for women is underpinned mainly by the economic calculation that more women in the labour market results in an increase in gross national product (GNP) through the introduction of new activities and through the recording of activities (such as informal childcare) that were hitherto unrecorded and protected from taxation and regulation (Boeri et al., 2005). Thus, the treatment of lone mothers has moved from policies based on assumptions a generation ago that their primary task is motherhood, to assumptions that they will increasingly be in the labour force (Kiernan et al., 1998). The Netherlands and the UK, like the US, signalled the shift in policy assumptions by applying limited welfare-to-work policies to this group from the mid- to late 1990s, and the trend has continued, with the Netherlands introducing a new part-time work obligation supplemented by means-tested benefits for lone mothers with children under 16 in 2007, and the UK government introducing a work obligation for lone mothers with children of over 12 years of age in 2008 with the intention of extending it to those with children over seven in 2010 (DWP, 2007). In the case of couple families, the decline of the male breadwinner model, the changing nature of risk, an increasing degree of economic independence for women, and the desire to modernise social protection systems to match the goal of a less standardised and more flex-ible working life has given rise to more discussion as to the desirability of more individually based 'drawing rights' in social security systems (Supiot, 2001), but without sufficient attention to gender inequalities.

The new principles underpinning social provision have neatly piggy-backed onto the erosion of the male breadwinner family. For the shift in ideas and practices in regard to social welfare systems is both instrumental, serving the competition and growth agenda of the European Commission and member states, and is also in keeping with 'individualisation'. This is defined by social theorists as the processes whereby people's lives come to be less constrained by tradition and custom and more subject to indi-vidual choice (Beck, 1992; Beck and Beck-Gernsheim, 1995), but is usually understood at the policy level simply in terms of increasing economic independence on the part of women. In this analysis, both the changes in the contributions that men and women make to households and the fluidity of family forms mean that there can be no firm normative assumptions regarding the ability of women and children to depend on a male breadwinner. It therefore becomes additionally convenient for policymakers to assume progress towards an 'adult worker model' family and increasingly to treat men and women the same: as fully individualised (Lewis, 2001).

However, there is a danger that the new set of assumptions about the desirability and inevitability of an adult worker model family is outrunning the social reality. This is chiefly because there are still profound gender divisions in both paid and unpaid work, albeit that these vary between countries and within countries, between regions, social classes and between people of different ethnicities (for example, in the UK, Asian women are much less likely to be in the labour force than white or black Afro-Caribbean women). Policymakers have been eager to encourage greater private responsibility for risk – especially in regard to provision for old age (Hacker, 2006, Taylor Gooby, 2004; Brush, 2002) – which again links to the emergence of an adult worker model family. But to assume the existence of this family model is no more accurate a description of the behavioural reality than was the idea of a male breadwinner model family in the early twentieth century. Women have always engaged in the labour market, but on different terms to men: they have lower pay rates, shorter working hours and periods of exit (foregoing earnings and often pension contributions), usually in order to do care work. Furthermore, the issue of care work in and for itself in terms of how to compensate it, how to organise it, and how to ensure greater equality between men and women, figures only rarely on the agendas of most governments.

The increased attention given to work and family balance policies has tended in most countries to be in the main about something else: primarily the need to promote employment, but also fertility and children's early learning, again often as a means of making the necessary investment in human capital to secure future economic growth and competitiveness. However, the wide variety of goals for work and family balance policies are not necessarily compatible. For example, these policies are held to be good for business: by promoting working patterns that lead to reduced absence due to casual sickness; improving employee retention, productivity, morale and commitment; and by making it easier to manage a 'diverse' workforce – but this may mean that policies are less focused on social goals to do with prioritising family well-being (Perrons, 1999). Policies that are aimed at maximising mothers' employment may work to the detriment of children's welfare in the light of the evidence that exists to support the idea that very young children need a one-to-one relationship (Waldfogel, 2006). There may be difficulty in squaring the best interests of the very young child with support for parents' choices, let alone with the interests of both fathers and mothers, or indeed of the broader economy and of business.

The impetus to move towards an adult worker model family has been strengthened by academic analysis of the need to 'modernise' social policies and by the prescriptions of transnational organisations, including the European Commission and the Organisation for Economic Co-operation and Development (OECD), which has shown considerable interest in work and family policy in the 2000s, albeit that the prescriptions from different parts of that organisation have not always tallied (Mahon, 2006). The next section illustrates the way in which the development of work and family policies has been approached since the 1990s at the EU level. What happens at the EU level has been significant for those member states, like the UK, which had done relatively little in the work–family field until the late 1990s, but much less so in other countries, particularly in Scandinavia, where work–family balance policies were developed from the 1970s. The purpose of exploring the development of work and family policy at the EU level briefly here is that it provides a particularly clear-cut illustration of a shift away from work and family policies as part of an approach to equal opportunities, which have occupied a large place in EU policymaking, and towards a more instrumentalist, employment-driven approach that is more in line with wider welfare state restructuring.

ILLUSTRATING POLICY CHANGE: THE EU LEVEL

The implications of the shift to an adult worker model for policies to do with paid and unpaid work and for women in particular are clearly apparent at the EU level (Lewis, 2006a). In most countries, economic policy has tended to take priority over social policy. At the EU level, this has also been a function of the role of the Commission as above all a market-maker; social policies have developed as an adjunct to market-making. However, one of the few commitments to social policy at the time of the 1957 Treaty of Rome was to securing equal pay between men and women. While this was intended primarily to secure an even playing field between member states in respect of pay rates, it also provided a basis for building policy interventions in the work–family field.

Since the late 1990s, social policies have been promoted in terms of their potential to further both employment and economic goals, with employment policy seen as the pivotal point in this triangular relationship. As a result, social policy at the EU level has increasingly become 'employment-led' (O'Connor, 2005), and the focus on 'market integration' has tended to confirm the subordination of social to economic policy (for example Hodson and Maher, 2001; Leibfried, 2005). Considerable concern has been expressed about the extent to which the European Social Model is equipped to promote rather than impede economic growth, the comparator being the better economic performance experienced in the US, at least prior to 2007/8 (CEC, 2004). It is possible to trace growing EU concern to push member states to address the problems of high levels of unemployment and relatively lower labour market participation rates – particularly among women – compared to the US, together with the accompanying perceived need to 'modernise' social protection systems in line with these challenges.

In a major social policy document issued in 2000, the European Commission defined social policy as 'a productive factor' and gave it a new role (CEC, 2000: 5). While in the past its task had been 'minimising negative social consequences', in the future its focus would be on 'modernising the European social model and investing in people' (CEC, 2000: 6). Employment policy became the major preoccupation of both social policy (in order to secure the viability of the work–welfare relationship) and economic policy (in order to promote competition and growth). Particular attention was paid to women's employment rates in the context of the European Employment Strategy (EES); in 2000 the Lisbon Council set a target of 60 per cent for female labour market participation in member states by 2010 (CEU, 2000), albeit without any specification as to the number of hours to be worked. Indeed, as early as 1993, the European Commission identified the formal care sector as a source of new jobs (CEC, 1993), the implication being that women workers might trade the work of informal care for paid work in the formal care sector. As the High Level Group reviewing the Lisbon Strategy put it, the aim has been to 'embed' Europe's commitment to social cohesion 'in the core of the growth and jobs generation process' (High Level Group, 2004: 16).

It is instructive to see how the approach to work and family policies has shifted in relation to the determination to modernise social policy and to make it 'fit for purpose' in terms of supporting the core goals of economic growth and competitiveness and, more recently, higher fertility rates. It is possible to see a shift: first, from concern with equal opportunities between men and women, towards a greater preoccupation with opportunities for mothers to engage in paid work; and second, regarding the choice of policy instruments away from parental leave, which enables labour market exit (usually by women), towards more concern about the provision of childcare services, which would seem to promote labour market attachment (although, as Chapter 3 shows, these commonly understood outcomes are not as clear-cut as might be supposed). Since the late 1990s, work and family policies have been conceptualised in relation to the goal of increasing women's employment rates, and since 2005 additionally in relation to the goal of increasing fertility in the face of population ageing. Indeed, by the late 2000s, these policies were increasingly understood not just in terms of underpinning the crucial employment strategy within the social policy, economic policy and employment triangle, but as: first, part of a new more highly specified 'flexicurity' strategy that linked 'modernised social policies' – mainly in the form of active labour market policies in preference to employment protection – firmly to the promotion of flexible labour markets; and second, as the link between economic and demographic policies. To this extent, work–family policies have become more visible, both at EU and member state levels.

Work–family reconciliation policies were explicitly addressed from the early 1990s. Most of the key documents issued on the subject during the early and mid-1990s made reference somewhere, if only in passing, to the desirability of men and women sharing employment and family responsibilities. In 1992, a European Council recommendation was issued on childcare and recommended that member states develop and/or encourage initiatives to enable women and men to reconcile their occupational, family and child-raising responsibilities (CEU, 1992). The recommendation also defined childcare broadly and proposed that measures were needed in four areas: childcare services, leave for employed parents, family-friendly policies at the workplace, and measures to promote the increased participation by men in the care and upbringing of children. It thus covered all the main dimensions of work and family balance policies under the heading of 'childcare' and also addressed the role of men and fathers. Even the 1994 White Paper on Social Policy, which provided an early endorsement of the need for higher 'adult' labour market participation, referred to the need for 'greater solidarity between men and women' at the same time as it prioritised the role of social policies in promoting women's employment (CEC, 1994: 43).

In 1996 a directive on parental leave (CEU, 1996) was adopted, which laid down minimum individual rights to three months parental leave for men and women. Member states were left to determine the conditions of access, whether the leave should be compensated and whether it should be full- or part-time. The leave was to be non-transferable – fathers could not transfer it to mothers – in order to promote gender equality. However, the fact that no minimum remuneration requirements were specified (a victory for the employer's side) made it much less likely that men would take it (as proved to be the case; Bruning and Plantenga, 1999), and that it would in practice be reconciliation for women (see Chapter 3).

Since the late 1990s, there has been a significant change in the way in which work–family reconciliation policies have been talked about.

As the then Social Affairs Commissioner Padraig Flynn, commented in his foreword to the Employment and Social Affairs Directorate's 1998 report on reconciliation, the issue 'is an integral part of the European Employment Strategy process' (CEC, 1998). From 1998, work–family reconciliation has been more firmly integrated into the guidelines accompanying the European Employment Strategy. The result has been: first, that the goal of promoting gender equality by changing the behaviour of men has tended to slip out of the picture; and second, that the policy focus has narrowed substantially to the provision of childcare services, which are often considered to be more likely to promote female employ-ment than measures that provide time to care, particularly long childcare leaves. Following the Lisbon targets for women's employment, the 2002 Barcelona Council set targets for the provision of childcare services to reach 90 per cent of children between three and school age, and 33 per cent of under-three's.

By the early 2000s, arguments for the need to reform 'work organis-ation' by increasing flexibility, in which the provision of childcare was recognised to play a part, were made without any reference to equal opportunities (for example CEC, 1997; Webster, 2001). This signalled the extent to which work–family reconciliation had become increasingly tied to the new flexicurity agenda, and to be conceptualised as an important component of the commitment to enhancing flexibility by, for example, encouraging part-time work in order to increase the mothers' employment rates, but also to the goal of promoting 'social quality' at work (CEC, 2001). Work–family balance policies were conceptualised as increas-ing the attractiveness of work, but there was insufficient attention paid both to guaranteeing the conditions of such work (which often remained precarious despite the 1997 Part-Time Work Directive 97/81 designed to improve its quality) and to issues to do with unpaid care work. In 2003, work–family reconciliation was included under the 'quality and produc-tivity' objective in the EES Guidelines (CEU, 2003), the equal opportuni-ties pillar, under which it had appeared from 1998 (CEU, 1998), having been abolished as gender equality became a 'horizontal principle' to be mainstreamed across all policy fields. There was as a result rather less mention of gender equality, which in the sense of 'equal sharing' of paid and unpaid work between men and women was given reduced priority (Rubery et al., 2003).

However, the European Commission has long recognised that 'the new gender balance in working life [meaning women's entry into paid work] is at odds with traditional family policies', and reform was viewed as a necessary part of the modernisation of social protection (CEC, 1997a). Esping-Andersen, who co-authored an influential policy document for the Belgian Presidency in 2001, went further in his indictment of the 'familialism' of the old welfare settlement, arguing that policies based on assumptions regarding the traditional roles of men and women in families and the male breadwinner model family had become the 'Achilles heel' of welfare states, running counter to both family formation and labour supply (Esping-Andersen, 1999: 70). Work–family reconciliation policies have long been a part of the EU's mainstream concern about economic policy and access to labour markets. But in the early and mid-1990s they were clearly nested within equal opportunities policies as well as employment policies. They have increasingly been absorbed into employment policy, and the approach to them has been above all instrumental, linked to strategies to raise women's employment rates and to policies to promote adequate security for workers in post-industrial, flexible labour markets. A 2006 Commission consultation document on extending EU legislation on childcare leaves, services and working time reiterated: 'the need for a better work–private life balance in order to achieve economic growth, prosperity and competitiveness' (CEC, 2006a: Introduction).

With the adoption of the strategy of flexicurity, work–family policies have been seen as a component of both employment policies and of a modernised social security system. But this has proved a difficult balancing act for policymakers, and in 2007 the Commission warned – albeit in a document on gender equality rather than on the mainstream policy issue of flexicurity – that flexicurity policies 'should avoid stressing the "flexibility" aspect for women [mainly in the form of reduced working hours and short or fixed-term contracts] and the "security" aspect for men' (CEC, 2007b: para. 3.1). Nevertheless, a few months later it was still possible for the European Expert Group on Flexicurity (2007) to issue a document on 'flexicurity pathways' with no reference to gender equality issues. Even in Denmark there is evidence to show that men have enjoyed better access to active labour market policies – a crucial dimension of the flexicurity strategy – than women (Hansen, 2007).

By the mid-2000s, the issue of fertility was also being joined to that of employment, with the High Level Group on the Future of Social Policy in an Enlarged European Union (2004) promoting work–family reconciliation additionally as a means of allowing couples 'to have the number of children they desire' (see also CEC, 2006b). In this context, work and family policies were again linked more explicitly to gender equality and also to the promotion of solidarity between the generations, as it was recognised that caring responsibilities were increasingly borne by the young and intermediate generations, and mainly by women (CEC, 2007a,c). In 2006 both the European Council and the Commission advocated measures to promote the use of parental leave by men (CEU, 2006; CEC, 2006c), and the Commission launched a consultation process with the social partners on how to improve reconciliation policies (CEC, 2006a, 2007a). But in the main, EU-level policy has focused much more attention on the need for reconciliation policies for women – harnessing them to employment policy and making them a measure of social quality – than for men.

GENDER EQUALITY

Gendered patterns of paid and unpaid work are fundamental to the problem of gender inequality. But the term 'work–*family* balance' has not passed without criticism. First, academic commentators working mainly on what happens at the level of the firm and particularly on flexible working have long used the term 'work–*life* balance' (for example Rapoport et al., 2002; Gambles et al., 2006). This is generalisable to all workers and may therefore be considered by employers to be less divisive, in addition to serving the wider workplace agenda of how to manage an increasingly diverse workforce. Thus, work–life balance, which has also penetrated government documents in the UK and at the EU level, goes beyond the need to address the gendered issue of paid and unpaid work. Many, including trade unionists as well as managers, think that a wider focus will also benefit the pursuit of gender equality; others fear that it will dilute it (see Chapters 3 and 5). Rapoport et al. (2002) have advocated the use of the term 'work–personal life integration', which they suggest will address a dual policy agenda of improving workplace performance and pursuing gender equality (see also Thomas, 1990; Guest, 2001). Second, as in this last example, the idea of 'balance' has also been questioned. Gambles et al. (2006) have suggested that balance implies a trade-off: as one element goes up the other goes down (see also Jones et al., 2006). Better, it is argued, to call for the 'harmonisation' of paid work with other parts of 'life' (Gambles et al., 2006). However, from the point of view of research in the work and family field, Crompton and Brockman (2006) have suggested that the notion of work–life 'articulation' is a more neutral and more appropriate focus than the idea of balance as a means to achieving and harmonious accommodation.

Nevertheless, in respect of the territory of paid and unpaid work, parents as well as policymakers regularly speak about employment and childcare issues in terms of 'juggling' and 'balancing'. From a gender perspective, it makes more sense to talk about work–family balance policies, than work–life policies, which take in the issue of leisure as well as care, and which may apply to all workers rather than being focused on the issue of combining paid and unpaid work.

Whether and how gender issues warrant explicit consideration by policymakers has proved problematic in most EU member states. In any case, there is a big debate about what might constitute gender equality in relation to such policies. Gender equality has often been defined by academics chiefly in relation to women's opportunities in the labour market (for example Korpi, 2000) as well as by policymakers. If this definition is adopted, certain policy prescriptions follow, and are likely to give priority to measures that encourage female access to employment. To go further and to ensure equal treatment in the labour market would, of course, require much more political will to implement a wide range of policies on pay and conditions, and on workplace discrimination.

But gender inequality is also present in the division of unpaid work. Given that the unpaid work of care is necessary to the well-being of society, other analysts have asked whether there should not also be a right to give and to receive care for men and women (Knijn and Kremer, 1997), which in turn raises issues to do with how care is rewarded in the formal and informal sectors and how it is shared between men and women at the household level, as well as between the individual and the state. There is tension between policymakers' desire to promote female labour market participation and the continued expectation on the part of most governments (and people) that it will be women who will continue to take primary responsibility for care work. Indeed, family policies are often about competition between different values and their incorporation into policies (Strohmeier, 2002), probably to a greater extent than in other policy fields. For example, Hertz (1999) has noted the extent to which the whole idea of balancing work and family may be a euphemism for competing ideologies about child-rearing. Using cross-national evidence, Kremer (2007) has also stressed the importance of the way in which different ideals of childcare (for example professional care, surrogate mothering or parental sharing) prevail at different times in different countries and influence policymaking.

Most Western and Northern European welfare states rely on ideas about what constitutes best practice in terms of caring for children. Usually, some form of leave (taken mainly by mothers) will cover the child's early years, followed by the provision of childcare services. The Scandinavian countries introduced 'daddy quotas', whereby men are obliged to take some parental leave or lose it altogether. This avoids compulsion, while encouraging men to do unpaid work. However, even in these countries, where work–family balance policies are most developed and gender equality has been explicitly promoted, it is more accurate to describe policy as supporting a 'gender participation model' (Hobson, 2004) – that is, enabling women to enter the labour market and to leave it 'for cause' (namely, to care) – rather than enabling women and men to be able to make a real choice to engage in paid and/or unpaid work. In these countries, as at the EU level, work–family balance policies largely have been, and remain, policies to ease the burden on women who undertake paid and unpaid work.

All this raises issues about how gender difference and gender equality matter for policy. Some feminist commentators have pointed out that because social policies of all kinds increasingly assume the existence of an individualised, adult worker model family, priority needs to be given to policies that promote women's equality in the workforce (for example Orloff, 2009). Indeed, many feminists have long argued in favour of women's financial autonomy as a crucial means to equality (Orloff, 1993), which involves considerably more than mere access to the labour market. But if women report that they want to do care work, should this not be respected? Even when academic writers eschew comment on what might be 'good' or 'bad' for women, they nevertheless tend to reflect deep-seated and very different national traditions as to what constitutes gender equality. Thus Trzcinski (2000) has called attention to the continued strength of a 'maternalist' tradition in Germany. The danger at the policy level is that a decision to opt for care work is treated as private, and that society fails to compensate fully or otherwise accommodate it. Women who express a preference for the informal work of care may be expressing ideas about their own identities: as mothers rather than workers (Akerloff and Kranton, 2000); about what they consider 'the proper thing to do' (Finch and Mason, 1993), in which case their behaviour probably has much to do with normative expectations which may also be influenced by economic pressures; or about their assessment of what their options are. For example, a choice to do care work may be influenced by a belief based on historical reality that childcare provision in their neighbourhood is either too expensive or of insufficiently high quality. Cultural differences between countries, social classes and ethnicities are likely to be important in all this (Pfau-Effinger, 1998).

But it remains a problem as to whether women in particular should be 'allowed' to make the choice to do care work rather than paid work if it disadvantages them. For example, mothers may choose to stay at home to care for children without realising that this will impose costs in terms of their career advancement and pension entitlements. Should government merely applaud such altruism (which may not be fully understood by mothers themselves), seek to inform the choice, or compensate mothers for it? It is surely dishonourable to do the first without attempting either the second or third of these. In addition, what should be done about the fact that men's choice not to care constrains women's choice to work? It may be, as Bianchi and Casper (2004) have suggested, that further enlargement of choices for women depends on men changing their behaviour, and in particular on changes to the male career norm.

The goals of governments in promoting work–family balance are diverse, but gender equality in and for itself is rarely a priority outside Scandinavia, and even those countries are not immune from debate about what constitutes gender equality and what constitutes 'choice'. In the UK, gender equality has hardly been discussed; rather, policy documents have striven for gender neutrality. But it is very difficult to define gender equality in the context of work–family balance policies. The age-old problem of equality-as-sameness or equality-as-difference (Lister, 1997) is central to this problem. If the aim is sameness, in the context of work–family balance this translates into an equal division of paid and unpaid work between men and women: a citizen worker/carer model. This has been espoused by Fraser (1997) on the basis of philosophical argument, and by Gornick and Meyers (2003) as a result of their empirical research. But if equality consists of recognising difference or diversity, then policy may seek to reward women's disproportionate amount of care work, albeit at the risk of perpetuating this work as women's responsibility. If some form of gender equity rather than equality has been reached, then this second option may appear to be legitimate. In the UK, for example, total work hours, paid and unpaid, are similar for men and women, but men work long hours and do less unpaid work, while women work part-time hours and do more unpaid work. However, there is still the problem that care work materially disadvantages those who choose to do it in Western societies, even when it is compensated, as the relative rates of poverty for men and women testify. Whether it takes place in the formal or informal sectors, care work is poorly rewarded financially. This is a problem that is likely to increase in significance as governments seek to make people more responsible for their own welfare, especially in old age, and to privatise risk.

While the goal of a citizen worker/carer model is very attractive for those, myself included, anxious to see more progress towards gender equality, the difficulty of disentangling gender equality and gender equity, and of accommodating very different ideas about what adult men and women should contribute to families, particularly in increasingly pluralist societies, has meant that a different approach to defining gender equality has been used in this book. It focuses not on equality of outcome, but rather on the importance of agency and the possibilities different policies and policy packages hold for permitting a 'real choice'. Derived from the work of Sen (1999) on capabilities, it is an approach that eschews prescription and instrumentalism, and permits the reframing of the current policy debates over the nature of choice – for whom and about what – that have become increasingly dominant in a number of member states, including Scandinavia (Ellingsaeter and Leira, 2006). The idea of 'real' or 'genuine' choice goes beyond choice as a simple expression of preferences and acknowledges the important role of policy in addressing the constraints on choice. If care is a universal human need (Nussbaum, 1999), then arguably it should be possible for anyone to choose to do it (Lewis and Giullari, 2005). Truly genuine choice can only exist in a perfect universe of fair and adequate wages, generous family policies, and secure work and family situations. However, it is employed here to indicate a possible policy direction that is oriented towards equal opportunities and which eschews a wholly instrumental approach. This does not constitute a rejection of the desirability of a universal worker/carer model, which it is assumed will produce less of a double burden for working mothers, more egalitarian family and gender relations, and a reduction in women's poverty. But the main concern of this book is with the patterning of policy packages and with policy trajectories, rather than policy outcomes, and a major task will be to explore the definitions of gender equality used by policymakers, and the meanings of choice that have increasingly been used in various countries in relation to gender neutrality and gender equality.

Defining gender equality in terms of real choice for the purposes of the analysis cuts the Gordian knot of equality versus difference and provides a yardstick for reaching conclusions about policy trajectories. From this definition, it follows that work–family balance policies must address a wide range of concerns and focus on both unpaid and paid work. Thus policies must deal with: both working time and time to care; the cash transfers needed either to buy care in order to enter the labour market, or to buy the time to exit the labour market to care; and the provision of care services. Time – and indeed the gendered politics of time, at the household as well as the societal level (Baldock and Hadlow, 2004) – is as important as money (at least in the richer Western and Northern European member states), and the interaction between the different components of policy packages in this respect is difficult to gauge. Neither care services nor parental leave alone is sufficient to secure 'real choice'. Indeed, the nature of the policy package is crucial in terms of the range of policies it offers and the fine-tuning of each policy in the package (for example in respect of eligibility, compensation rate and duration). Working time also involves employers and what happens at the level of the firm. As the OECD (2001) reported, in countries with good state provision on work–family balance, some firms did little, but where the state did nothing, firms failed to fill the gap (see also Evans, 2002). Long working hours, or inflexible working hours set in the interests of the employer rather than the employee, run counter to a real choice to care.

THE BOOK

The main purpose of this book is to understand the nature of the work and family balance policy packages that have developed in different countries, together with their implications for the pursuit of gender equality. These packages have addressed the care of children, which is also the focus of this book. Several commentators have argued that care for the old and for children should be considered together (Anttonen and Sipilä, 1996; Leitner, 2003; Anttonen et al., 2007). In terms of the impact of care work at the household level, and in terms of debates about the future of policy, this is an important point, even though it is crucial to delineate carefully the very real differences in the nature of care work for the old and the young. However, policymakers have tended to treat elder care and childcare separately, in terms of policy approaches and mechanisms. This book is confined to looking across the range of policies dealing with children.

The first part is broadly comparative, focusing mainly on the EU15 member states with reference to the US. It reviews the context for the development of work and family policy, first in terms of labour market behaviour and family formation at the aggregate level and at the level of the household, and in relation to people's attitudes and preferences. Crompton et al. (2007) have sought to understand the way in which work and family responsibilities are 'articulated' by situating them in their economic and policy context, 'filtered' by varying norms and values. Equally, context matters when the focus is on policy rather than behaviour. For example, similar labour activation policies in Denmark and in the UK look very different in practice because they have been inserted into different institutional arrangements. Neyer (2006) has also shown the extent to which similar family policies are likely to have different effects in different contexts.

As Chapter 2 shows, context also matters for policy formation, although exactly how is a matter of debate; it is remarkably difficult to establish clear causal relationships. Thus, while most commentators are agreed that there are external challenges to welfare states, above all in the form of globalisation, it has not proved easy to find any clear-cut pattern of responses, and a strong strand in the literature argues that domestic challenges have been more important in provoking reform (Pierson, 2001; Timonen, 2003). The changes in the contributions men and women make to families, which revolve largely around changes in labour market participation (especially of women), together with the changes in family form, which are crucial to demographic change, are key dimensions of these domestic challenges. A review of these changes shows how much of a gap exists in different countries between assumptions regarding progress towards the individualised adult work model family and higher fertility rates endorsed by policymakers on the one hand, and the social reality on the other. In addition, policymakers face difficulties in understanding the relationship between these factors and people's attitudes and preferences, which cannot be ignored in liberal democratic states. Recent case studies of childcare have made a convincing argument that there is an iterative relationship between attitudes and behaviour, and that policies can help to change both (Himmelweit, 2005; also Kremer, 2007). Policy may seek deliberately and radically to change attitudes and behaviour, or to instigate only moderate reform while nevertheless initiating change.

Much depends on how the nature of the challenges is interpreted. Feminist analysts have consistently argued that the way in which policies are represented is underpinned by normative assumptions regarding the gender order and gender differences (for example Lewis, 1992; Mazey, 2000; Bacchi, 2004). The existing gendered patterns of work and care bear testimony to the fact that the countries of Western Europe started the twenty-first century in different places in terms of patterns of female labour market participation and attitudes towards whether mothers should work, as well as in regard to policies (as Chapters 3 and 4 show). There seems to have been substantial convergence between countries in the 2000s in terms of the overarching instrumental policy goal of work–family balance policies as a means to promoting women's employment, and in many countries as a means to achieving higher fertility rates. But there remains ample space for differences between countries in terms of the attention paid to other policy goals: for example the desire to promote children's cognitive development; the balance between policies in the total policy package; and the policy instruments that are actually used.

Influential work by political scientists on policy development has stressed the importance of 'path-dependence' and the tendency to continuity rather than change (Pierson, 1994; but also Crouch and Farrell, 2004). But the work and family policy field has been marked by change in the sense of both reform to existing policy instruments and the introduction of new instruments, rather than continuity. Policy development in this field has amounted to more than the kind of change at the margins that is often directed towards patching up existing arrangements, but which may in the end result in significant reform (Streeck and Thelen, 2005; Clegg, 2007). Nevertheless, the fact that policymakers do not start with a blank slate is important to an understanding of the different policy priorities, packages and trajectories. Sociologists have also recognised the importance of societal effects deriving from the policy orientations of major interest groups (Gallie, 2003). Thus, for example, in the Scandinavian countries the pursuit of gender equality has become normative, while in the English-speaking countries the historical strength of the public–private boundary has to be negotiated by a government wishing to intervene in the work and family field. The first section of the book cannot explore in any depth the part played by the policy actors and institutions in different countries (this is attempted only for the UK in Part II). Rather, it focuses particularly on coming to some understanding of the nature of the ideas and rhetoric that are used to make the case for policy development and/or change (Schmidt, 2001, 2002; Campbell, 2002) and their relationship to policy instruments, which is explored for four countries in more depth in Chapter 4.

The second part of the book focuses on the UK and on the policy goals, instruments and politics of policymaking since the late 1990s, tracing policy development in the three main areas of flexible working time, leaves and childcare services. The UK is an oddity in Western Europe in that it started in 1997 with close to a blank slate in terms of explicit work and family policies. Chapter 5 first elaborates labour market behaviour and what we know about attitudes towards work and family responsibilities in the UK, and then examines the nature of provision, looking at the way in which policies have been framed, the interests of other policy actors, particularly employers, and what has been achieved. The UK case is a good example of profound continuity as well as change. The conclusion returns to the issue of gender equality: what has been achieved and what needs to be done. Work–family balance policies have a number of objectives and have been pursued using a variety of policy instruments. The balance between instruments differs within and between countries in line with the priority accorded different goals, with the result that there have also been welfare trade-offs between adults (particularly mothers) and children, and between men and women.

NOTE

1. Of course, as Brody (1981) recognised more than quarter of a century ago, 'women in the middle' – in their fifties and sometimes in their forties – may be called upon to care for older dependent children and elderly parents.

PART I

2. The policymaking context: behaviour and attitudes

Since the late 1990s, the main concerns of European Union (EU) member states in relation to work and family policies, as well as the broader challenges facing welfare states, have centred on raising employment rates (particularly of women) and, in many countries, on low fertility rates. This chapter begins with an aggregate picture of these two issues in order to show the wide variations between countries, and indicates the difficulties in interpreting the relationships between them. The different national contexts in terms of these two dimensions of behaviour together with attitudes mean that different policy approaches are to be expected, even though policymakers often tend to consider only those aspects of these very complicated issues that seem directly relevant to the policy goal they have set. Nor is the context for policymaking limited to behaviour and attitudes. Policy packages on work and family have existed for some time in most European countries and, together with the variable strength of different policy actors in the different countries, exert important influence on what policymakers decide to do (see Chapters 3 and 4).

Employment and fertility rates are related to one another, even though the mechanisms are far from clear. Before the mid-1980s it was assumed that the more women were in paid employment, the lower would be the fertility rate. But, beginning in the mid-1980s, this assumption ceased to hold. Some (but not all) Northern and Western European countries have high female labour market participation rates and relatively high fertility, while in Southern Europe, both rates are low. As Castles (2003) has commented, this amounts to 'the world turned upside down' and also raises major issues as to what an appropriate role for policy might be. It is suggested that the gendered division of paid and unpaid work may be having an effect on fertility rates, and that Western states are increasingly facing a 'care gap'.

It is additionally necessary to review what is happening at the level of the household: in terms of how paid work and the unpaid work of care are combined by men and by women, and what the domestic division of labour looks like. In all countries, women have changed more than men, increasing their paid work to a much greater extent than men have increased their unpaid work. These gender divisions underpin the issue of work–family balance. The policy response in most EU member states has tended to focus on ways of 'reconciling' responsibilities for 'work and care', particularly for women. But some see this as merely 'papering over the cracks' rather than addressing ways in which incompatibilities between work and care are underpinned institutionally, economically and ideologically.

What people think should happen, and what they say their preferences are, matter to policymakers. Ideas about 'the proper thing to do' (Finch and Mason, 1993) in respect of having jobs, having children and doing the unpaid work of care are likely to be strongly held. It is no easy matter to work out what people think or want, or the extent to which there is a gap between ideas, beliefs, attitudes and behaviour. But in liberal democratic states policymakers must be cautious about the rapid and determined pursuit of policy goals that are out of kilter with what significant numbers or groups of people think or want.

Policymakers rarely consider all the elements of behaviour and attitudes in the round. As the previous chapter indicated, attention often focuses on a particular policy goal that is unrelated to the issue of combining paid and unpaid work per se, but which – as in the case of raising employment rates – is intimately connected to it. Thus work–family balance policies are often instrumental. In any case, academic understandings of the causes of the changes in labour market and fertility behaviour, and of the relationships between these and policies in terms of both cause and effect, are hotly contested. This chapter only begins to indicate how behavioural and attitudinal contexts are important for understanding the issue of the conflicting demands emanating from those different contexts, and for the potential role of work and family policies.

PAID WORK

The increase in women's (and particularly mothers') employment in the post-war period has been large. During the 1950s in many Western countries the status of mother and paid worker was separate for a majority of women; the male breadwinner model was perhaps at its strongest in most countries during this decade. During the 1960s and 1970s, more mothers worked, but often part-time or sequentially (following a substantial period out of the workforce in order to care for children). In the EU, only the Nordic countries have a long history of high levels of female employment; Finland had already exceeded the EU's 60 per cent target for women's employment in the mid-1960s and, with Sweden, had more women in paid work at that time than Italy, Spain and Greece do today. Furthermore, the time at which women entered the labour market in significant numbers matters. This had happened in the Nordic countries before welfare state spending came under pressure, and therefore at a time when expenditure on policies like childcare and care leaves was much more likely to occur. The expansion of female employment in a country like Spain in the 1990s was much more likely to be characterised by precarious employment that is also likely to be more intensive (Burchell et al., 2007), and took place with little by way of state policy supports.

Almost all other member states have seen an (often substantial) increase in women's employment since 1970. The Netherlands has shown a particularly striking 35 percentage point increase, although, as we shall see, the majority of women work rather short part-time hours. Indeed, few countries have a long history of full-time employment for women; Portugal, Finland and France are notable exceptions. From the 1980s, women's labour force participation has become more continuous, even among mothers with preschool children. Indeed, from the 1990s economic conditions made it much more costly to interrupt employment because of the effect on human capital (Boeri et al., 2005). But in many Western European countries the mothers of young children in particular are likely to work part-time. In the UK, the Netherlands and Germany, particularly large proportions of all adult women work part-time. However, the meaning of part-time work in terms of the number of hours worked and the conditions of employment varies considerably.

There are many reasons for the increase in women's employment. Classical economic theory predicted that increasing male wages and affluence would strengthen the male breadwinner model family, but the relationship between incomes and prices made women's contribution to the household economy more and more necessary, especially in relation to rising housing costs (Goldin, 2006). In addition, greater possibilities for consumption have resulted in the supply of more paid labour; in Schor's (1991) view the desire to consume has driven the long-hours culture in the US. On the demand side, the advent of a predominantly service economy has opened up many more opportunities to draw women into jobs in both the public and the private sectors. While women are very likely to work in public sector service industries in the Scandinavian countries, in the US similar jobs are much more likely to be located in the private sector, with concomitant implications for conditions of employment. In addition, there are social and cultural reasons for the greater financial contributions that women now make to households. Technological change in the form of the birth control pill has made it possible to control the timing of reproduction in relation to career. As the average age at first marriage has increased (from 23.1 for women in 1961 to 29.7 in 2006 in the UK; *Population*

Trends, 2008), so the majority of women have an established identity as a worker before they have children. A majority of women in full-time work are likely to report a financial need to do so, but they are also likely to say that if financial need were to be removed they would still choose to work. This is hardly surprising given their steadily increasing level of educational achievement.

However, the position of lone mothers is more variable. Young, never-married mothers, who are more numerous in the UK than in other Western European countries, are more likely to be poorly educated, with little by way of career prospects and low employment rates. As Phoenix (1991) pointed out many years ago, for these women having a child rather than getting a job is often the way to make the transition to adulthood. In the case of older lone mothers, Lehmann and Wirtz (2004), using 2001 data from the European Community Household Panel Survey, show that the proportions of those aged 25–49 in paid work (including part-timers and the self-employed) were above the average for all women of that age in the EU15. The lowest employment rates for lone mothers in this age group were found in the Netherlands (53 per cent) and in Belgium, Germany and the UK (58–60 per cent). Lone mothers' employment rates also tend to be higher than those for partnered mothers (Saraceno, et al., 2005; OECD, 2007), particularly in Southern Europe, where there is little by way of social assistance safety nets and where lone mothers are 'pushed' into the labour market, but also in many Western European countries, which reflects the fact that lone mothers cannot count on the social insurance protection that is available to women in couple families by virtue of their dependence on a male breadwinner husband, for example in Germany (Daly, 2000). The UK and the US used to be exceptional in having very much lower employment rates for lone mothers than for partnered mothers, but since the mid-1990s welfare-to-work policies have narrowed the gap. Only in Ireland and the Netherlands in the EU15 do lone mothers still have substantially (more than 10 percentage points) lower employment rates. In the Scandinavian countries, where employment rates for lone mothers have been high for longer, it is tempting to make a link with the way in which social policies make it easier for all mothers to earn and care.

Table 2.1 looks at the position of men and women in the labour market over the last decade. It shows men's employment rates rising slightly in most countries since 1994, and more substantially (more than 5 percentage points) in Finland, Ireland and Spain. Women's employment has risen everywhere, with large increases of around ten percentage points in Belgium, Finland, Greece, Italy and the Netherlands, and double that in Ireland and Spain. By 2006, eight countries had achieved the EU's Lisbon target of 60 per cent female employment. Women's employment is particularly low in Italy, and the average female employment rate for the EU15 remains well below that in the US.

In addition, part-time work (defined in Table 2.1 as under 30 hours a week) is much higher in EU15 member states than in the US. It is very important in the Netherlands (above all), but also in Germany, the UK, Ireland and Belgium, where over a third of employed women worked part-time in 2006, with Austria and Italy close behind. The proportion of employed women working part-time has increased in eight countries and substantially so (more than seven percentage points) in Austria, Germany, Ireland, Italy and Spain. Nevertheless in Spain, as in Italy and Greece, the tendency is still for women either to work full-time or be out of the labour market altogether. In some countries part-time employment has fallen, notably so in Sweden, and perceptibly in the UK. In addition, there are differences between countries in the extent to which women without children or with grown-up children are also likely to engage in part-time work – in other words, the extent to which part-time work is the norm for women in the labour market. Anxo et al.'s (2007) survey of working time in European companies suggests that this seems to be the case in Denmark, Germany, Ireland, the Netherlands, Sweden and the UK, but less so in Austria, Belgium, France, Italy and Luxembourg.

The full-time equivalent (FTE) employment rates in columns (g) and (h) of Table 2.1 indicate the relative importance of women's employment: for example, the figure for the Netherlands, which has a high employment rate but also a high rate of part-time work, is lower than that for Greece, which has the second-lowest female employment rate. In addition, FTEs show the extent of the gender employment gap, which is bigger when women's employment rates are lower (or men's rates higher) and/or women's part-time employment is higher. Since the mid-1990s, the extent to which women are doing less paid work than men has declined in all countries except Sweden, where lone mothers' employment rates in particular have failed to recover since the economic recession of the early 1990s (Skevik, 2006). However, in FTEs, the gender employment gap (in columns j and k) has long been much lower in the Nordic countries than elsewhere, and is at its highest in the Netherlands, Ireland, Greece, Luxembourg, Italy and Spain. With under a fifth of women working part-time, the gender employment gap measured in FTEs in the US is below that in the EU15.

Thus the trajectory for women's employment is generally upwards. There have been hiccoughs: for example it fell particularly sharply in Finland during the economic recession of the early 1990s and has still not quite regained its mid-1980s level of 70 per cent. Indeed, patterns are hard to predict. In the Nordic countries, which have had high levels of female employment for a long time, more women now work full-time,

Table 2.1 Employment rates for men and women and gender employment gap, 1994, 2000 and 2006* (% of men/women aged 15–64 years)

	Men's employment		Women's employment						Gender employment gap	
	All		All		Part-time		FTE		FTE	
	(a) 1994	(b) 2006	(c) 1994	(d) 2006	(e) 1994	(f) 2006	(g) 2000	(h) 2006	(j) 2000	(k) 2006
Austria	77.5	76.9	58.8	63.5	26.2†	31.4	51.0	49.9	25.2	22.7
Belgium	66.5	67.0	44.8	53.6	30.0	34.7	44.2	45.2	27.8	21.7
Denmark	77.6	80.6	67.1	73.2	26.2	25.6	62.2	62.5	14.8	13.6
Finland	61.1	70.5	58.7	67.3	11.5	14.9	60.5	62.9	8.8	6.6
France	66.1	67.5	50.8	57.1	24.5	22.9	48.7	50.7	20.4	16.0
Germany	74.0	72.9	54.7	61.5	28.0	39.2	46.1	46.5	25.0	22.9
Greece	72.2	74.6	37.1	47.5	13.1	12.9	40.5	45.4	31.4	29.3
Ireland	64.8	77.3	38.9	58.8	25.5	34.9	45.1	47.1	30.9	27.9
Italy	67.8	70.5	35.4	46.3	20.6	29.4	36.7	41.4	30.3	28.5
Luxembourg	74.9	73.3‡	44.9	53.7‡	25.7	27.2	44.6	46.1	31.3	27.4
Netherlands	74.9	78.7	52.6	66.0	54.5	59.7	40.5	42.9	34.2	29.4
Portugal	73.5	73.9	55.0	62.0	15.2	13.2	57.3	59.1	19.3	14.9
Spain	63.3	77.3	31.5	54.0	14.3	21.4	37.5	46.8	33.0	27.8
Sweden	72.2	76.8	70.7	72.1	24.9	19.0	60.2	61.0	9.8	11.4
UK	75.3	78.4	62.1	66.8	41.2	38.8	49.7	51.7	24.5	21.3
EU15	70.5	73.5	49.4	58.5	28.3	31.7	45.4	48.2	25.7	22.6
USA	79.0	78.1	65.2	66.1	20.4	17.8	n.a.	n.a.	n.a	n.a.

Notes: * Because almost all countries have revised their series since 1994, comparisons over time and between countries are not directly comparable. In this table, 'part-time' employment refers to persons who usually work less than 30 hours per week in their main job. Columns (e) and (f) show the percentage of women who work PT as percentage of all employed and self-employed women in the OECD sample who declare their usual hours of work. FTE = Full-time equivalent: i.e. total hours worked divided by the average annual number of hours worked in full-time jobs in each country, calculated as a proportion of total female population in the 15–64 age group. The FTE employment gap is the difference in employment rates measured in full-time equivalent between men and women in percentage points.
†2003 figure. Using a different definition, part-time employment of women in Austria is reported to have risen from 28 per cent of total female employment in 1997 to 40 per cent in 2004 (www.eiro.eurofound.ie/2006/10/articles/at0610049l.html, accessed 16 January 2007).
‡2005 figure.

Sources: Columns (a)–(f): OECD (2007), *Employment Outlook: Statistical Annex*, Paris: OECD Tables **B** and **E**; columns (g)–(k): European Commission (2007), *Indicators for Monitoring the Employment Guidelines including Indicators for Additional Employment Analysis*, European compendium, Brussels: DG Employment, Social Affairs and Equal Opportunities Tables 17.A1 and 17.A2.

but the Finnish recovery since the early 1990s seems to have been partly based on part-time jobs. Among the countries with historically high rates of women's part-time work, the Netherlands and Germany – but not the UK – are continuing to increase this form of employment. The pattern of development in Southern Europe is also difficult to interpret. The expansion of female employment in Spain and Italy has been based significantly on part-time work, but this is not the case in Greece and Portugal. Part-time work is often in human services and tends to be sexually segregated and low-paid: in the UK, occupational segregation has been shown to be key because workers in highly segregated occupations suffer a wage penalty irrespective of the hours they work (Manning and Petrongolo, 2005).

Women's employment rates vary considerably by education level and age (Table 2.2), although there are more similarities between countries. In all countries, more highly educated women have jobs than do those with less education. Moreover, for women with tertiary education, employment rates vary rather little between countries – from 75.3 per cent in Italy to 86.7 per cent in Sweden (among 25–64-year-olds). These Organisation for Economic Co-operation and Development (OECD) figures suggest that EU15 employment levels of the most educated women are above those in the US and not far behind those of men. The range is somewhat wider at a lower overall employment rate for those with secondary education, with the exception of Greece, where the rate is particularly low. Among those in the lowest educational category (equivalent to less than upper secondary school education) women's employment rates range from well under 40 per cent in Belgium and Italy to over 55 per cent in Portugal and Sweden, but the EU15 figure (46.2 per cent) is still above that for the US. The differentiating effects of education on women's propensity to work can be intensified by the presence of children. There is continuing evidence that women with tertiary education and children are even more likely to have jobs than lower-educated women with no children (Franco and Winquist, 2002; Aliaga, 2005).

As for age, Table 2.2 shows that women's employment has grown substantially in the age range most likely to have dependent children (25–54), and that here the EU15 has virtually caught up with the US. However, the employment of older women has tended to grow as fast or faster still, except in Greece. In contrast, the employment of younger women in the EU15 has actually fallen in some countries (most notably in Austria, Germany and Luxembourg). While some of this fall may be attributable to increases in women's education levels, EU15 women's employment lags behind that of the US in this and the older age group. The employment rate for young men in particular in the EU15 also lags well behind that for the US.

The employment rate of mothers varies hugely between countries; Table 2.3 shows that for mothers aged 20–49 with children under 12, it is 80 per cent in Denmark, and 50 per cent in Italy. This table shows that the presence of children continues to be an important factor associated with women's exit from employment in many countries (but note that the figures in this table are affected by differences between countries in how they classify people taking maternity and parental leave). In all EU15 countries except Denmark, mothers are less likely to be employed than women without children. The difference between the employment rates for mothers and non-mothers is particularly striking in Germany, Luxembourg and the UK, and exceptionally low in the Nordic countries, Portugal and Greece. The presence of even one child has a marked effect on employment rates in the UK and Germany above all. In households with two or more children under 12, women's employment was lower everywhere except Denmark, but in most EU countries, the steepest decline in mothers' employment rates occurs with the third child; the decrease is particularly striking (20 percentage points or more) in Belgium, France and the UK. In contrast, the presence of children results in a rise in fathers' employment rates in all countries. The employment impact of children is far less variable for men than for women, although it tends to be rather higher in Southern European countries and in France and Finland (OECD, 2007).

There is also a relationship between mothers' employment rates and the ages of their children. In Finland, where homecare leave (with job protection) lasts until a child reaches three, the employment rate of mothers when the youngest child was under three is the lowest at 52 per cent, but rises to 81 per cent when the youngest child was aged 3–5 (OECD, 2007), thus showing that long care leaves do not necessarily result in long-term female labour market exit (see Chapter 3). Employment rates among mothers of very young children are also particularly low in Germany. As children get older, mothers' employment rates tend to rise, especially in the UK and the US.

While part-time work for women increases in most countries with the arrival of children, Table 2.3 shows that it is recognisably *the* way of reconciling work and family in the UK, the Netherlands, Germany and Austria. Part-time work also remains important for mothers in Sweden (which is not available in this data set), albeit with longer hours (see Table 2.4).

As Torres et al. (2007) have noted in their analysis of 2003/04 data from the First European Quality of Life Survey, the presence of children results in very different patterns of labour force attachment for partnered mothers. Mothers tend to work 'continuously' in Denmark, Sweden and Portugal, and – at a somewhat lower level – in France and Belgium also. In the other Southern European countries, mothers either leave the labour market or

Table 2.2 Women's employment levels by education and age*

Women's employment to population ratios, %	By education level, 2005, women aged 25–64			By age, 1994 and 2006					
	Lower	Middle	Higher	15–24		25–54		55–64	
				1994	2006	1994	2006	1994	2006
Austria	46.9	67.7	81.8	56.2	49.9	68.9	77.0	18.0	26.3
Belgium	35.7	65.5	80.6	25.3	23.0	59.7	70.8	12.4	22.7
Denmark	51.2	75.1	84.3	59.1	64.5	75.2	81.7	40.2	53.5
Finland	53.6	71.5	82.4	28.5	41.4	73.5	79.7	32.1	54.3
France	50.7	68.6	78.3	18.8	21.6	66.7	73.4	28.1	37.8
Germany	44.7	65.2	78.1	48.6	41.3	65.3	72.7	24.5	40.6
Greece	38.1	53.6	76.2	20.6	18.8	48.1	60.6	22.4	26.7
Ireland	39.6	64.9	82.0	30.6	44.0	46.5	68.1	19.7	40.0
Italy	32.4	63.4	75.3	21.8	20.1	46.3	59.3	13.7	21.9
Luxembourg	48.7	59.0	78.1	41.8	21.3†	53.5	68.4†	13.2	24.9†
Netherlands	47.1	71.5	82.7	55.0	62.7	59.4	75.1	17.5	37.1
Portugal	62.9	76.5	86.3	35.7	31.6	69.0	75.3	33.4	42.8
Spain	39.1	63.6	77.5	21.8‡	37.7‡	39.0	63.7	17.5	28.7
Sweden	56.7	77.8	86.7	42.7	44.6	81.1	81.5	59.3	67.1
UK	45.2	74.1	86.0	56.9‡	56.5‡	69.3	74.9	38.5	49.0
EU15	46.2	67.9	81.1	35.2	37.1	60.3	70.2	24.9	37.2
USA	43.4	66.5	77.7	55.3‡	52.3‡	71.5	72.5	47.0	56.5

Women's employment to population ratios, %	By education level, 2005, women aged 25–64			By age, 1994 and 2006					
	Lower	Middle	Higher	15–24		25–54		55–64	
				1994	2006	1994	2006	1994	2006

Men's employment to population ratios (comparable figures)

	Lower	Middle	Higher	1994	2006	1994	2006	1994	2006
EU15	70.1	82.9	87.9	42.6	43.2	85.0	86.9	47.9	54.4
US	69.6	79.3	87.8	61.0	56.2	87.2	87.3	62.6	67.5

Notes:
* Definitions and methodology: Lower education level = 'less than upper secondary'; Middle = 'upper secondary'; Higher = 'tertiary'. Figures are not directly comparable. Definitions of education levels are not fully comparable between countries, and almost all countries have revised their series since 1994.
† 2005 figures.
‡ Aged 16–24.

Source: OECD (2007), *Employment Outlook: Statistical Annex*, Paris: OECD Tables C and D.

Table 2.3 Women's employment rates with and without children, 2003* (Ratio of employed women aged 20–49 without/with child(ren) under 12 to all women of that age (%))

	Without child(ren)	With child(ren)	1 child	2 children	>3 children	PT working (% of all women)	
						No child	With child(ren)
Austria	83	72	78	66	57	16.8	32.3
Belgium	75	68	70	69	49	21.8	27.2
Denmark	77	80	80	82	67	[]	[]
Finland	78	72	75	74	56	10.2	7.8
France	77	66	73	64	40	14.1	17.6
Germany	80	60	66	55	38	21.3	35.1
Greece	57	53	54	53	40	4.9	6.7
Italy	60	50	53	46	35	12.3	15.2
Luxembourg	75	59	69	53	[35]	15.5	26.1
Netherlands	82	70	72	70	59	33.0	54.7
Portugal	77	76	78	75	60	7.7	7.2
Spain	62	51	54	48	41	8.7	9.7
UK	83	62	68	61	38	18.5	36.2
EU25	75	60	65	58	41	15.2	22.7

Notes:
* Data for Ireland and Sweden not available. Part-time is defined as under 30 hours. The part-time working figures refer to part-time women and mothers as a percentage of all women aged 20–49 in each country, including unemployed and inactive (for PT as a percentage of employed women, see Table 2.1).
Brackets [ ] indicate small sample sizes, in the Danish case, too small to be reliable.

Source: Eurostat (2005). 'Reconciling Work and Family Life in the EU25 in 2003' *News Release* 49/2005, pp. 2–3. Luxembourg: Eurostat.

work full-time, resulting in rather low employment rates. In Germany, Ireland and the Netherlands, and to some extent in the UK, women drop their working hours sharply with the arrival of children and continue to work part-time hours (a diminishing trend in the UK) as their children get older. However in Finland, mothers leave the labour force while their children are under three, but then return to full-time work. Furthermore, as Chapter 3 will make clearer, there is no easy fit between these patterns of participation during women's adult working lives and policy packages to promote work–family balance. For example, while there are extensive state supports for working mothers in Sweden and Denmark, there are very few in Portugal, which nonetheless has a long history of full-time continuous work for women. Historical traditions regarding the opportunity for, and prevalence of, full- or part-time employment for women are important: they are key to the differences between Finland and its Nordic neighbours, for example.

Indeed, the terms and conditions of employment vary enormously between countries, and variation in working hours is a particularly import-ant dimension. The 2005 European Working Conditions Survey reported the volume of hours worked to be the main determinant of 'work–life balance' (Parent-Thirion et al., 2007; Burchell et al., 2007). OECD data for 2006 show that all women working full-time in the EU15 work on average two hours a week less than all full-time men, with Austrian and UK male and female full-time workers putting in the longest average hours. Among all women working part-time, Eurostat figures for 2006 show the part-time average for women in Germany, the UK and the Netherlands to be between 18 and 20 hours, between 20 and 21 hours for Austria and Denmark, 23 hours in Belgium and France, and 27 hours in Sweden.

Table 2.4 uses European Social Survey (ESS) data (which has much smaller sample sizes than OECD or Eurostat data) for mothers with chil-dren under seven and under 16, and shows that there are wide variations in the working hours that mothers report. It also shows the proportions of mothers and fathers with children under 16 working long (more than 46) hours per week. The long hours worked by over a third of Greek mothers and 13–19 per cent of Spanish and Portuguese mothers provide additional evidence for a Southern European long-hours culture. Self-employment is also high among women in Greece and Portugal above all (accounting for just over 20 per cent of all women workers), and somewhat less so in Italy and Spain. Self-employed workers tend to work longer hours (Eurofound, 2006). Taken together with the relative lack of opportunity for part-time work, a long-hours culture may help explain the lower female employment rates that characterise most of these countries.

At least a third of fathers in the ESS sample report working more than 46 hours in Austria, Belgium, Germany, Greece, Britain, Ireland and Spain:

Table 2.4 *Working hours (mothers) and parents' long-hours working, 2004–05* (%)*

Hours 'normally' worked, including overtime	Partnered mothers								Long-hours working (>46 hours)	
	With children aged 0–15				With children aged 0–6				Mothers	Fathers
	0	1–19	20–34	>35	0	1–19	20–34	>35	>46	>46
Austria	25.7	10.9	31.2	32.2	32.1	6.5	27.5	34.0	9.0	34.0
Belgium	22.4	9.3	31.7	36.6	22.6	8.8	31.4	37.3	9.9	33.2
Denmark	8.0	3.2	24.1	64.7	6.9	3.0	25.7	64.4	11.1	25.3
Finland	13.7	1.4	12.8	72.0	21.1	1.8	14.9	62.3	9.3	29.9
France	17.1	5.9	22.7	54.3	14.4	2.5	24.7	58.3	9.7	28.9
Germany	33.0	18.4	25.0	23.5	38.0	24.9	17.0	20.1	4.7	35.1
Great Britain	30.8	20.9	25.8	22.5	31.0	25.4	20.2	23.4	10.3	43.5
Greece	46.7	2.5	9.4	41.4	50.4	3.3	8.9	37.4	33.2	33.1
Ireland	39.4	11.8	22.3	26.5	34.0	12.2	22.6	31.2	4.9	42.1
Netherlands	21.1	33.3	34.1	11.5	21.9	28.8	38.5	10.8	1.9	27.7
Portugal	33.8	6.5	3.5	56.3	29.6	9.5	5.0	55.9	18.9	30.4
Spain	38.0	4.2	12.3	45.5	37.9	3.9	11.7	46.6	12.6	43.4
Sweden	9.4	2.4	25.8	62.4	12.8	0.9	26.6	59.6	8.3	24.1
Total	27.8	12.8	22.6	36.8	29.2	14.4	20.0	36.5	9.3	35.7
	N = 3002				N = 1624					

Notes:
* Data from ESS. The hours breakdown allocates mothers in paid work in 2003–05, many of whom are likely to be on formal or informal maternity or parental leave, according to the hours they most recently worked.

Long-hours figures are a percentage of working mothers and fathers with children aged 0–15.

'Mothers' and 'fathers' = partnered women and men with children 0–15 in same household.

Source: Lewis et al. (2008), Table 3.

more than 40 per cent in the last three countries. These self-reported figures must be treated with caution. Looking at all full-time working men, the 2005 European Working Conditions Survey found that only in Greece did a very large proportion of men work over 48 hours; in Britain, Ireland and Spain the figure was over 20 per cent, and in Germany 15 per cent (Burchell et al., 2007). It is well established that fathers are likely to be working the longest hours, but on this issue as with so many relating to workplace behaviour, there is wide disagreement between surveys. In Austria, Greece, Britain and Spain the long hours worked by fathers reflects a long-hours labour market culture for all men aged 30–50 (and particularly for employees in Britain, where there are relatively low proportions of self-employed). Even in the Nordic countries, around a quarter of fathers appear to work long hours. In the Netherlands, the proportion of fathers working long hours, although high by the standards of Dutch men in general, is low by EU15 standards. Indeed, Gornick and Heron (2006) showed that, on average, US dual-earner married and cohabiting parents work 16 hours more per week than Dutch parents. Nickell (2006) has calculated that Americans also work over 14 per cent more weeks per year than the French and Germans, but only 8 per cent more hours per week, suggesting that in these cases the longer hours worked in the US are accounted for mostly by shorter annual holiday entitlements.

The break-down of part-time hours for mothers in Table 2.4 shows important differences between countries. Many more Dutch mothers work under 19 hours than do those in Germany and Britain, though considerably fewer leave the labour market altogether. Even in these countries where a significant proportion of mothers of young children work part-time, a majority work over 20 hours. Indeed, this is now more true of the UK than was once the case (and is reflected in the FTE figures in Table 2.1). Table 2.4 also illustrates differences between Nordic countries for mothers with children under seven. In Finland, many more mothers stay at home for long periods when children are small than in Denmark or Sweden.

These figures raise the issue of the quality and security of part-time work. If part-timers are not treated on the same basis as full-timers, then mothers' use of part-time work as a way of reconciling paid work with childcare implies gender inequalities which may have long-term consequences: for pension entitlements, for example. The EU's 1997 Directive on part-time workers, jointly formulated by employers' and trades unions' representatives using the process laid down in the 1992 Maastricht Treaty's Social Chapter, set out minimum standards of equality in relation to full-timers that member states were required to transpose into their national legislation. However, the Directive permits considerable latitude in the details (Kilpatrick and Freedland, 2004) and implementation may be variable.

Moreover, as Anxo et al. (2007: 2) comment: 'part-time work can be either a response to employees' demands . . . or a means for companies to increase flexibility, sometimes to the detriment of employees'.

In the Netherlands, there seems to be a longstanding predisposition for shorter working hours on the part of both men and women (Visser, 2002); nearly half of all jobs are part-time, three-quarters of women's jobs and nearly a quarter of men's, but these jobs are more secure and of much higher quality than in the UK especially (CEC, 2006; Vlasblom and Schippers, 2006). Anxo et al. (2007) found that among the countries with significant proportions of part-time work, negative perceptions about career prospects were highest among part-time mothers in Britain (nearly 50 per cent) and Germany (48 per cent), and lowest in Finland (2 per cent), Denmark (13 per cent) and Belgium (16 per cent). The gender pay gap for part-timers is particularly large in the UK: at 38 per cent compared to 17 per cent for full-time workers, which is also the highest in the EU (Plantenga and Remery, 2005; Grimshaw and Rubery 2007; see also Manning and Petrongolo, 2005, 2008). Short-hour part-time work has also been deliberately expanded in Germany, as part of the effort to increase labour market participation, with the creation of nearly 7 million 'mini-jobs' by 2006, 70 per cent of which have been taken by women. These jobs involve short part-time hours, low pay, and are not eligible for social protection (Anxo et al., 2007).

There is evidence that part-time employment is voluntary in the Netherlands, and in Denmark and Sweden, where part-time hours are much longer and where mothers who are working part-time are likely to be exercising their legal entitlement to do so while their children are small. But it is more difficult to know how far those working in the German 'mini-jobs', for example, are doing so voluntarily. In the UK, the unavailability and/or unaffordability of childcare may constrain the 'choice' of mothers to work part-time. Similarly, working atypical hours may be a positive choice, for example in the UK, where such hours are particularly common (see Chapter 3, Table 3.5). Parents may wish to work shift patterns in order to maximise the amount of time they can care for their children. On the other hand, they may again see this as the only way to manage, given the high cost of formal childcare in the UK (see Chapter 5). Then again, such flexibility may be entirely employer-led – rather than employee-led – with employees being increasingly required to vary their work patterns, especially in more deregulated labour markets and in a country like the UK where trade unions are relatively weak (Rubery et al., 2005).

Relatively unprotected short-hour, part-time work is only one dimension of insecurity. In Southern Europe, the expansion of female employment has been recent and has thus taken place under entirely different macroeconomic conditions from the expansion in the Scandinavian countries, which began in the 1970s, when welfare policies of all kinds were still expanding. In Spain in 2006, about a third of the workforce as a whole was on fixed-term contracts (Eurofound, 2007), including almost a quarter of women workers; furthermore, the available attitudinal data suggests that these are not desired (Flaquer, 2000; Petrongolo, 2004). The use of short-term contracts has also grown sharply in France, where it is estimated that 60 per cent of the new salaried jobs created since 1983 are 'precarious' either in terms of being part-time or short-term contracts. In short, the pay and conditions attaching to working hours, together with patterns of flexible working, vary enormously between countries, particularly in respect of part-time hours, but also other forms of 'atypical work'. This matters for gender equality, because it is women who have always tended to deviate more from the notion of a 'standard (male) career path'. But if non-standard work is genuinely voluntary it may not be a policy issue. Nevertheless, it is difficult to understand why such large numbers of Dutch, UK and German women would 'choose' much shorter working hours than women in other EU15 countries, all other things being equal. Historical patterns and cultural understandings doubtless play a major part in explaining differences, but so might the incentives and disincentives to different types of arrangements provided by state policies and at the level of the firm.

Women's more marginal position in the labour market, together with their lower pay, means that they are not able to exercise the economic autonomy that is increasingly assumed to exist by policymakers. Sigle-Rushton and Waldfogel's (2006) analysis of Luxembourg Income Study data show that the cumulative earnings (to age 45) of the mothers of one or two children, born when the mothers were in their late twenties, are lowest relative to non-mothers for German, Dutch and UK women, and lowest relative to those of men in Germany and the Netherlands. Gornick and Meyers (2009) have shown that while in Denmark and Sweden married and cohabiting mothers take home on average 34–38 per cent of families' earnings, this figure drops to 28 per cent in the US and 18–19 per cent in Germany and the Netherlands. Indeed, there is a 'family penalty' attaching to employment, which matters much more in some countries than in others. In the UK, pay is 39 per cent lower for mothers compared with childless women born in 1958 (Joshi, 2002), and the penalty is particularly high for low- and medium-skilled women (Harkness and Waldfogel, 2003; Davies et al., 2000). Some of this has to do with the conditions of part-time working in the UK. In the Scandinavian countries the family penalty is negligible.

Even this limited exploration of the patterns and characteristics of women's employment shows how complicated they are,[1] and how they have seemingly little to do with kinds of work and welfare regime types that have usually formed the basis for analysis since Esping-Andersen (1990) presented his classification of the three worlds of social democratic (Scandinavian), corporatist (Western European) and liberal (English-speaking) welfare (see also Daly, 2002a). For example, in the Nordic countries, which are often lumped together, Finnish mothers of very young children are much more likely to be at home, making use of the long homecare leave that exists in that country, although, as Table 2.1 shows, on an FTE basis women's employment is as high in Finland as in Denmark or Sweden. Indeed, Finland and Portugal are the two countries with the strongest traditions of female full-time employment. From this we begin to get a sense that the incentives and disincentives to work and/or care offered by different sorts of policies may be important, but then again, countries like the US and Portugal have long achieved high rates of female full-time employment with a small fraction of Scandinavia's state-supported care services. Indeed, labour market factors, for example the availability of part-time work or the size of the gender pay gap, are likely to be as or more important in many countries as state work–family balance policies.

CHILDBEARING

Low fertility rates have become a larger issue at the EU level since 2005, but are a major policy issue only in some member states. Why this is so becomes clear from Table 2.5 which shows fertility rates in the EU15 and the US, none of which reach the level necessary for replacement. In the English-speaking countries, the Nordic countries, and French- and Dutch-speaking Western Europe, fertility rates are between 1.7 and 2; in Southern Europe and in the German-speaking countries they are at 1.4 or below. Again, these patterns do not map onto Esping-Andersen's three worlds of welfare capitalism. There is remarkably little by way of comparable cross-national data showing which groups of the population are having more or fewer children. Fertility rates now tend to be higher in countries where women's educational achievements and employment rates, and also extra-marital birth rates, are higher. However, the better-off, who are usually also the better-educated, tend not to be having as many children (Fahey and Speder, 2004). Low fertility and differential fertility rates (between social classes, ethnicities and regions) have sparked considerable debate in some Western European countries, particularly in Germany, where 36 per cent of all women aged 41–44 are childless. In the UK, it is clear that if government succeeds in its goal of reducing the relatively high number of births to young, unmarried, teenage women the fertility rate would drop

Table 2.5   Fertility rates, 1980–2005*

	Total Fertility Rate (children per woman)			Total Fertility Rate
	1980	2003	2004	2000–2005
Austria	1.65	1.38	1.42	1.39
Belgium	1.68	1.64	1.64	1.66
Denmark	1.55	1.76	1.78	1.75
Finland	1.63	1.76	1.80	1.72
France	1.95	1.89	1.90	1.87
Germany	1.56	1.34	1.37	1.32
Greece	2.21	1.28	1.29	1.25
Ireland	3.25	1.98	1.99	1.94
Italy	1.64	1.28	1.33	1.28
Luxembourg	1.49	1.63	1.70	1.73
Netherlands	1.60	1.75	1.73	1.72
Portugal	2.18	1.44	1.42	1.47
Spain	2.20	1.30	1.32	1.27
Sweden	1.68	1.71	1.75	1.64
UK	1.90	1.71	1.74	1.66
EU25	1.88	1.48	1.50	n.a.
USA	1.80	2.07	2.07	2.04

Note: *Some figures are provisional or estimates.

Sources: Cols 1–3: Kyi (2005), Table 3; col. 4: UN Social Indicators (2005) *Indicators on Child-bearing*. New York: UN. (http://unstats.un.org/UNSD/Demographic/products/socind/childbr.htm, accessed 7 March, 2008).

closer to the EU15 average (Coleman and Chandola, 1999), although the increasing proportion of births to non-UK-born mothers accounted for a rise in the birth rate in 2007, a matter that received considerable press attention.

Between 1970 and 1980, fertility rates in OECD countries declined for both younger and older women; between 1980 and 1990, the fertility rates of these two groups of women moved in different directions in most countries, with the rate for older women increasing; and between 1990 and 2000 the two rates kept moving in opposite directions in most countries, but at a slower pace (d'Addio and d'Ercole, 2005). This suggests that the postponement of partnership formation and childbirth, which may well be related to the longer time women spend in education and their greater commitment to employment, are key factors in low fertility. The fertility rates for the period 1990–2000 seem to indicate that there has been some recuperation, but given that the higher number of children women are having when older does not fully compensate for the fewer children they have when young, low levels of fertility are unlikely to be a temporary phenomenon. The postponement of childbirth is likely to affect finished family size, and increases the probability of more one-child and childless families.

The causes of low fertility are a matter for intensive debate and are remarkably difficult to unravel: there are no easy, straightforward or undisputed answers. Given that labour market and fertility decisions are often made together, it is difficult to explain one by the other (Meulders and Gustafsson, 2004). Nevertheless particular characteristics of labour markets may be important. While high female employment does not seem to be associated any longer with low fertility, there is the possibility that careers for women, as opposed to 'jobs', increase labour market attachment and may result in postponed childbearing. Increased earnings may also adversely affect fertility (for example Ahn and Mira, 2002; d'Addio and d'Ercole, 2005; see also Blossfeld, 1995). And, as Table 2.3 shows, the presence of children does affect employment rates.

On the basis of comparative data, Gustafsson and Kalwij (2006) have concluded that work–family reconciliation policies matter for fertility: while motherhood is now postponed in all EU member states, the size of the effect differs between the countries and is associated with the development of such policies. Fagnani (2007) has also concluded that, above all, the availability of affordable, high-quality childcare and the statutory regulation of care leaves and flexible working patterns have had a positive impact on fertility. Similarly, Olah's (2003) comparison of second births in Hungary and Sweden – countries of similar size and both with overwhelmingly dual-earner families – shows that 'policies matter'. It is interesting that in Sweden, with its long history of reconciliation policies, women with relatively high levels of education do not appear to be having significantly fewer children than the average. However, Björklund's (2006) analysis of the completed fertility of Swedish women born between 1925 and 1958 finds that the negative relationship between women's educational level and fertility did persist, despite the fact that work–family policies were developed in that country from the late 1960s.

Lower fertility among better-off and better-educated women in many countries suggests that the cost of children is not the main issue, but material insecurities may still play a part. Insecure employment may be particularly important. The fertility rate in Sweden dropped at the beginning of the 1990s, when the sharp economic downturn and rising unemployment may have made women too nervous to leave the labour market to have children (especially given that generous parental leaves and benefits depend on the mother having been in full-time work for almost a year), or may possibly have made women more inclined to invest in education than in children (McDonald, 2002; see also Neyer, 2006). However, Finnish women reacted to a more precipitous economic downturn in the opposite way. Short-term contracts (see above p. 27) may have a similar effect on the fertility behaviour of Southern European women, because they create uncertainty among young people about their future income (Adserà, 2004; de la Rica and Iza, 2006). Bovenberg (2005) has argued that employment stability can be achieved by either flexibility and deregulated labour markets on the US model, with little security beyond ease of entry and exit for the worker, or by institutionalising leaves from the labour market with the guaranteed right of return, as in Finland. But a 'middle way' of 'flexicurity' advocated by the European Commission (CEC, 2006) with the goal of achieving both labour market flexibility and a measure of security for workers – and put into practice most rigorously in Denmark and the Netherlands – may be another way of securing higher fertility rates. The birth of children increasingly represents a risk for their parents, particularly their mothers, which suggests that their opportunity costs should be redistributed (Folbre, 1994). So, while women's employment per se may not be a problem for fertility, the terms and conditions of that employment do matter, including the allowances that are made for combining paid with unpaid work.

However, social and cultural factors are also important: for example, high cultural expectations for intensive parenting, or the nature of peer and kin pressure for more or fewer children. The way in which people estimate the 'value of children' is complicated: Bernardi (2003) has noted that opposite choices can be made with reference to the same dominant value of parenthood. Thus valuing motherhood or parenthood may not be enough to result in the birth of children if, say, mothers and fathers feel that they cannot invest materially and emotionally to the extent that is expected in their community, or if they believe that childrearing demands too great a sacrifice. Young German women now have an ideal family size of 1.7 and young German men of only 1.3, which may be due to raised expectations of parenting, but also to the importance attached to self-realization, or to increasing acceptance of the new low-fertility norm, in which case the ideal may fall lower in Germany and in other Member States. Lutz (2006, 2007) has pointed out that the German-speaking countries were the first to see fertility fall to very low levels in the 1970s and are now the first to show below-replacement ideals of family size among younger people, which may signal a further fall in birth rates in the future. He attributes this to the tendency of young Germans to be both more consumerist and more pessimistic. If this is so, it may be that it is as much the lack of motivation to have children as the barriers to doing so that are important in some countries (Klein and Eckhard, 2007). Yet in Southern Europe, where fertility is lowest, ideal family size remains more than two children (Goldstein et al., 2004; Fahey and Speder, 2004; d'Addio and d'Ercole, 2005). High rates of youth unemployment and the tendency to leave home later (at an average age of 29 in the case of Italian men) may be particularly significant. But unemployment is also high among young people in France, where fertility remains high in European terms.

The household context is probably crucial for understanding the nature of decision-making in respect of fertility. Social theorists have drawn attention to the difficulty of combining two careers with child-rearing; there is a disjuncture between increasing individualisation and family-building (Beck and Beck-Gernsheim, 1995). In Northern and Western European countries, a domestic division of labour built on full-time work for both men and women in the household is likely to characterise cohabitation and marriage prior to childbearing. The arrival of children forces established patterns to be re-evaluated and may be perceived as risky, by women especially, in terms of the effects on career and a period of greater economic dependence on men in the context of high separation and divorce rates (Lewis, 2005). This is particularly likely to be the case in countries where the responsibility for managing career and family have historically been private and usually assumed by mothers. 'Gender systems' (Pfau-Effinger, 1998; Oppenheim Mason, 2001), defined in terms of the beliefs, norms, common practices and sanctions that shape notions of the rights and obligations of men and women, vary considerably even within Western Europe. It is reasonable to propose that the gap between actual and desired family size reflects to some degree both the perceptions and the reality of opportunity costs for mothers in terms of time-use and career advancement. Securing women's employment prospects matters for them as individuals and has become a precondition for family formation now that households need two incomes.

Historically, explicit pro-natalist policies providing incentives to parents to have more children, most crudely by rewarding mothers with especially large families, have had little effect on fertility (Gauthier, 1996). However, removing obstacles to higher fertility has been shown to have some success: thus Bradshaw and Mayhew (2006) have shown that fertility is lowest in countries with the least generous child benefit packages, even though motivation seems to be a more important factor than removing barriers in the German case. D'Addio and d'Ercole (2005) suggest that total fertility rates are higher in countries with wider childcare availability and lower direct costs of children, and also where there is higher availability of part-time work for women and longer childcare leaves. Chesnais (1996) and McDonald (2000, 2002) have argued that governments need to accommodate all dimensions of family change: as Sleebos (2003) has argued, there is no one magic policy bullet for raising fertility. But where women are able both to have children and to continue to be attached to the labour market – by making use of cash benefits in respect of children and work and family balance policies in the form of leaves, childcare services and flexible working patterns – fertility rates are higher (see also Meulders and Gustafsson, 2004). For as McDonald (2000, 2002) has argued, if women have educational and employment opportunities similar to those of men and then find that these are curtailed by children, they may well opt not to have children.

This argument suggests that both gender equality and state intervention are important in relation to fertility. Bonoli's (2008) examination of the reasons for differing fertility rates in the Swiss Cantons, which set their own family policy, has shown that the provision of childcare services and, to some extent, family benefits are important explanatory variables. Nevertheless, in the US, women's fertility and labour market participation rates are high, with little intervention to 'reconcile' work and family on the part of the state and no universal child benefits, although legislation to secure equal opportunities in the labour market tends to be stronger than in European countries. Market provision of cheap childcare, often using migrant labour, is also part of the answer in the US, and more emphasis has been placed in the American literature on the need for change at the level of the firm (Rapoport et al., 2002). But in the EU context, state intervention via family policies and the regulation of the labour market has been historically important as part of the established context within which fertility decisions are made. As we shall see (in Chapter 3) the nature of state intervention takes many different forms, and given that gender attitudes, the domestic division of labour, and the nature of the labour market are also crucial, concentration on any single policy is unlikely to be successful.

THE HOUSEHOLD LEVEL

Patterns of Paid Work: An Adult Worker Model?

The Eurostat couple data analysed by Franco and Winquist (2002) and Aliaga (2005), and ESS data (Lewis et al., 2008) permit the construction of households with and without children according to whether each of the adults works part-time or full-time. Franco and Winquist's data from the European Labour Force Survey for the year 2000 show that the majority of families with children in a third of Western European countries outside Scandinavia still relied on a single earner, and only in a third were both adults usually working full-time, even among couples without children. Comparison of Eurostat figures for 2000 with those for 2003 (Aliaga, 2005), and with the ESS data for 2004 (Lewis et al., 2008), shows that within four years this situation had changed. In all but three countries (Belgium, Italy, the Netherlands) a majority of couple households without children were dual full-time earners by 2003 (over 70 per cent in Finland, Sweden and the UK). Even in Italy, the proportion of households with children and only one earner had fallen below 50 per cent (and without children to under 40 per cent), although in Greece, Spain and Luxembourg the male breadwinner model still accounted for over 40 per cent of couples with children.

With or without children, therefore, the male breadwinner model family has now been hugely eroded in all EU15 countries. However, the bulk of the change in the 2000s occurred among couples without children and took the form of a shift from male breadwinner couples to dual full-time earning (especially in Austria, Belgium, France, Greece, Italy, Portugal, Spain and the UK). Insofar as these couples are young, this may signal a rapid change for patterns of parental employment in future, particularly in labour markets without a large part-time component. Among couples with children, the outcome of the relative fall in the number of male breadwinner families varies from country to country. The incidence of the male full-time/female part-time model of families with children increased particularly in Austria, Germany and the Netherlands (and remains strong in the UK). The incidence of dual full-time earning by parent-couples increased particularly in Luxembourg and Spain. Table 2.6 uses ESS data to show that in 2003/04 the male FT/female FT model accounted for over 30 per cent of couples with children under 16 in seven countries, and in the Nordic countries, France and Southern Europe this pattern was more common than all forms of male full-time/female part-time work. The male sole-earner model continues to characterize over 30 per cent of households in Germany, Greece, Ireland and Spain.

Does this signal a shift from the one-and-a-half-earner model to a dual, full-time earner model? Caution is needed here. First, the issue is very susceptible to definitions of full-time and part-time work. OECD and Eurostat data use more than 30 hours to define full-time work, while the analysis of ESS data in Table 2.6 uses more than 35 hours. But ten or 15 years ago more than 40 hours might have been deemed a more appropriate definition of 'full-time', which would eliminate from the full-time category a lot of women now counted as full-time. Men's full-time working hours are still longer than women's, and a father working 46 hours and a mother working 35 hours are both classified as full-time in Table 2.6. Second, the one-and-a-half-earner model has not traditionally been characteristic of labour

Table 2.6 *Household structure according to working hours, 2004–05*
(partnered adults with child aged 0–15, %)

	MFT+ FFT*	MFT+F longPT*	MFT+F shortPT*	Male sole earner*	Other*
Austria	21.9	23.4	7.2	27.2	20.4
Belgium	29.3	22.9	8.7	24.7	14.4
Denmark	55.0	22.4	1.4	12.6	8.7
Finland	59.6	8.7	1.6	20.9	9.3
France	44.8	18.3	7.1	18.1	11.8
GB	19.6	22.0	14.2	25.5	18.7
Germany	19.1	17.4	15.6	33.7	14.2
Greece	32.4	6.1	2.8	40.9	17.8
Ireland	22.2	17.5	7.5	35.5	17.3
Netherlands	6.3	27.5	27.7	23.3	15.2
Portugal	50.2	3.2	2.4	27.3	16.9
Spain	37.2	8.9	2.4	38.3	13.3
Sweden	53.8	24.8	1.8	12.2	7.5
Total	30.3	17.7	10.3	27.3	14.5

N = 5412

Notes: * MFT+FFT = both male and female partners normally work for >35 hours per week; MFT+FlongPT = male partner normally works >35 hours and female partner 20–34 hours; MFT+FshortPT = male >35 hours, female 1–19 hours. 'Other' includes female sole earner or main earner (e.g. Austria and Portugal 9 per cent), dual part-time household (e.g. Netherlands 7 per cent), not in paid work (e.g. Greece 5 per cent). This variable was constructed from ESS data on working hours of the main respondent and what she/he said about her/his partner's working hours. It counts the working hours of mothers according to their most recent paid work in 2003–05.

Source: Lewis et al. (2008), Table 4.

markets in Finland, Greece, Italy, Portugal and Spain, but part-time work is growing in Finland, Italy and Spain. There is, in short, large variation among countries. Finally, outside the Nordic countries, between 10 and 20 per cent of households do not fall into any clear category. Nevertheless, the fact that almost a third of households with children in the EU15 now have dual full-time earners, and that this working pattern has grown so fast among couple households who do not (yet) have children, is important. It should also be noted that EU enlargement has taken in many more dual full-time and male breadwinner households (Aliaga, 2005), which means that the one-and-a-half-earner model is currently exceptional in the EU27 (see also Haas et al., 2006).

Broadly speaking, the divisions we see in Table 2.6 are:

- Countries where dual full-time working is more usual than any other arrangement in couple households and represents a clear majority of partnerships with children: Denmark, Finland and Sweden. These countries have few single-earner couple households. (The Baltic countries also fall into this category though with less part-time work Aliaga, 2005.)
- Countries that polarize between dual full-time earning and single-earner families, and where part-time work accounts for only a small proportion of couple households: Spain, Italy (not in the ESS data set), Greece and Portugal, although the last of these has a much higher proportion of dual full-time earner households than the other two. (This pattern also tends to apply across Eastern Europe; Aliaga, 2005; see also Haas et al., 2006.)
- The rest are countries where some form of the one-and-a-half-earner model is more usual than any other: this is distinguished by substantial quantities of female part-time work, but nonetheless consists of a spectrum ranging from close-to-majority dual, full-time (France), to the Netherlands where well over half of households are one-and-a-half earners, and Ireland where male breadwinner families were still the largest single category in 2004 but where there was a substantial proportion of female part-time/male full-time households.

There is a majority of dual full-time earner households only in the Nordic countries and Portugal. But while women in Denmark and Sweden are either working full-time or long part-time hours, in Finland they are either working full-time or not at all because of the widespread use of long homecare leaves on the part of mothers with children under three. At the other extreme, in Southern Europe, Ireland and Germany, there are still relatively high proportions of male breadwinner families. In the Netherlands, there are very few full-time dual-earner households and a high proportion of male full-time and female short part-time households, although men also work relatively short full-time hours compared to the UK (see above, p. 31).

The Domestic Division of Labour

At the household level, patterns of employment and fertility affect the way in which unpaid housework and care work are arranged, although a more equal domestic division of labour, for example in Sweden, may also influence fertility and women's labour market participation. Indeed, influences on the domestic division of labour are complicated, and are also related to ideas about gender-appropriate work, and the nature of bargaining at the household level. The way all these various factors come together for mothers and for fathers differs in respect of childcare and housework, and varies considerably between countries. Nevertheless, it looks as though there are more broad similarities than differences in the gendered divisions of unpaid work across countries.

The issues for men and women seeking to juggle their paid and unpaid contributions to their families revolve around time and money; Daly (1996: 9) has suggested that 'time has become the dominant currency in families' (see also Mutari and Figart, 2001). This is in large part because total working time, paid and unpaid, in dual-earning households has created 'time pressure' (Jacobs and Gerson, 2004). Many surveys report that people, especially mothers, feel more rushed (Folbre and Bittman, 2004). Yet, time-use data show no decline in the amount of leisure time (Gershuny, 2000), and furthermore, many calculations of 'total workload' show a rough equality between men and women in a number of Western European countries. For example total workload appears to be almost equal in Germany, but this is achieved at the expense of one of the most unequal domestic divisions of labour, with men concentrating on paid work and women working short part-time hours and doing most of the unpaid work (Finch, 2006). The gap between the total work of women and of men in households is particularly wide in Southern Europe and in France. Furthermore, the European Working Conditions Survey suggests that on the whole women have a significantly longer paid and unpaid working week than men, whether they work part- or full-time (Parent-Thirion et al., 2007).

But working hours alone, whether paid or unpaid, are not the end of the story. Recent data that include answers to questions about 'secondary activities' show women's workload to be higher than men's (Sayer, 2007; Bryson, 2007). For example, women are much more likely to be combining childcare with leisure activities than are men. In addition, Southerton and Tomlinson (2005), using UK data, have shown the extent to which time pressure represents multiple experiences of time. These encompass not just the number of things to be done, but also the problem of coordinating the way tasks are tackled with others in the household who may be working different shifts, for example, and juggling different tasks or, in the end, multi-tasking. Studies of the domestic division of labour have long shown that mothers in particular tend to assume more of the responsibility for coordinating and allocating tasks (for example Pleck, 1997).

Table 2.6 shows the different household arrangements regarding paid work among couples, which are the basis for understanding the nature of the divisions of unpaid work. Generally speaking, women have reduced their hours of unpaid housework, while increasing the amount of paid work they do. Men now do slightly more unpaid work, particularly in respect of childcare, which nevertheless continues to impact much more heavily on women than on men, and more so than elder care (CEC, 2007c: 13).[2] Men's paid work hours have decreased over time. However, this is due mainly to young men spending longer in education and older men taking early retirement; fathers tend to work the longest hours. These comments refer to couple families. But as Furstenberg (1988) pointed out in the late 1980s for the US, while there is some evidence of greater 'father involvement' in two-parent families, there are also far more 'absent fathers' who have very little involvement with their children.

Gershuny (2000) has suggested that there are signs of convergence between men and women over time, although change on the part of men is slow – amounting to 'lagged adaptation'. There has been continuous, albeit slow, change on the part of men in respect of doing more domestic labour (Sullivan, 2006), so we might expect men to continue to increase their unpaid contribution if women continue to increase their paid working hours. But in couple families, women have increased their hours of employment much more rapidly than men have increased their contributions to unpaid work, and as Bianchi and Caspar (2004) have pointed out for the US, mothers may not be able to increase their paid work any further unless fathers do more (see also Stier and Lewin-Epstein, 2007). Dual-earner households tend to be able to rely more on buying in household and childcare services, especially where both partners work full-time, although Bianchi et al. (2006) report that in order 'to make time', mothers have reduced the time they spend on housework, on volunteering, time spent with friends, relatives and husbands, and their free time. Fathers have reduced the time they spend on personal care. Mothers feel more rushed and do more multi-tasking than fathers

In Europe, state policies to provide parental leave, for example, may make it possible for mothers to remain in the labour force and care for young children, but may also give fathers little incentive to do more unpaid work (Windebank, 2001; Hook, 2006; Stier and Lewin-Epstein, 2007; and see Chapter 3). Gendered inequalities in paid and unpaid work certainly remain. Baldock and Hadlow's (2004) cross-national European study found, as in the US, that mothers report feeling more rushed. Furthermore, it is likely that the preservation of their free time reduces men's perceptions of feeling rushed compared to those of women (Mattingly and Sayer, 2006).

Men in couples do more housework and routine childcare when they are employed fewer hours and mothers more hours; when they are more highly educated; when mothers earn more; and when mothers are employed full-time and have been employed for longer (Coltrane, 2008). UK data also show the burden of housework to be more evenly split where women earn as much or more than their partners (Harkness, 2003). According to Torres et al.'s (2007) analysis of the 2003–04 data from the European Quality of Life and Eurobarometer surveys, exceptionally low amounts of unpaid work seem to be done by working fathers in Portugal – although Stier and Lewin-Epstein's (2007) findings from the International Social Survey Programme (ISSP) data, which control for age, education and presence of children, cast some doubt on this result. Austria, followed by France and Germany, were also low, with a significant amount of unpaid work being performed by working fathers in Italy and Spain. In France, commentators are agreed that fathers combine few unpaid hours with relatively low hours of paid work: a 2005 survey showed that in couples with one child under 14, housework was done almost entirely by mothers in France. Fathers who did unpaid work were more likely to contribute to childcare (Letablier, 2007).

Table 2.7 shows comparable time-use statistics collected by Eurostat for all employed men and women and for those with a youngest child aged 0–6 and 7–17. Employed men do more paid work and have more leisure in all countries. Working women do around twice as much domestic work as men in all countries except Sweden (where they do significantly less than this) and Italy and Spain (where they do much more). Working women with children aged 0–6 spend the longest time on childcare in Sweden, the UK and Finland, and men in Sweden and Finland. While the time spent on childcare by men and women falls sharply when the youngest child is aged 7–17, the last section (D) of Table 2.7 shows that domestic work excluding childcare actually increases. This is important, not least because state policies have historically done little to address reconciliation policies for families with children in this age group, and do not in any case attempt to address the issue of housework.

While academic studies report different amounts of paid and unpaid work by men and women, they tend to agree that there are increased feelings of time pressure, especially among mothers. These might more accurately be termed 'care pressure', certainly in the case of households with preschool children (Ellingsaeter and Leira, 2006), in which both men and women seem willing to reduce and/or 'contract out' housework, but where attitudes towards who should be responsible for the care of children are far from clear-cut. There is evidence that both mothers and fathers have increased the amount of time they spend on childcare in spite of longer paid work hours. The gendered division of labour at the household level remains unequal in all countries; UK data have shown that when a

Table 2.7 Time use of employed men and women, 1998–2003* (minutes per day)

	Women			Men		
	Employment	Domestic work	Free time†	Employment	Domestic work	Free time†
A. All working men and women						
Belgium	228	232	231	298	135	263
Finland	247	201	278	324	119	306
France	270	220	188	342	113	231
Germany	213	191	289	294	112	311
Italy	275	231	197	370	70	246
Spain	285	209	214	363	80	260
Sweden	235	212	267	310	143	291
UK	234	208	261	333	114	281
	Employment	Domestic work	Of which: childcare	Employment	Domestic work	Of which: childcare
B. Dual-earner couples, youngest child 0–6						
Belgium	212	293	100	304	174	50
Finland	218	308	122	348	162	61
France	227	288	101	329	142	37
Germany	138	314	104	298	171	57
Sweden	162	321	128	311	199	67
UK	197	320	128	356	156	58

Table 2.7 (continued)

	Women			Men		
	Emplymt	Dom. wk	Of which: childcare	Emplymt	Dom. wk	Of which: childcare
C. Dual-earner couples, youngest child 7–17						
Belgium	192	270	29	303	139	16
Finland	258	224	17	333	129	9
France	252	253	25	345	122	9
Germany	196	248	26	318	121	14
Sweden	256	236	38	322	152	25
UK	231	242	23	345	131	12

D. Time spent by man+woman on paid and unpaid work according to household situation, minutes per day

	Singles no ch.		Couple no ch.		Couple youngest ch. 0–6			Couple youngest ch. 7–17		
	Emp.	Dom.	Emp.	Dom.	Emp.	Dom.‡	Childcare	Emp.	Dom.‡	Childcare
Belgium	551	276	540	328	516	317	150	495	364	45
Finland	525	227	588	290	566	287	183	591	327	26
France	651	229	627	321	556	292	138	597	341	34
Germany	516	198	514	309	436	324	161	514	329	40
Sweden	561	247	559	309	473	325	195	578	325	63
UK	557	195	578	320	553	290	186	576	338	35

56

Notes:
* Diary data: Italy and Spain 2002–03; other countries between 1998 and 2002. Figures show averages for each category over seven days.
† Includes small amounts of 'unspecified', but excludes commuting and personal care (i.e. sleep, hygiene etc).
‡ 'Domestic work', which includes childcare in sections B and C of this table, here excludes childcare, which is shown separately.

Source: Eurostat (2006). *Comparable Time Use Statistics: Hetus Pocketbook*. Luxembourg: Office for Official Publications of the European Communities.
Country files at http://forum.europa.eu.int/Public/irc/dsis/tus/library?1=/comparable_statistics&vm=detailed&sb=Title.

man and a woman have equivalent pay, the same social class and working hours, women still do more unpaid work (Bond and Sales, 2001).

But, again, it is not clear whether, how or to what extent this is a policy issue. First, the domestic division of labour is a difficult issue for policy to address: are men to be 'forced' to do more unpaid work? Or should it be more a question of addressing women's position in the labour market and of securing greater equality and autonomy, which may in turn have an impact on the gendered division of unpaid work? After all, as we have seen, many studies have shown that the more a woman earns, the more domestic work the man is likely to do. Breen and Prince Cooke (2005) have used game theory to suggest that the proportion of autonomous women has to increase before men will increase their share of unpaid work, and before 'hardline men' will change the nature of their unpaid work contributions rather than seek separation and divorce, although the basis of such negotiations at the household level are likely to be rather more complicated than this (Folbre, 2008: 38). Gershuny's (2000) picture of slow convergence in men's and women's paid and unpaid work patterns might suggest that efforts to shorten men's working hours would speed up change, but Folbre and Bittman (2004) have questioned the validity of the idea of lagged adaptation and thus whether shortening men's working hours would in fact result in them doing more domestic labour as opposed to, say, more leisure activities. Certainly in France, where legislation was passed in 1998 limiting working hours for men and women to a 35-hour week (albeit that this maximum could be calculated over the whole year, permitting longer working hours during some periods), there has been little evidence of men doing more unpaid work (Crompton and Lyonette, 2006); the 35-hour legislation was abandoned in the summer of 2008.

Second, gender inequalities in the domestic division of labour must in any case be perceived as inefficient or unjust to warrant intervention. As Thompson and Walker (1989) noted in the late 1980s, such inequalities may be consistent with people's ideas about 'doing gender', and Hochschild (1989) has elaborated the complicated ways in which women seek to justify inequalities and to preserve their marital bargains (see also Major, 1993). It cannot be assumed (as do Breen and Prince Cooke, 2005) that all men and women seek to avoid unpaid work; some men, particularly in Northern European countries, are increasingly claiming the right to care (Gavanas, 2002; Burgess, 2007). If the division of domestic labour is perceived as just, or if the partners appreciate each other's efforts in this regard, relationship satisfaction is likely to be higher, which in turn has implications for the degree of conflict over work–family balance (Maximiliens and Schneewind, 2006).

However, recent studies have found that work–family balance conflict is often related to the kind of arrangements that couples make regarding their domestic division of labour and to gender ideology. Using ISSP data, Crompton and Lyonette (2006) have reported that a traditional division of labour is associated with higher levels of reported conflict between work and family responsibilities in full-time dual-earner families. Thus in France, where women are more likely to work full-time than in many Western European countries, but where men do less by way of domestic work, full-time employees report high levels of work–family conflict. Yet, using original data, Strandh and Nordenmark (2006) found that, paradoxically, work–family conflict was higher among women in Sweden, where fathers tend to do more by way of unpaid work, than in Hungary and the Czech Republic. They attributed this to the high expectations that Swedes have for achieving gender equality in relation to the domestic division of labour. Gender equality has long been a part of the social justice agenda in Sweden, as it has at the EU level. But elsewhere it may be easier for governments to meet their employment goals by addressing the reconciliation needs of women alone.

ATTITUDES AND PREFERENCES

Evidence of changing attitudes towards paid and unpaid work and of conflict or dissatisfaction on the part of men and/or women in respect of work–family balance may be important signals for policymakers that at least some people want change, while also underlining the point that the interests of different groups in the population may differ. This makes policymaking in the field of work and family tricky. Psychologists (for example, Alwin, 2005) suggest that attitudes reflect beliefs, relate to specific situations, and are general evaluations of an action. They are held to be good predictors of intentions, which in turn predict behaviour. Preferences are linked to values, a particular type of belief, and are therefore generally thought to be more stable and, Hakim (2000) has argued, better predictors of behaviour than are attitudes. However, Brooks and Manza's (1999) study of the influence of mass opinion on social policy suggested that policy preferences are embedded above all in social structure, institutions and collective memory. Crompton (2006) has argued that neither attitudes nor preferences are the major determining factor in respect of mothers' employment; type of job and cost of childcare are likely to be more significant. For example, mothers in professional and managerial jobs are much less likely to identify themselves as home-centred. People may well 'adjust' their attitudes to their institutional situations (Uunk et al., 2005), although a preference in the abstract – about childcare for example – may also be rather different from that expressed when a child actually needs care and childcare institutions are visited (Schwartz, 2004). Van Peer (2002) and Fagnani (2007) have further suggested that highly educated women in particular adapt their desired family size over the life cycle as the realities of pursuing a career become evident.

Attitudinal data are very difficult to interpret on many counts. The same people may express seemingly contradictory attitudes, and similar questions asked by different surveys often elicit very different results. Deeper understanding can be achieved only by a more refined analysis of the data (Ostner and Schmitt, 2007). For example, younger women tend to have less negative attitudes towards the employment of mothers (d'Addio and d'Ercole, 2005). Such a shift has been particularly pronounced in the case of Norwegian women (Korpi, 2000), who used to be far more traditional than other Scandinavian women on the matter of women staying at home to care for young children (Leira, 1992) than is now the case. In the UK, attitudes towards women's paid employment have shown a greater degree of change among older age groups (even though they remain more conservative than younger women), making it more likely that behavioural change will endure (Crompton et al., 2003).

As Table 2.8 shows, responses to the ESS questions directly relating to mothers' employment tended to vary much more between countries than between men and women in each country. Over 50 per cent of mothers with a child 0–15 in Portugal, Spain, Germany, Britain and Ireland, but fewer than 25 per cent in the three Nordic countries, agreed or strongly agreed that 'a woman should be prepared to cut down on paid work for the sake of her family'. The countries where the subset of mothers with young children was noticeably (around 5 or more percentage points) more likely to agree with the statement than the whole sample of mothers with children under 15 were Austria, Finland and Germany, while in France and Portugal somewhat fewer mothers with young children agreed. The difference in attitudes among Finnish mothers with younger children fits with the sharp rise in employment rates there when children reach the age of three (see above, p. 60). Further analysis[3] suggested agreement or strong agreement with this statement by 46 per cent of mothers in the ESS sample who report only an earning role, 53 per cent of mothers who say they combine earning with housework, and 66 per cent of the few in the sample who were non-earners.

Proportionately, the second set of responses in Table 2.8 show even more intercountry variation than the first. Very few parents in the Nordic countries agree or strongly agree that 'men should have more right to a job than women when jobs are scarce'. Countries where the highest proportions of mothers with children 0–15 agree (or strongly agree) are Greece (40.5 per cent), Portugal (35.3 per cent) and Spain (30.3 per cent). Interestingly,

when children are under seven, it seems from these data that lower proportions of both parents (but more consistently mothers) in several countries
(particularly Britain) think that men should have more right to a job than
women when jobs are scarce. As against the 21.3 per cent average figure
for all mothers with children under 16 agreeing or strongly agreeing with
this statement, the comparable figures for the subsets of: (1) mothers who
identify themselves only as earners; (2) mothers who report earning and
doing housework; and (3) 'housework-only' mothers, were 16.5 per cent,
20.3 per cent and 45.0 per cent respectively. So, even among mothers who
do not earn, only a minority think that men should have more right to a
job when jobs are scarce.

Thus, in countries where women's and mothers' employment has been
the norm for decades, the attitudinal data in the ESS survey suggest much
more egalitarian views on male and female paid work in the context of
child-rearing, whereas in Southern Europe more mothers express the gendered attitudes usually associated with a traditional family model. Wall's
(2007) analysis of the 2002 International Social Survey Programme data
has stressed that while attachment to the male breadwinner model has
eroded, it has done so in different ways in different countries. She found a
wide range of attitudes regarding the kind of contributions men and women
should make to households. In particular, significant minorities of respondents favoured what she termed a 'modern moderate motherhood' model,
with support for both stay-at-home and part-time working mothers; and a
'modern unequal caring model', with support for mothers' paid work, but
not for the sharing of unpaid work. D'Addio and D'Ercole's (2005) data
extracted from the World Values Survey suggest continuing ambivalence
about working mothers' relationships with their young children, particularly in Italy, Portugal, Germany and the UK. Across countries, the labour
market behaviour of mothers is related to their attitudes, with those who
are not earning and who have less by way of educational achievements
more likely to accord priority to men in breadwinning and to women in
caring (Crompton, 2006), albeit that this is a minority view.

There is evidence of change in attitudes over time towards women's
paid work in particular. Men's attitudes towards the contributions that
they should make are relatively rarely reported, but are almost certainly
subject to less change, as might be expected given the rather slow change
they report in their use of time. Thus Warin et al. (1999) reported that UK
fathers still tend to identify as breadwinners first and foremost, and therefore to think that the most important responsibility of fathers is to earn.
In the Netherlands, Visser (2002) has argued that Dutch women changed
their views on the desirability of part-time work during the 1980s, and that
the Dutch one-and-a-half-earner model family is very much a bottom-up

*Table 2.8 Attitudes of mothers and fathers on work–care prioritisation, 2004**

% that agree or strongly agree:

	'A woman should be prepared to cut down on paid work for the sake of her family'				'Men should have more right to a job than women when jobs are scarce'			
	Mothers: child(ren) aged 0–15	Fathers: child(ren) aged 0–15	Mothers: youngest child 0–6	Fathers: youngest child 0–6	Mothers: child(ren) aged 0–15	Fathers: child(ren) aged 0–15	Mothers: youngest child 0–6	Fathers: youngest child 0–6
Austria	48.3	51.4	55.8	59.5	18.0	28.2	16.5	30.1
Belgium	42.3	31.6	41.6	33.0	24.6	23.3	21.6	21.5
Denmark	18.1	13.0	16.8	14.1	4.8	2.4	3.0	3.3
Finland	23.7	22.0	28.1	20.4	6.7	7.1	7.9	8.8
France	49.2	47.1	44.1	38.6	22.7	24.6	19.8	15.2
GB	52.1	44.0	50.1	49.0	16.9	13.7	9.9	13.4
Germany	57.9	56.1	61.9	62.1	19.1	18.8	12.0	20.8
Greece	44.0	48.3	46.3	50.8	40.5	53.9	41.1	58.0
Ireland	50.7	36.4	52.3	34.2	22.2	16.2	20.9	16.3
Netherlands	32.1	30.6	34.6	26.8	14.2	12.5	11.7	8.7
Portugal	74.5	66.9	71.3	66.8	35.3	35.5	42.1	41.9
Spain	58.2	51.5	61.2	53.7	30.3	25.9	27.8	28.0
Sweden	14.1	13.5	14.7	16.9	4.3	2.9	3.7	3.9
All	50.5	46.1	51.0	47.4	21.3	20.4	17.5	19.4
No. observations:	3035	2500	1636	1360	3034	2503	1638	1361

Notes:
* Answers given by partnered mothers and fathers from over 5500 different households to questions G6–G10 in European Social Survey, 2004 edition.
I am grateful to Dr Carmen Huerta for the calculations.

Source: European Social Survey, Round 2. http://ess.nsd.uib.no

creation. Nevertheless, the precise nature of the relationship between attitudes and behaviour remains contested, although this is not the main issue here. Rather, it is to emphasise that the problems for policymakers centre on the gaps between what people think ought to be the case, what they say they want and what actually is, in relation to what kind of behavioural changes policymakers want to see.

The importance of preferences has become more controversial in the debate over work and family balance and whether there is a role for state intervention. Hakim's (2000) argument has centred on the idea that women in affluent, modern societies are now in a position to make real choices about work and care based on their values. She argues that the availability of contraception, the existence of equal opportunities legislation, the expansion of white-collar jobs, the creation of jobs for secondary earners and the increasing importance attached to attitudes, values and preferences mean that women can exercise control and make choices. In this conceptualisation, behaviour results from choice, and is thus also construed as being what women want. If this is indeed so, then there is very little for policymakers legitimately to do beyond respecting, and perhaps further enabling, the kind of behaviour that exists. Using the answers to questions about which ideal family model corresponds most with respondents' ideas about the family, Hakim identified a home-oriented group of women, a work-oriented group and a large (60 per cent) group of 'adapters', who tend to hold complex and contradictory attitudes about paid and unpaid work, shaped by external events. But there are many problems with this classification: for example, the mother who works short part-time hours may well identify as home-centred, but is not necessarily less committed to her job. Indeed, using ISSP data, Luck and Hofäcker (2003) found that work and family orientations were not mutually exclusive.

People do have choices within systems, but how much? As we shall see in the next chapter, the nature and extent of choices has become central to policy rhetoric. All manner of constraints may affect how far attitudes and preferences influence work and childcare choices; Nussbaum (2000) rejected an approach based on the importance of preferences because it fails to take into account the extent to which people act out of habit, fear, low expectations and unjust background conditions. People often do not do what they intend to do because they are constrained by a lack of resources and opportunities; indeed Liska (1984) concluded that in everyday life, behaviour is more dependent on resources than motivation. Social provision can supplement an individual's resources. Thus Kangas and Rostgaard's (2007) comparison of the Nordic countries with Germany, the Netherlands and the UK has indicated that longer and better-paid parental leave and affordable, good-quality childcare both make it more likely that women will work full-time. Yet, mothers in Portugal tend to work full-time despite the lack of formal childcare, because of high economic need and low per capita income (Crompton and Lyonette, 2006a). Certainly, mothers who are not financially constrained will have a larger choice set and may be in a better position to realise their preferences. As McRae (2003) has pointed out, women may have similar attitudes and orientations but different capacities for overcoming constraints. It may also be difficult to express a preference for something known to be not readily available, or which runs counter to social norms and existing provision. Thus, mothers in the UK, who have a long experience of formal childcare services as being expensive, often not very accessible and often not of very good quality, may be more likely to express a preference to care for their children at home. In the case of Italy, low fertility and low female labour market participation are located within a strong family-oriented value system, and there is evidence that responsibility for providing family-based care has inhibited fertility: more than three-quarters of disabled elderly people get family help and it is common for children not to leave home until their late twenties (Simoni and Trifilleti, 2005). In addition, family care, which has reduced the demand for female labour and inhibits the supply of formal services, makes larger families a less attractive prospect (Bettio and Villa, 1998; Del Boca, 2000; Bettio and Plantenga, 2004). There is thus a structural vicious circle that is hard to break.

Indeed, it seems likely that preferences are usually compromises between what is desirable and what is feasible, and may therefore change depending on circumstances (Naegele, 2003). Women with preschool children may experience constraints in terms of their choices around work and care in terms of their need for money, for childcare, and how they feel about their identity as a worker and a carer. It is not that values are unimportant, far from it. But it is unlikely that preferences are as stable as Hakim's work suggests, certainly among women, whose circumstances and identities often change massively over the life-course as a result of motherhood in a way that men's do not. Akerloff and Kranton (2000) have suggested that identity is fundamental to behaviour and may change over time, and Crompton and Harris (1998) identified no fewer than six orientations to combining paid work and mothering: 'domestic', 'satisficer' (whereby paid and unpaid work is combined without maximising either), 'maximiser' (of paid or unpaid work), 'careerist by choice', 'careerist by necessity' and 'undecided'. Women in their sample made transitions over the life-course between these. As we have already seen (see Chapter 1) Himmelweit (2005) has made a convincing argument that there is an iterative relationship between attitudes and behaviour, and also that while policies can only affect behaviour directly, this will have an affect on attitudes and have a multiplier effect, thus helping to change both.

Recent studies have sought to establish what people want in regard to working hours and number of children. National-level studies in the UK (Dex, 2003) and the US (Jacobs and Gerson, 2004) have shown considerable dissatisfaction with the number of paid hours worked. A large survey conducted by the European Foundation for the Improvement of Working and Living Conditions (Eurofound) in EU15 and Norway sought to quantify the number of hours that women and men preferred to work, taking into account the need to earn a living (Atkinson, 2000; Bielenski et al., 2002; see also OECD, 2001). It concluded that the EU's strategy of bringing employment rates in Europe up to the US level was consistent with people's preferences, but that since most employees also wanted shorter working hours, 'the preference in Europe is for a combination of high labour market participation rates and short individual working times rather than the American combination of high employment rates and long working times' (Bielenski et al., 2002: Foreword). Already by 1998 employees were questioning the distinction between full-time and part-time work, with 'growing interest in a reformed or variable full-time norm located in the range of what actually constitutes "short" full-time and "long" part-time employment – that is, around 30 hours' for women and 35 hours for men (Bielenski et al., 2002: Chapter 4). It is interesting that these survey data reporting what kind of hours people would like to work show less difference than might be expected between men and women, although there remains considerable variation between countries. Drawing also on more recent data, Eurofound (2006) has concluded that most men and women would like to avoid the extremes of marginal part-time work (under 20 hours) and long (over 45) hours of work.

There are also gaps between actual and preferred arrangements between men and women at the household level (for the actual arrangements, see Tables 2.6 and 2.7). At the end of the 1990s in the EU15, while 35 per cent of households (defined as couples with at least one partner in work) were male breadwinner model families, only 15 per cent reported wanting this arrangement. The greatest degree of fit was achieved by couples who both worked full-time: 33 per cent of households reported doing this and 32 per cent preferred this arrangement. Twenty-five per cent of households were in a one-and-a-half breadwinner model family and 32 per cent preferred this (Bosch and Wagner, 1998; see also Jaumotte, 2003).

As for fertility, an attitudinal study based on Eurobarometer data concluded that there was a degree of mismatch between people's aspirations and what they achieve (Fahey and Speder, 2004). In the vast majority of Western EU member states, younger (under 35), middle-aged and older (55+) women wanted between two and three children, with only Austrian and German women preferring fewer than two. Younger men all had rather lower ideals of family size, falling below two in Austria, Germany and Belgium, with the highest aspirations (2.2 or 2.3 children) being expressed by respondents in Ireland, the Scandinavian and Southern European countries. The mismatch between ideal and reality was particularly pronounced for men (somewhat less so for women) in Southern Europe. Van Peer (2002) has concluded that higher educational attainment among women has more effect on actual reproductive behaviour than on preferences, with better-educated women scaling down the number of children they want over the life-course.

THE IMPLICATIONS FOR POLICY

The issue for policymakers is not so much the precise nature of the relationship between attitudes and preferences on the one hand, and behaviour on the other. While there is increased concern about making policy 'evidence-based', the nature of causality is in any case a matter of huge debate. Rather, the issue is: first, the extent to which there is a gap between attitudes and preferences and behaviour; and second, whether attitudes and preferences are in tune with policy goals. In respect of fertility, there is some evidence that people in the vast majority of countries would like to be able to have a family that would ensure population replacement, although the preferences for very small families expressed in Germany and Austria may suggest that preferences are catching up with behaviour (Fahey and Speder, 2004; Dey, 2006; Lutz, 2006, 2007). Recent EU-level documents have commented on the need to enable people 'to have the number of children they desire' (CEC, 2005, 2006b, 2007c). Respect for private choices regarding intimate relationships and childbearing has been conspicuously absent in large tracts of Western Europe within living memory, but is crucial for liberal, democratic states and the European Commission's choice of wording in this regard is important. In any case, specific and often rather crude pro-natalist policies – for example, rewarding women for having a large number of children – have been shown to be ineffectual. Ideal family size does seem to be higher than what is achieved and thus in line with policy goals, but if it is indeed the better-off who have the highest gap between ideal and achieved fertility, any policy intervention to help this group would be regressive (Fahey and Speder, 2004).

While comparable cross-national data on fertility behaviour and attitudes are relatively scarce, much more is known about labour markets and the differences in behaviour, attitudes and preferences for women and men, particularly in terms of working hours. There is argument about how far there is a gap between behaviour and what people, especially women, would like to see happen. Hakim (2000) argues that observed behaviour reveals preferences. But both sides of the debate provide evidence to suggest that attitudes and preferences may not be as in tune with employment-led social policies as they seem to be in respect of fertility policy, whether because of Hakim's view as to the existence of a significant minority of home-oriented women, or her critics' insistence on variation in women's behaviour over the life-course in accordance with circumstances.

What matters for policy is what policymakers prioritise, how they frame the issue, and whether and how they pay attention to the different dimensions of behaviour, attitudes and preferences. Paid work, unpaid work and fertility issues are related to each other, but in very complicated ways that are poorly understood. Nevertheless, many contributors to the academic literature and the wider debate have a particular view about the direction for policy. Thus, Hakim argues that policy is currently determined by the needs and wants of career-oriented women and therefore suits what her analysis suggests is a minority group. At the most, all that is needed for this group of women in this formulation is information, so that the women who want to work can make informed choices. If policymakers are interested in the issue of fertility, then they should give greater attention to those women who are home-centred and more likely to want larger families.

However, if there are structural causes of, for example, low fertility and low female employment, as has been strongly argued in the case of Italy, then there may be a clearer role for the state, although where to try to break the circle of normative expectations regarding family care and low demand for female labour is difficult. The OECD (2007) has stressed the importance of policies that provide 'a continuum of support', rather than fertility-specific policies, citing work and family policies in the Nordic countries as a successful example. However, the Italian government has tended to see family change as a problem to be addressed by strengthening family values (Saraceno, 2002), which runs counter to academic analyses (see above, pp. 65). Policies to reconcile work and care tend to be seen as an answer to problems of fertility and labour market participation. But even if policy can be used effectively in such an instrumentalist fashion, where to put the emphasis is far from obvious: on the terms and conditions of employment, on childcare services or on entitlements to exit the labour market in order to provide care? In any case, much depends on the precise way in which each policy instrument is designed. For example, according to classical economic theory, childcare leaves should raise fertility, but their effect on mothers' employment is more debatable, depending largely on duration and level of compensation (see Chapter 3).

Policies do not bear directly on attitudes. But they can have an impact on social norms (Boeri, 2005; Gallie, 2003), for example, if they assume the achievement of gender equality to be an ideal. In her examination of family policies and fertility in Europe, Neyer (2006) stressed the importance of the symbolic meaning of policies: a lack of childcare provision signals to women that it may be difficult or impossible to combine employment and motherhood. Hook (2006) has argued convincingly (*pace* Gershuny and Sullivan, 2003), that context, particularly in regard to the extent of women's labour force participation, and policies (because they change societal norms) are especially important in determining the domestic division of labour. For example, Brighouse and Olin Wright (forthcoming) have suggested that there will be a 'tipping point' in respect of men taking parental leave: at some point, perhaps when 20 per cent do so, or perhaps 40 per cent, it will become normative behaviour. Himmelweit and Sigala (2004) have also stressed the need for enabling rather than coercive policies if governments are to reap the reward of positive effects on attitudes of policies designed to encourage behavioural change. This has obvious importance in regard to welfare-to-work policies designed to increase employment. These have often tended to the punitive in the US, but in Europe have been more enabling under the banner of 'active labour market policies', above all in Scandinavia, but also in the UK in respect of lone mothers, although recent proposals have sought to tighten work obligations for those with children over seven by 2010 (DWP, 2007), which may risk running counter to popular attitudes about the primacy of the care work provided by these mothers (Duncan and Edwards, 1999). If policies are centred on work and care arrangements and focused on securing 'social quality' (Beck et al., 2001) that enhances the terms and conditions under which an adult worker family model is achieved, then they are more likely to secure a positive feedback loop with behaviour and attitudes of the kind Himmelweit and Sigala (2004) feel that it is possible to secure (see also Himmelweit, 2005). Policies that are merely instrumental and designed to secure greater labour market participation among mothers or higher fertility are less likely to ensure this positive feedback.

The pursuit of gender equality, which is rarely an explicit policy goal in relation to work and family policies, requires policymakers above all to consider issues to do with both employment and care work. There is the tendency to design policies for mothers, but as we have seen, the gendered division of labour in households can be a source of conflict between men and women, and may impede both labour supply and fertility. This raises the issue of whether policies should also be directed towards men as fathers, given that their choices help to structure those of their female partners (Lewis and Giullari, 2005). But the choices that different groups of men and women make will be different and probably relate to values and structures: to the desired and the possible. An enabling policy goal – to maximise the choices of men and women – is the easiest to justify in democratic states in this very complex field, and this requires attention to both sides of the issue: to paid work and unpaid work. Gambles et al. (2006) have argued that this goes beyond the capacity of state policies, and they have prioritised what happens to work cultures at the level of the firm. There is certainly a role for agencies beyond the state, and employers are key, but state policies matter in terms of both their direct effects and indirectly in terms of the influence they exert on social norms and the decision-making environment. Most analysts allow that state policies make a difference, although how much is disputed. But at the most general level, it is always going to be difficult for people, especially women, to negotiate systems in which neo-liberal economic policies effectively penalise childbearing, while conservative family ideas demand sacrifices. The next chapter explores further the nature of the existing policy packages in the work and family balance field in different countries, and the issues arising from the different policy options.

NOTES

1. They would become more so if the data were to be disaggregated by region as well as nation-state and if variables such as ethnicity were to be explored. For example, in the UK, women with Pakistani and Bangladeshi family roots are less likely to have jobs than other British women (Lindley and Dale, 2004).
2. Again, these statistics need to be treated with caution. Three decades of feminist research have repeatedly shown that women do more heavy, personal care for older people than do men.
3. These results are not shown in Table 2.8 because sample sizes for the individual countries were often small.

3. Work–family balance policies: comparisons and issues

There is a range of policy choices that have been made in the field of work and family balance. Governments have focused on promoting flexible working, particularly in terms of the hours worked, and on care issues, by enabling parents to care themselves or by financing and/or providing childcare services. There is also considerable variation as to how much states have elected to do and what has been left to parents or to employers. The detailed provisions of each policy instrument also matter in terms of how far they enable genuine choice on the part of mothers and fathers to engage in paid and unpaid work and what effects they have on men's and women's decisions in this respect. The nature of the policy priorities and policy packages developed in different countries depends in large measure on the policy goals. Gender equality has not figured largely in these outside the Scandinavian countries. Nevertheless, even the existence of work and family balance policies can play an indirect role in legitimising the changes in the balance of paid and unpaid work that men and women aspire to, as well as a direct role in helping them to achieve their goals.

This chapter begins by examining the broad differences between the kind of policy 'logics' that exist in different countries, and the broad nature of the incentives and disincentives for men and women to work and to care. It then explores what the issues of care and care work represent; after all, recent social policies have been largely employment-led. In many countries increasing attention has also been paid to the problem of low fertility rates, and to the welfare and development of children, particularly in those Western European countries where government interest in the work and family field has been substantially stepped up. However, there has been little attempt to take a more 'care-centred' perspective, which directs attention to how care work is rewarded and how it is shared between men and women, and between the state, employers and households, as well as to ways in which the changes to the organisation of paid work can enable unpaid work. The second main part of the chapter looks at the nature of policies on childcare services, care leaves and working hours in turn, the issues arising from them in regard to the pursuit of gender equality, and the welfare trade-offs between men and women, and adults and children.

POLICY LOGICS

Just as governments differ significantly in terms of the nature of the labour market and fertility challenges they face, and the kinds of popular attitudes they must accommodate, so also their policy inheritances are very different. These are remarkably difficult to describe simply. Gøsta Esping-Andersen's (1990) typology of 'three worlds of welfare capitalism' distinguished between the English-speaking, 'liberal' welfare states with their heavy reliance on means-testing and targeting help to the poor; the corporatist, continental 'Bismarckian' models reliant on social insurance with the aim of status-maintenance; and the social democratic (Scandinavian) countries with their more universal approach. It is still used, notwithstanding the rather rapid development of 'hybrids' since the late 1990s, which tend to focus on different kinds of employment-led social policies and approaches to 'flexicurity' (see above, p. 7). Esping-Andersen used social insurance data to measure the extent to which people were permitted to leave the labour market for cause, but if the recent development of tax credits in some countries (particularly the UK), changes in the operation of means-testing, and the extent of service provision – in education, health, housing and social care – were to be included, the conclusions as to the nature of 'worlds of welfare' would be rather different.[1] As we saw in the last chapter, it is also difficult to fit data on women's employment patterns or fertility into Esping-Andersen's typology.

There have been a number of efforts by scholars interested in gender and social policy to develop alternative approaches to classifying or understanding welfare regimes, building on the first two attempts to focus explicitly on gender in relation to 'welfare regimes' (Lewis, 1992; Orloff, 1993), and on early work pointing out that once gender was inserted into Esping-Andersen's 'worlds of welfare', his broad characterisations did not hold, even in the Scandinavian case (Leira, 1992). Some have stressed the importance of culture as well as institutional structures in influencing the assumptions that policymakers make about how adult women in particular should spend their time, and how young children should be cared for (Pfau-Effinger, 1998; Haas, 2005; Kremer, 2007). Others have focused more on outcomes in order to construct new patterns of differentiation between countries: Korpi (2000) followed Orloff's (1993) insistence on the importance of autonomy for gender equality and hence the capacity to form an independent household, and investigated the extent to which policies supported women's continuous paid work or encouraged their unpaid care work. Mutari and Figart (2001) took a rather different approach, following Fraser's (1997) definition of gender equality as equal divisions of paid and unpaid work between men and women – the citizen worker/

carer model – and focused on policies in relation to time, albeit again with a central focus on paid working time.

In fact it is often difficult to avoid what amounts to a normative position in approaching the issue of gender and welfare regimes, and what might constitute gender equality as a policy aim. A present-day American sociologist may have considerable difficulty divorcing herself from the long history of US feminism's emphasis on 'equality-as-sameness' (to men), just as a West German sociologist is likely to be affected by that country's long feminist tradition of 'maternalism' and respect for gender difference (Wikander et al., 1995). Consideration of gender and 'welfare' demands a working definition of gender equality in relation to both paid and unpaid work (as well as many other policy issues lying outside the scope of this book, as various as transport, education, violence). Gender equality has been conceptualised for the purposes of this book as the possibility of making a 'real choice' to engage in paid and/or unpaid work (see above, pp. 18–19). While such a definition raises difficulties in respect of some people's choices having the potential to limit the choices of others – for example, men's choice not to do unpaid work limiting women's choice to do paid work – it does recognise the importance of agency and avoids treating policy simply in terms of prescription.

A rigorous exploration of the incentive and disincentive effects of all dimensions of tax and benefit systems and services affecting paid and unpaid work for men and for women is beyond the scope of this book. This chapter focuses on the three dimensions of work and family balance policies that were specified in Chapter 1: childcare services, leaves to care and flexible working arrangements. But, first, it is useful to outline in broad terms the principles informing the policy logics that have underpinned different approaches to gender, paid and unpaid work in different countries. Only in the US and in some of the Nordic countries have models been based on the assumption that men and women will be fully engaged in the labour market. In Finland a male breadwinner model never took root in a country that made a rapid transition from an agricultural to a service economy, but the Norwegian situation has, until relatively recently, looked more like that of the UK in respect of women's balance of paid and unpaid work.

The US and Nordic work and welfare models operate in very different ways. In the US case, the obligation to enter the labour market is embedded in a residual welfare system that often borders on the punitive, whereas in the Nordic countries, it is supported by an extensive range of cash benefits for children and care entitlements in respect of children and older people. The position of lone mothers – always a border case for the study of social policy (Kiernan et al., 1998) – is particularly instructive in this respect, because as a group these mothers focus the problem of combining unpaid care work and employment. Since 1996, the US has treated these women as citizen workers, mandating work-first policies and imposing time-limited welfare benefits. Employment rates for lone mothers are high in the US; the push factor is strong. But employment rates are higher still in Sweden and Denmark and lone mothers' poverty rates are much lower than in the US, because they also get a significant proportion of their income from state transfers. The Nordic model treats women as workers, but then makes allowance for difference, grafting on transfers and services in respect of care work for partnered and unpartnered mothers alike (Lewis and Aström, 1992).

Thus, the US operates a fiercely gender-neutral, equality-defined-as-sameness adult worker model, with very few state supports for the unpaid work of care, although the overall level of tax allowances and credits is comparable to European levels of family benefits (with the largest proportional benefits going to those with higher taxable incomes), and the market provides good access to affordable (but not necessarily good quality) childcare. But there is no public support for paid family leave from work (Folbre, 2008). Günter Schmid (2000) has referred to this as the reinvention of domestic service, using, as it often does, migrant workers (see also Ehrenreich and Hochschild, 2003). Scandinavia operates what is in practice, but not in name, a gender-differentiated 'supported adult worker model' (Hobson, 2004), with high penetration of services for the care of children and elderly people and cash transfers during parental leave. In Sweden, moderately high proportions of mothers work (long) part-time hours, exercising their right to work a six-hour day when they have preschool children, as well as having the possibility of leaving the labour market for up to three years if they have two children in rapid succession. But the Swedish and Danish labour markets are among the most sexually segregated in the Western world. Swedish women have more choice about combining work and care, but at the expense of considerable inequalities in respect of labour market segregation. The introduction of the 'daddy quota' in the Scandinavian countries, whereby men are obliged to take part of the parental leave allocation (usually a month, but two in Sweden) or lose it altogether was aimed at promoting greater gender equality in unpaid work, and hence at tackling labour market inequalities (Leira, 1998).

Other Western European countries have moved substantially towards assuming the existence of an adult worker model family, but in practice still operate a mixed model of 'partial individualisation'. Thus the Netherlands and the UK began to change the nature of entitlements for lone mother families in the mid-1990s, such that women with school-age children have been increasingly encouraged to seek employment. The main motives have been the wish on the part of governments to limit cash transfers to this group and to address the issue of child poverty. However, incentives to partnered women to enter the labour market may be ambiguous, depending on the operation of the tax and benefit system, the cost of childcare, and the length and remuneration of care leaves, as well as the nature of the labour market. In the UK, the operation of a welfare system for adults that relies mainly on household-based, means-tested social assistance rather than social insurance provides an inbuilt disincentive to the partners of unemployed men to enter the labour market (Rake, 2000).

In all these policy logics, it is possible to discern ideas about what is appropriate for women in particular to do in respect of work and care. In some countries the desire to promote an adult worker model family is stronger in respect of some groups of women (particularly lone mothers) than others. Thus, in the UK and the Netherlands, the pendulum shift in the treatment of lone mothers – from mothers to workers – has affected the behaviour of this group of women. Policymakers in different countries effectively operate with somewhat different assumptions about the contributions that men and women in general, and particular groups of women, make and should make to families, even though there is evidence of convergence towards the promotion of an adult worker model family. So, for example, in Germany recent increases in social expenditure on care have been focused as much or more on stimulating services as on increasing cash benefits, with the aim of promoting female employment. This means that choice in all these models is in part structured by social policies. In the US and Scandinavia it is assumed that adults will be in the labour market, but in Scandinavia sufficient 'policy supports' in the form of leaves and cash compensation for care as well as childcare services are provided to permit women to choose to care as well as to work, with the result that these countries effectively operate something close to a 'one-and-three-quarter-earner model family'. To the extent that the 'policy supports' are gender neutral, men are also permitted to choose to care, but labour market segregation means that men are likely, as in other countries, to be in better-paying, private sector jobs and, again as is the case elsewhere, to experience work cultures that are often unsympathetic to taking care leaves. In the US, women can choose to work (there is stronger anti-discrimination legislation and an ample supply of affordable, but not necessarily high quality, childcare), but it is much harder to choose to care, especially for lone mothers.

Policies have thus grown up in very different ways in different countries, in respect of their form, extent and concentration; for example, the UK has historically done somewhat more to provide for care for elderly people than for children, whereas in France, Belgium and Italy the reverse has been the case (Anttonen and Sipilä, 1996; Bahle, 2003). Such differences cast long shadows over what are considered to be appropriate areas for, and modes of, state intervention. In the US, where the state has not intervened much at all on the issue of care, it would be very difficult for government to play a major role in promoting service provision. The 1993 Family and Medical Leave Act covers a broad range of care work, including for elderly people, and is available to men and women (Orloff, 2009), but it is unpaid and while many women have access to occupational benefits, even among the 100 'best employers for working mothers', one-quarter provided four or fewer weeks of paid leave in 2006, and just over half six weeks or less (Lovell et al., 2007). In contrast, in European Union (EU) member states, there is for the most part a strong tradition of intervention to support care in terms of both cash transfers and services, even though the mechanisms differ according to context. It would, for example, be very difficult to introduce a German-style long-term care insurance for elder care in the UK, where social insurance has dwindled dramatically in importance as a policy instrument since 1980. Both the UK and Germany have expanded the number of childcare places since the late 1990s, but in the UK this has been done relatively quickly by central government offering pump-priming money to (mainly) private sector providers, whereas Germany has used the long-established system of local finance and local consensus between public and voluntary providers to determine the way in which services should develop. Service development has been slower than in the UK, but the places created have proved much more sustainable (Evers et al., 2005).

When Gauthier (2002) examined trends in a broad range of family policies (defined in terms of direct and indirect cash benefits, and state support for care leaves for working parents) between 1970 and 1999 across 22 industrialised countries, she concluded that while state support had increased in all countries, the nature of particular policy responses in the different countries had been so different as to increase divergence between them. However, since the late 1990s, there has been considerable convergence in policy goals towards the desirability of an adult worker model family and employment-led social policy. But Gauthier's observations, which pertain to a somewhat different set of policies from those examined in this book, reinforce the point that differences in the extent to which policies had already developed in the work–family field and in the nature of the instruments used are likely to continue to exert influence on policymaking. To some extent then, policies will be path-dependent (see above p. 21).

Policies to make provision for care work are additionally complicated by the needs and wants of carers and care-recipients, which are not necessarily compatible, and are further constrained by the nature of the social welfare system. The next section considers briefly some of the problems posed by care work for policy. Care and enabling a choice to care has not been the policy priority, rather policy agendas have focused much more heavily on enabling employment.

PROBLEMS OF CARE WORK FOR POLICY

The logic of the shift in policy assumptions towards the desirability of an adult worker model family is that care work will be substantially 'commod-ified', that is, put into the paid work arena. As early as 1993, the European Commission identified the formal care sector as a source of new jobs (CEC, 1993), the implication being that women workers might trade the work of informal care for paid work in the formal care sector. By the turn of the century, the number of care workers (in elder and childcare) as a propor-tion of the total workforce had reached around 10 per cent in Sweden and Denmark, and around 5 per cent in the UK (Cameron and Moss, 2007). But the notion that a large proportion of informal care can easily be trans-formed into paid work is problematic and prompts consideration of the nature of care work. While reference to care in policy documents at the national and EU levels is usually only in relation to employment, there is a huge literature on the nature of care and caring which merits attention if gender divisions are to be addressed, and, indeed, if policy goals and approaches are to be realistic.

There are several reasons why paid care work is unlikely to be fully substitutable for unpaid care work. First, care is more than tending, more than a task. It involves emotional labour and relationship (Finch and Groves, 1983). Indeed, it is passive as well as active: a carer has to make sure that a frail elderly person does not fall, or be around while a young child plays with another child. The shift in emphasis from passive to active welfare that has underpinned the recasting of the work–welfare relation-ship makes the valuing and rewarding of care work even more difficult. It is noteworthy that the concept of 'active ageing' used in policy documents in the 2000s (CEC, 2002; Lewis, 2007) means longer participation in the labour market and ignores the informal work of care carried out by large numbers of grandparents for children, and by the 'young old' for the 'old old'. Informal care for and by grandparents is crucial in the vast majority of member states (see below Table 3.2).

Second, even when care is commodified it neither fully substitutes for women's care work in the home, nor does away with their need to rely on the informal care provided by relatives and friends. The restructuring of welfare states since the late 1990s, resulting in more mixed economies of provision, has also resulted in more fragmentation in some countries (particularly the UK) with the gaps in formal provision being plugged by informal care. For example, a child must often be taken from part-time nursery care to a day care centre or a childminder. Third, the obligation to care is experienced differently by men and women (which throws additional doubt on ideas about women's simple preference to care). Women's reputations as carers are often socially and culturally important, which may weaken their negotiating power at home and in the labour market. The notion of the 'proper thing to do' (Finch and Mason, 1993) is often very different for men and women in respect of what constitutes an appropriate balance between employment and care work. Women also experience stronger pressures to care than do men: what Land and Rose (1985) termed 'compulsory altruism'.

If it is not possible (or desirable) to commodify large amounts of informal, familial care, then policies directed towards achieving a 'balance' between paid and unpaid work, which may help men and women to make genuine choices about how they combine employment and care, become more important. But there are major problems about the rewards that are attached to care, whether paid or unpaid, and about the extent to which policies promote the sharing of care between men and women at the household level.

The issue of monetary rewards for care work, via the wage system or via state benefits, has been widely addressed. No matter where care work takes place, it is undervalued. The main solution favoured by the UK's Women and Work Commission – to encourage young women to aim higher – will not help in this regard (Communities and Local Government, 2007). Indeed it bodes ill for societies such as the UK which are going to have ever greater numbers of elderly people needing care. England (2005) suggests that care is undervalued because it is considered to be 'women's work', and because of the work's emotional content, which results in carers becoming 'emotional hostages'. However, many women in particular feel a deep obligation to care for children and (specific) adult relatives (depending on the quality of family relationships, on social class, ethnicity and nationality). Informal care may also be experienced as bringing positive emotional and relational rewards that are preferable to a low-paid, low-status, insecure job. Indeed, it may well be considered to be preferable to look after one's own children or mother than take a job looking after other people's. But from the view of governments, this means that payment for informal care is often regarded as 'deadweight' cost (meaning that the state is paying for something that would be done anyway) and at worst is held to undermine 'natural reciprocity' in the family (for example, in the UK, see Royal Commission on Long-Term Care, 1999).

However, from a rather different political and disciplinary perspective, Deacon (2007) has argued that citizens should not be able to 'free-ride' on those doing unpaid care work. As England (2005) has also argued, care produces public goods for society that are not recognised and hence not rewarded. For example, if parents do a good job in bringing up their children, then the children, neighbours and the wider society all benefit (see alsoVan Staveren, 1999; Folbre and Bittman, 2004). But this also makes it possible to argue that such state benefits that are tied to children – for example, in the UK, child benefit – should depend on a particular standard of care being reached (Carnoy, 2000).

Paid care work is also low-paid in the majority of member states. The output of care, wherever it takes place, is the labour involved in caring, which gives rise to a productivity problem (Himmelweit, 2005a): a productive childcare unit would have a high child–staff ratio, but that would result in low-quality care. Thus there is little alternative to public subsidy if the quality of care on offer is acknowledged as a key policy and welfare issue. The problem is that an hour of informal care work is not substitutable for an hour of paid work time (Glucksman, 1998; Harvey, 1999). Feminist analysis has also long insisted that commodified labour is often embedded in, and depends upon, unpaid labour: research in the 1980s explored various occupations in which women appeared to be 'married to the job' (Finch, 1983) – as the wives of diplomats or clergymen, for example.

This brings us back to the issue of time and the politics of time. Informal care work is above all time spent by someone on behalf of somebody else: 'time is translatable into money, but the same quantity of time means something very different for those who live in different circumstances or who have different possibilities of shaping their time' (Nowotny, 1994: 127). The 'rationality of care' (Waerness, 1984) means being other-oriented and often waiving rules and routines which are grounded in linear and commodified time, and in bureaucratic rationality.

This prompts the need for attention to the moral and philosophical debates about what care is and why it matters. According to Eva Feder Kittay (1999); and Kittay and Feder (2000), care consists of meeting the needs of someone who cannot meet them himself or herself. It therefore necessarily involves relations of dependence. Such a definition makes it easy to see the potential for tension arising in respect of the shifts underpinning welfare restructuring towards 'active' welfare and greater insistence on the labour market participation of all adults. Kittay's formulation poses a rather stark opposition between relations of dependence and the 'independence' that comes from reliance (some might say dependence) on a wage. Her characterisation of care is undoubtedly accurate in the case of a profoundly disabled person, but may be less apt when it comes to describing the care needed by an early teenager, or indeed in respect of an able-bodied adult. Martha Nussbaum (2003: 51) offers a larger definition of care and makes the case for care as a universal human need: 'Any real society is a caregiving and care-receiving society, and must therefore discover ways of coping with these facts of human neediness and dependency that are compatible with the self-respect of the recipients and do not exploit the care-givers', even though her main preoccupation is also the care-receiver.

Knijn and Kremer (1997) have insisted on the right to give care as well as the right of the dependent person to receive it. The human relations of care involve both the caregiver and care-receiver and may be as (or more) accurately characterised by interdependence and reciprocity, as by dependence (which then tends to be pitted against the need to promote independence, defined by policymakers in terms of wage-earning). This point has particular purchase when it comes to the intergenerational aspects of care relations which, interestingly, have been ignored in the debate over intergenerational accounting (and in particular, whether pension provision can be afforded in the future) (for example Kotlikoff, 2003).

Joan Tronto's (1993: 174) argument for an ethic of care suggests that it is the denial of interdependence that effectively devalues care, whether it is carried out in the public sphere as paid work, or in the private sphere of the family and (weakly) compensated by the state:

> Disdain of 'others' who do caring (women, slaves, servants) has been virulent in our culture. This dismissal is inextricably bound up with an attempt to deny the importance of care. Those who are powerful are unwilling to admit their dependence upon those who care for them. To treat care as shabby and unimportant helps to maintain the positions of the powerful vis-à-vis those who do care for them.

A disproportionate amount of care is given by women to children, and by women to women (not least because a majority of frail elderly people are female), whether formally or informally. But the reality of interdependence should not obscure either the power relations that may exist in the care relationship, which the addition of a cash payment in respect of one party to the relationship may disturb or reinforce, or in the relationship between both carer and care-receiver and the wider society.

The relations of care may thus involve dependence, interdependence and power, as well as trust and love. Early analysis of the care relationship in the informal, unpaid sector insisted that care is embedded in personal relationships of love and obligation and the process of identity formation. Graham (1983: 30) highlighted the conflation of care as exploited labour (with significant opportunity costs) and care as love rather than mere tending (and as such a key part of female identity): 'Caring is experienced as a labour of love . . . The experience of caring is the medium through which women are accepted into and feel they belong to the social world'. Laura Balbo (1987: 51) also stressed the emotional content of care – what she called women's 'servicing work':

> Unless something is added to material goods in order to link them to what a specific individual expects or wants, personal needs are not satisfied . . . Being there to wait, to listen, to respond; to attend to the needs and desires of others; to worry when difficulties are anticipated; to deal with one's own sense of guilt when problems are not successfully resolved: this is servicing.

This means that care work is often a matter of 'passive' attendance involving emotion and relationship, as well as 'active' tending. How much these dimensions of care can, do, or should enter the arena of paid care is a matter of controversy (for example in respect of the 'content' of nursing, see Davies, 1995; see also Himmelweit, 1995; England, 2005). How far they can become the province of men is also a major issue.

If care is a universal human need, then it has to be done and warrants a central place in policymaking. This strengthens the idea that there has to be a real 'choice' for all adults to do it (Lewis and Giullari, 2005). Furthermore, given that there is so much difficulty in increasing the rewards for care work, promoting a less unequal division in this respect between men and women may be crucial for achieving gender equality. But sharing care at the household level poses particularly difficult issues, for there is a tension between the individual's real freedom to choose and gender equality. Historically men have chosen to do much less care work than women, which is bound to affect women's choices about care and employment. There are group inequalities between men and women in respect of the gendered division of care and employment that have to be addressed (Phillips, 2001). As Nussbaum (2003: 51) has observed, given the human need for care and the gender inequalities arising from the responsibility for care work, care becomes 'a central issue for gender justice' (see also Moller Okin, 1989). Yet 'compulsion to care' threatens the moral qualities of attentiveness, responsibility, competence and responsiveness identified by the feminist theorists of care (see especially Tronto, 1993). In addition, it is politically difficult for employment-led social policy to permit people to choose unpaid work over paid work, other than for short periods of exit from the labour market. It is therefore not surprising that care work remains undervalued, or that care policies continue to be aimed more at women, whose labour market position is weaker, than at men.

WORK AND FAMILY BALANCE POLICIES

The focus of this book is on work and family balance for parents and on the three main sets of policies – childcare services, leaves from the labour market to care, and state intervention to promote flexible working patterns – that have been developed in this field. Different countries have tended to focus on different policy areas. Historically, some have focused more on the provision of cash, via wage replacement, benefits or tax allowances, and some more on services (de Henau et al., 2006). For example, the Scandinavian countries are distinguished above all by the level of their public expenditure on service provision, especially in Sweden and Denmark, which spend a third more on services than on cash transfers (Rostgaard, 2002). In regard to flexible working, some countries have had no hesitation in seeking to extend legislation on hours of work, while others have tended to regard this as a matter for employers and unions. Indeed, policies directed towards balancing or reconciling work and family responsibilities are complicated, lying, as they do, at the intersection of public and private (in the sense of both state–family and state–market provision), formal and informal, and paid and unpaid work, as well as involving provision in the form of cash and services (Daly and Lewis, 2000).

Each dimension of work–family balance policies may involve the state in the provision of either or both cash and services. For example, vouchers may be given to parents to buy childcare. This was tried (unsuccessfully) in the UK in 1996/7 (Sparkes and West, 1998), and has been under discussion in parts of Germany. Policies may also involve public, independent (market and voluntary) sector, and private (family) finance and provision. The choice of policy instruments and the details of their implementation – for example, the precise percentage of wage replacement during a care leave – varies enormously and results in different incentive effects. An individual entitlement to parental leave would seem on the face of it to offer a genuine choice to men as well as women to take time to care: Pfau-Effinger (2004) has argued that it represents a new kind of social right. But if the level of wage replacement is very low, then it is unlikely that families will be able to afford a decision on the part of fathers to care. Leitner (2003) has proposed the need for a new classification of welfare systems according to an assessment of how far they explicitly or implicitly promote care by the family (familialism), and how far they have promoted 'defamilialisation', by providing alternatives to family care via state or market services.

Policy instruments therefore involve more complicated choices than just cash transfers versus services, and indeed throw up additional difficulties in regard to the complicated relationship between informal and formal care.

It may be helpful to conceptualise policies in the work and family balance field, which may be regulated, financed, and/or provided by the state (and topped up by employers), as encompassing:

- Time: the regulation of working time and the provision of time to undertake informal care.
- Money: cash for carers to buy formal care, cash for carers while they are on leave, and direct expenditure on services.
- Services: for child and elder care that are directly provided by the state, or provided by the independent sector and employers.

This list indicates some of the complicated policy choices that must be made in each of the three fields discussed in the rest of this chapter. The mix and nature of policies are different in different countries and may tilt the balance between paid and unpaid work for men and for women at the household level to varying degrees, even though it is important to remember that gender equality has not figured largely and consistently as a policy goal anywhere other than the Scandinavian countries, particularly Sweden. Even in Scandinavia, there are large differences in the nature of the particular instruments that have been developed and in the incentive structures they provide for mothers and fathers. Ellingsaeter and Leira's (2006) recent edited book on Scandinavia has shown the extent to which Denmark has focused support on working mothers and provides the least support for fathers; Finland supports both mothers who work and mothers who care, also with relatively little for fathers; while Sweden alone provides support for working and non-working mothers and for fathers. Such policy differences seem to be reflected in family practices. Thus, in Finland, mothers of very young children are much more likely to be at home than working part-time, making use of the long homecare leave (although, as Table 2.1 showed on a full-time equivalent (FTE) basis women's employment is as high in Finland as in Denmark or Sweden).Thus the trade-offs between the interests of men and women, and between adults (often women) and children also make gender equality a difficult issue.

Childcare Services

The development of childcare policies since the late 1990s has focused on formal care and particularly on early-years education in many (but not all) countries. However – as we shall see in more detail in Chapter 4 – in France, where virtually all children over three have been assured a childcare place for a generation, new public money has tended to go into home-based care by parents or childminders in the 2000s. In fact informal care, usually by kin and disproportionately by grandparents, remains very important in most countries, especially for younger children.

Table 3.1 presents Organisation for Economic Co-operation and Development (OECD) and Eurostat data on preschool day care and early education enrolments, public expenditure on these, and the hours young children spend in formal care per week. The Nordic countries and France have the highest rates of public expenditure, which have had a positive impact on not only the levels of provision, but also its quality. The table also shows the hours spent in care or education by children between school age (six in most member states) and 12 years, an issue that has become increasingly significant as more mothers work for longer hours.

The proportion of under-threes in formal care is particularly high in Denmark (61.7 per cent), with the only other countries recording percentages higher than 30 being Sweden and Belgium. In the OECD data set, only these countries meet the EU's Barcelona Council target of provision for one-third of under-threes, although it should be noted that it is not entirely clear as to how far this target may be reached by also taking into account provision for childcare leaves. However, there are important differences in usage within countries that have high levels of enrolment: for example, in Denmark, minority ethnic families tend not to use formal childcare (Kremer, 2007). Figures for the proportion of under-threes in formal care are particularly low for Italy and Greece (but not Spain), and for Austria and Germany. In all these countries the tradition of family (maternal) care for young children has been particularly strong.

By age five (when school begins in the UK[2]), the vast majority of children attend some kind of formal provision in all countries except Finland, which is surprising given the high rates of return of mothers to full-time work (even after taking homecare leaves which are often as long as three years), and the high educational achievement rates of Finnish children. However, Nordic data for 2004 show a much higher proportion (73 per cent) of Finnish children aged five in formal care (see note to Table 3.1). Finnish parents have a legal entitlement to a childcare place (as do parents in France, Germany, the Netherlands and working parents in the UK since 2008), but long care leaves are popular. The US is also something of a laggard at this point in the child's life. Unsurprisingly the variation between countries in regard to three- and four-year-olds is greater. Again, Finland is very unlike its Scandinavian neighbours. The English-speaking countries have provision for only 50 per cent or fewer three-year-olds, with Austria, Finland, Ireland, the Netherlands and Luxembourg falling below that. Some countries – France, Belgium, Italy, Spain – have virtually all 3–5-year-olds in institutional provision. The nature of entitlements to different forms of care varies between countries. In the UK, subventions for day care are largely confined to working parents by virtue of the way in which such care is funded: parents who claim the childcare element of working tax credit must be working more than 16 hours per week, whereas in a country such as Sweden the right to a place attaches to the child.

Table 3.1 also shows that young children in some countries spend long hours in formal care; the figure for under-twos in Denmark is particularly striking, as it is for children between three and school age. Preschoolers are also more likely to spend long hours in institutional care in Italy, where the nature of provision varies considerably between regions. Finally, the proportions of children between school age and 12 years who spend over 30 hours per week in education or care is very high in Italy, Sweden and the UK. This has much to do with the length of the school day, but in the UK, where a high proportion of mothers work part-time, the government has invested more money in 'wraparound care', meaning that more schools run breakfast and after-school clubs to accommodate the flexible hours worked by a substantial proportion of parents, many of whom work shifts. (On the variety of initiatives in respect of out-of-school care across EU25, see Reid and White, 2007.)

The recent European Social Survey (ESS) provides additional information on the use of childcare in member states and on what parents report as their childcare preferences. In Table 3.2, the data on childcare usage are restricted to young children of mothers who were in paid work within the previous seven days, because these are the mothers most likely to need childcare. The table sets out the responses of working mothers with a youngest child aged 0–6 to a question asking about the usual type of childcare that was used in their household. The responses of fathers who replied to the questions on both the use of childcare and demand for formal childcare were not very different from those of mothers in the same country, even though they were from different households.

It might be expected that in countries with high proportions of mothers employed full-time, the use of formal childcare would be high. Indeed, Table 3.2 shows that formal childcare is very important in the Nordic countries, where female employment is high, and in France, where there is a strong tradition of full-time work for women. All these countries have long-established provision for formal childcare that is accessible, affordable and high quality. Care by the mother or partner is particularly important in Britain where fathers working atypical hours (see below Table 3.5) provide significant amounts of care. However figures such as those in Table 3.2 may hide substantial complexities. For example, it is clear that use of formal care in Finland and Sweden is about twice as high for preschool children over three years of age as it is for babies and toddlers, while in Denmark formal care is used more from a younger age. Nearly half of

Table 3.1 Formal childcare and hours of education, children 0–12, 2004–05* (% of all children of same age group)

| | Pre-school care and education usage and public expenditure, 2004 (OECD) | | | | Expected years in education | Public expenditure % GDP | Hours in care or education, 0–12 yrs, 2005 (Eurostat) | | | | | |
| | Enrolment in day care | | | | | | 0–2 years | | 3 yrs to compulsory school age | | Compulsory school age to 12 years | |
	<3 yrs	3 yrs	4 yrs	5 yrs	3–5-yr-olds	2003	1–29 hrs	>30 hrs	1–29 hrs	>30 hrs	1–29 hrs	>30 hrs
Austria	4.1	45.9	82.1	93.1	2.2	0.6	4	0	53	16	66	32
Belgium	38.5	99.3	99.9	99.7	3.1	0.8	23	19	50	48	44	56
Denmark†	61.7	81.8	93.4	93.9	2.7	1.6	13	60	15	79	34	65
Finland† ‡	22.4	37.7	46.1	54.6	1.4	1.4	8	19	25	51	82	18
France†	26.0	100.0	100.0	100.0	3.2	1.2	16	16	56	39	48	52
Germany†	9.0	69.5	84.3	86.7	2.4	0.4	8	8	61	26	69	29
Greece†	7.0	[]	57.2	84.1	1.4	0.4	3	4	27	34	54	45
Ireland†	15.0	48.0	46.6	100.0	1.5	0.2	14	6	64	14	64	35
Italy†	6.3	98.7	100.0	100.0	3.0	0.6	9	16	21	70	13	87
Luxembourg†	14.0	37.9	83.5	96.9	2.2	0.9	14	8	51	12	74	23
Netherlands	29.5	32.3	74.0	98.4	1.7	0.5	36	4	82	7	89	11
Portugal	23.5	63.9	79.9	90.2	2.3	0.8	3	26	9	55	30	69
Spain	20.7	95.9	100.0	100.0	3.1	0.5	25	14	54	40	53	46
Sweden	39.5	82.5	87.7	89.7	2.6	1.3	22	31	35	52	1	95
UK	25.8	50.2	92.0	98.2	2.4	0.6	24	6	72	28	10	90
USA†	29.5	41.8	64.1	77.0	1.8	0.6	n.a	n.a.	n.a.	n.a.	n.a.	n.a.

Notes:

* Figures in this table are not directly comparable. Many of these data have started to be gathered only recently and inter-country comparability has not been achieved (see, e.g., footnote below on Finland). Note that compulsory school starts at different ages. Public expenditure figures: local public expenditure may or may not be fully included. OECD's definition of childcare includes, for 0–2-year-olds, centre-based care, childminders and care by non-family members in the child's own home; for 3–5-year-olds, all day care facilities and schools. Eurostat data refer to children cared for by formal arrangements other than family – EU-SILC Survey reply categories 1–4 (pre-school or equivalent, compulsory education, centre-based services outside school hours, a collective crèche or another daycare centre). For further information, see sources.

† Reference years for OECD enrolment data vary: 2005 – Denmark, USA; 2003 – Finland, Greece, Luxembourg; 2002 – France; 2001 – Germany; 2000 – Ireland, Italy.

‡ Although use of formal preschool childcare is lower in Finland than other Nordic countries, the OECD figures in this table appear to understate the proportions of children over three in daycare in Finland, where schooling starts at age seven. The Eurostat figures are much higher; *Nordic Statistical Yearbook* figures for 2004 show 73% of children aged five in day care, 69% aged four and 62% aged three (Ellingsaeter and Leira, 2006: Table 1.2); the European Commission's Joint Employment Report shows a figure of 77% coverage for preschool children over three in 2005 (Plantenga et al., 2008).

Sources: OECD Family Database (www.oecd.org/els/social/family/database, accessed 23/08/07); CEC (Commission of the European Communities) (2007), *Indicators for Monitoring the Employment Guidelines including Indicators for Additional Employment Analysis, 2007* compendium, Brussels: DG Employment, Social Affairs and Equal Opportunities, Table 18.M3.

Table 3.2 Childcare use and formal childcare preferences among mothers of young children in paid work, 2004–05* (percentage of mothers in paid work, child aged 0–6)

	Types of childcare used for youngest child						Mothers' views of formal childcare provision				
	Formal	Parent at home	Grand-parents	Other unpaid	Other	Obser-vations (no.)	Want 'much more'	Want 'slightly more'	Provision is 'about right'	Want 'less'	Obser-vations (no.)
Austria	26.6	13.7	41.9	16.1	1.6	51	5.8	17.8	76.4	0.0	72
Belgium	37.3	7.5	47.8	6.0	1.5	67	5.5	15.1	75.3	4.1	73
Denmark	67.8	8.1	16.1	5.8	2.3	87	2.3	9.0	84.3	4.5	89
Finland	60.9	10.9	23.4	1.6	3.1	64	0.0	11.2	74.2	14.6	89
France	67.8	15.6	10.7	0.0	6.0	94	15.3	37.1	47.7	0.0	102
GB	30.3	26.4	30.9	10.9	1.6	61	2.6	15.5	79.9	2.0	73
Germany	45.1	19.8	32.2	0.7	2.3	74	7.3	17.8	74.4	0.6	89
Greece	26.1	8.7	61.7	3.5	0.0	52	11.2	25.1	62.0	1.7	82
Ireland	40.2	11.0	31.7	17.1	0.0	92	5.4	21.0	71.0	2.6	106
Netherlands	32.5	22.3	34.5	9.6	1.0	98	1.0	10.4	86.7	1.9	105
Portugal	43.8	9.5	33.6	10.4	2.7	90	36.1	37.6	26.2	0.0	103
Spain	32.5	19.4	30.1	11.0	7.0	46	16.0	29.1	53.2	1.7	57
Sweden	69.1	21.0	6.2	2.5	1.2	81	2.2	7.7	83.5	6.6	91
Total	46.8	18.4	26.2	5.2	3.4	957	9.6	23.1	65.7	1.5	1,131

Notes:
* 'Formal' = all forms of paid childcare; 'Parent at home' = no childcare needed (e.g. don't go out to work, always one parent at home, I/my current partner care for children); 'Other unpaid' = ex-spouse, ex-partner, other family member and other unpaid carer at carer's or child's home (e.g. neighbours).
The data on usage are for mothers in paid work within the last seven days.
The data on views of provision of childcare also include mothers in paid work any time in 2003–05, many of whom may be on formal or informal maternity leave.

Source: Lewis et al. (2008), Table 7.

parents of 0–2-year-olds in Sweden and a third in Finland, but under 20 per cent in Denmark, said that their youngest child was cared for by a parent (or partner) at home.[3] However, Finch (2006) reported that mothers in employment in the UK and in Sweden do not provide more childcare for young children than do the mothers of all-age children. She suggests that this is because in Sweden mothers call upon formal care, while in the UK they increase their use of informal care by kin, especially grandparents. Nevertheless, the volume of unpaid, informal care of all types remains high for young (and old) people in all Western countries.

Bettio and Plantenga (2004) have endeavoured to construct an index of the intensity of informal care (for dependent children and elderly people) using 1996 European Community Household Panel data and have concluded that it is most intense in the Netherlands and the UK and lightest in Finland and Denmark, and also in France and Portugal. The ESS data in Table 3.2 suggest that grandparents (more often grandmothers) are a highly significant source of childcare everywhere (overwhelmingly so in Greece), except in Sweden, Denmark and France. In Sweden and Denmark, a high proportion of women aged 55–64 (67 and 54 per cent respectively) are in employment (see Table 2.2), which may help to explain the lack of grandparent care, but this is not the case in France, where the figure is 38 per cent. Wheelock et al. (2003) have drawn attention to the importance of redistribution between the generations in respect of care, and their concept of the 'family earning household' widens household boundaries to include the 'complementary economic activity' of grandparents. This kind of activity, which enables the employment of mothers in so many countries, tends to be ignored in the push to extend the years of formal employment: the European Employment Strategy adopted a target of 50 per cent labour market participation for those aged 55 and over.

Table 3.2 also shows the preferences of working mothers whose youngest child is under seven for formal childcare provision. Here responses from mothers who were in paid work up to two years before the survey are included, in order to record the childcare views of mothers who were on statutory or non-statutory maternity and parental leave. The responses of ESS fathers who chose to reply to the questions on childcare (both usage and demand for formal care) were again not very different from mothers in the same country (even though the male main respondents were from different households). In most countries, a substantial majority were content with the amount of formal childcare that is available.[4] The exceptions were Portugal, where a high percentage of mothers wanted 'much more' childcare, and, to a lesser extent, France and Spain. Portugal has a relatively high rate of mothers employed full-time and of dual full-time earner households (see Tables 2.1 and 2.6), and given this, relatively low levels of formal childcare provision (Table 3.1). In the case of Spain, the employment of childcare workers (often migrants) by households has become increasingly important (Flaquer and Navarro, 2005; Bettio et al., 2006). While part-time work is growing, the fact that the women who are in the labour market still tend to work full-time (and are concentrated in the younger age groups) helps to account for the wish for more formal provision. France, however, has relatively good provision of formal childcare. Dissatisfaction in this country may relate to the changes in childcare policy, moving away from subsidy for provision towards subsidy for households wishing to employ a childcare worker (as a labour activation measure – see Chapter 4), and/or to relative lack of participation by men in domestic work. In countries where enthusiasm for formal provision is relatively low, it would, of course, be useful to know to what extent current costs, quality, availability and short opening hours play a part. De Henau et al. (2006) have stressed the extent to which these factors affect take-up.

Apart from Portugal, France and Spain, there is no evidence in these data (for 2003/4) to suggest that ESS mothers would support expenditure on policies to provide universal childcare as a 'public good' in countries that do not already have it. However, the views mothers express on childcare may owe much (or little) to the nature of the care provided, or to culturally determined attitudes, which may change. Not shown in Table 3.2 is the fact that demand for more childcare provision appears to be slightly stronger among mothers with the lowest and with the highest educational qualifications – perhaps because the former need to work more for financial reasons and the latter want to work more. The ESS did not examine mothers' attitudes to the relationship between formal childcare and the health and developmental needs of children, which is also an important consideration for policymakers.

In fact, the policy goals in developing formal childcare provision have been many. The OECD (2001) set out the following aims for the provision of formal childcare: to promote the employment of mothers, to support children 'at risk', to promote children's development and educational attainment, and to tackle social integration and cohesion. Priorities for childcare have varied between countries and over time. Only in Sweden was the development of formal provision (beginning in the 1970s) linked strongly to the promotion of gender equality in the labour market. In Denmark and Finland, more emphasis was attached to child development issues. The increasing desire on the part of member states to make sure that social spending is directed towards 'social investment' (Lister, 2003; Jenson, 2006) has also made public spending on children attractive: they are the next generation of workers. Above all, investment in early-years education is expected to pay off. Thus, countries that have lagged behind in the provision of formal childcare, particularly the UK and Germany, have made huge strides in provision since the late 1990s (see Chapter 4 for more detail).

The proportions of preschoolers in care or education do not exactly predict public expenditure figures, suggesting that other factors, such as the qualifications of the formal carers, are important. This would certainly be the case in Scandinavia, particularly Denmark, which has a long tradition of employing highly qualified early-years professionals, and where public expenditure on childcare reaches 1.6 per cent of gross domestic product (GDP). The costs of childcare to parents vary enormously between countries. In continental European countries, parents usually pay between 20 and 30 per cent of the costs, but in the UK they pay at least twice that much – some figures for the UK suggest as much as 75 per cent (Daycare Trust, 2006).

However, estimates of costs to parents of childcare are difficult to make. OECD estimates using 2004 data for dual- and single-earner families are set out in Table 3.3. The first column of Table 3.3 shows the 'average typical parental fee' for one month of full-time care for a two-year-old, were the parent to be paying the full fee, in relation to each country's 'average wage'[5] (for the UK, this figure takes into account the childcare tax credit – see Chapter 5). The second and third columns show the net cost for two children aged two and three for a two-earner couple with 167 per cent of the average wage, first as a percentage of the country's average wage and then as a percentage of the family's own net income. The fourth and fifth columns show these same figures for a lone-parent family earning 67 per cent of the average wage and working full-time (albeit that lone parents are much more likely to have one child than two). Thus the second to fifth columns show the extent to which public subsidies reduce the cost for parents. Ireland offers very little help at all, while the UK helps lone parents much more than couple families (OECD, 2007). The costs to UK parents are shown to be very high compared to other Member States (Ireland excepted) and compared to US parents.

High childcare costs have been shown to have an impact on the hours mothers work (Cleveland and Krashinsky, 2003). Where the costs are low – in the Nordic countries – they moderate the negative impact of high marginal effective tax rates (OECD, 2007). In these countries, a parent can be described as 'a thief of one's own wallet' if he or she does not use childcare and enter paid work (OECD, 2007: 160). However, the high cost of childcare in the UK may act as a disincentive to second earners entering low-paid jobs. The cost of childcare also affects the choice of care: where a high proportion of the costs fall to parents they are more likely to choose a place on the basis of price than of quality (Melhuish, 2004), and are

Table 3.3   *Costs of childcare to parents, 2004* (figures are shown in relation to countries' wage levels)*

	Gross charge one child* % AW	Two-earner, two children*		Single earner, two children*	
		% AW	% net household income	% AW	% net household income
Austria	9.6	19.1	14.9	5.8	9.3
Belgium	19.7	4.7	4.2	1.9	3.5
Denmark	8.4	8.4	7.8	6.0	8.5
Finland	7.6	9.2	7.2	3.1	4.1
France	25.1	14.8	11.3	5.0	8.8
Germany	9.1	9.1	8.4	3.6	6.8
Greece	4.5	6.6	4.7	2.7	4.6
Ireland	24.8	44.6	29.2	44.6	51.7
Luxembourg	32.4	8.5	5.7	3.4	4.8
Netherlands	17.5	13.5	11.5	1.7	3.0
Portugal	27.8	5.9	4.2	1.3	2.0
Spain	30.3	n.a.	n.a.	n.a.	n.a.
Sweden	4.5	7.6	6.2	3.4	4.8
UK	24.7	43.1	32.7	9.9	14.4
USA	19.5	27.3	19.4	4.6	6.2

Notes:
*Average typical parental fee that the provider charges as a maximum for one month of full-time care without allowance for government subsidies, in relation to the country's gross 'average wage' (AW, OECD definition).
The first column is for a two-year-old (i.e. one child only) as per cent of AW.
The second and third columns show the cost after provider subsidies and tax/benefits for two children aged two and three to a two-earner couple with aggregate earnings of 167 per cent of average wage, first as a percentage of the country's average wage and then as a percentage of the family's own net income.
The last two columns show comparable figures for the same two children in a sole parent family earning 67 per cent of the average wage whilst working full-time. No data for Italy.

Source: OECD (2007), *Babies and Bosses. Reconciling Work and Family Life. A Synthesis of Findings for OECD Countries.* Paris: OECD, Charts 6.4 and 6.5.

more likely to use informal care. There is also a gender equality issue that attaches to the high costs of care: Harkness (2003) has shown that in the UK, the costs of childcare are borne entirely by women in 60 per cent of families where women work part-time and in 44 per cent of families where they work full-time. In other words, in some countries, particularly the English-speaking ones, where children have long been considered a private responsibility, childcare is still understood as a woman's responsibility and it has to be 'worth' her going out to work.

In the UK, with little history of state intervention, it continues to be important to be able to justify further public expenditure in this field. The idea of 'social investment' has made the case for childcare as a public good easier to make. Cleveland and Krashinsky (2003) in their paper for the OECD argued that both the importance of child development and of encouraging higher fertility make public expenditure on childcare economically efficient. The OECD (2005) suggested that investment in family-friendly policies generally pays off by increasing (women's) labour supply and aiding children's development. Indeed, there have been some optimistic findings to the effect that increases in economic productivity and output as a consequence of providing publicly subsidised childcare will meet the costs of provision (PricewaterhouseCoopers, 2003). How childcare is subsidised also matters. The UK sets greater store by demand-side subsidies to parents via tax credits than other member states, stressing the importance of choice of supplier, but state subsidies to providers do not necessarily restrict choice. Demand-side subsidies tend to cost less but will also tend to subsidise low-cost childcare, which is often of poor quality.

However, Cleveland and Krashinsky (2003) suggest that parents must seek high-quality care for there to be public benefit. Extensive research in the US and by the Effective Provision of Pre-School Education (EPPE) project in the UK (Sylva et al., 2004) tends to support the idea that quality in formal care settings matters and that care in such settings has positive effects on school readiness and on social and behavioural development, while also tending to support the idea that parental care is best for children in their first year, and that what parents do probably matters most of all. Among three- and four-year-olds in formal daycare, the US data show improvement in cognitive behaviour, but have raised issues about social behaviour (NICHD, 2005; Belsky et al., 2007; Waldfogel, 2006). However, the quality of care is particularly variable in the US context, where the market tends to deliver cheap care, often via migrant labour. There is little doubt but that the quality of formal childcare in terms of staff–child ratios and, particularly, qualifications of staff, as well as a considered mix of early-years learning and care, is high in some countries: particularly in Scandinavia, but also in France, Belgium and some parts of Italy (notably the Emilia Romagna). The provision of formal childcare in these countries is long-standing and was developed with the welfare of the child as a leading, often the leading principle. Provision in these parts of Europe is also trusted by parents; Danish parents who do not permit their children to attend a day care centre are generally believed to be depriving them of an important developmental experience. The situation in a country such as the

UK, with a very different history of day care provision – focused mainly on children 'at risk' (Randall, 2000) – has meant that parents are likely to be both less familiar with, and more suspicious of, formal provision, and that rapid expansion of the system is likely to pose difficulties.

Quality has always been a problem in the UK and the US, where provision tends to be largely private and regulation on anything other than health and safety grounds has been rather weak. De Henau et al. (2006) have also commented on the lack of guarantees regarding quality in Spain, where private providers are important. In the Netherlands too, where the expansion of childcare has been spearheaded mainly by employers, public debate on quality has been muted. The OECD (2007) has been enthusiastic about the private sector meeting the challenge of providing sufficient childcare places, adding that public funding for private providers must be tied to quality standards. But in the US in the mid-2000s staff turnover in market-provided day care centres was as high as 30 per cent or more per annum and was over 17 per cent in the UK (Melhuish, 2004), although this fell a little in the late 2000s. While 50 per cent of the childcare workforce in the UK has no training, this is true of only 3 per cent in Denmark and 6 per cent in Sweden (Cameron and Moss, 2007). On the other hand, the UK does register and inspect childminders, a large part of the childcare workforce, something that does not happen in Belgium, the Netherlands or Germany.

In recent years, the main policy drivers of childcare expansion have been the desire to promote women's increased labour market participation and children's early learning, rather than a more rounded approach to the child's developmental needs (Moss, 2006). In this situation, it is possible for tensions to develop between the needs of working mothers for childcare and the needs of the child, rather than the kind of 'win–win' situation in respect of both that characterises the Danish experience. Academic findings are reasonably clear on the benefits of good-quality nursery education and day care for children over three, but much more divided on the effects of formal provision on children aged 1–3. No explicit rationale has been offered for the EU's Barcelona Council target for provision in respect of this younger group (nor is the kind of provision envisaged made clear), but there are likely to be limits on the extent to which care for very young children can be 'commodified'.

Childcare Leaves

In practice, the vast majority of Western European member states, even laggards like the UK, have moved towards a pattern whereby very young children are cared for at home and older preschoolers attend some form of institutional care, either full- or part-time. The care of very young children is enabled in all EU15 countries by some form of statutory entitlement to leave. This is often supplemented by employers, especially in the public sector and in jobs covered by collective agreements. Statutory leave provision in all EU15 countries allows mothers to meet the World Health Organization's (WHO) recommendation that they breastfeed for the first six months. However, the policy goals of care leave policies have varied considerably between countries: for example, when Germany introduced parental leave in the mid-1980s it sought to enable female labour market exit in accordance with traditional attitudes towards the gendered divisions of paid and unpaid work, whereas in France the original policy goals combined labour market considerations with pro-natalism, while in Sweden and Denmark the conditions of women's employment and concern about children's welfare predominated.

The duration and payment of leaves take very different forms in different countries. This in turn raises difficult issues in terms of first, the welfare trade-offs between parents (usually mothers) and children: the extent to which longer leaves might be good for young children, but bad for the labour market attachment and/or careers and working conditions of their mothers. Second, there is the problem of the extent to which leaves perpetuate the gendered division of unpaid work. How far leaves to care (especially long leaves) should be seen as essentially 'familialist' policies, reinforcing traditional gender divisions (Morgan and Zippel, 2003; Morgan, 2006), or as part of the modernisation of the social policies that recognise the need to provide informal care and the right to choose to provide it (Pfau-Effinger, 2004, 2006) is a matter of considerable debate.

Maternity, paternity and parental leaves are the main types of provision, but some countries also have leaves to look after sick children, or an entitlement to emergency leave days in the case of illness on the part of close kin (Moss and Wall, 2007). All Western European countries have had some kind of provision for maternity leave since the late nineteenth or early twentieth centuries, but even today this form of leave varies in terms of length and is subject to different eligibility criteria and amounts of payment. In most countries outside Scandinavia, better-paid maternity leave is conditional on a substantial record of paid work. Contract workers (particularly numerous in Spain) and self-employed workers (particularly numerous in Greece) often have only limited rights to maternity leave. Maternity leave was not legislated in the US, where it was felt to run counter to strict feminist interpretations as to what constitutes 'same treatment' (Wikander et al., 1995). The 1993 Family and Medical Leave Act offers the possibility of 12 weeks' unpaid leave to mothers and fathers alike.

At the EU level, maternity leave is treated as a health and safety issue, but its shape and form has implications for parental leave. Nowhere is this more true than for the UK, where maternity leave has been dramatically extended to 12 months, and payments have been made much more gener- ous, but where there is only a very short, unpaid period of parental leave. In contrast, in Sweden, maternity leave is now 12 weeks prior to the birth, while post-natal 'maternity leave' is formally defined as a gender-neutral 'parental' entitlement which, including the leave taken prior to the birth, can run as long as 18 months and is generously remunerated. Similarly, while there is no paternity leave per se in Iceland, one-third of the nine- month parental leave is allocated to the father alone; in most countries paternity leave tends to be short, from two to 14 days.

It has become clear that the decision to take leave depends on a number of dimensions of any particular policy (Moss and Deven, 2006; Moss and Wall, 2007; Bettio and Plantenga, 2004; Plantenga and Remery, 2005; Plantenga et al., 2008). Behaviour is also associated with attitudes and beliefs about the extent to which mothers in particular should stay at home to care for young children, and the nature of the labour market, particularly the availability of part-time work and the female unemploy- ment rate.

When the European Commission issued its 1996 Directive on Parental Leave, it laid down a minimum individual right to three months' parental leave for men and women, but Member States were left to determine the conditions of access, whether the leave should be compensated and whether it should be full- or part-time. The leave was to be non-transferable – fathers could not transfer it to mothers – in order to promote gender equal- ity. However, the fact that no minimum remuneration requirements were specified (a victory for employers) made it likely that men would not take it (as proved to be the case: Bruning and Plantenga, 1999), and that it would tend in practice to be 'reconciliation for women'. In law, parental leave is a 'family right' to be divided between parents as they see fit in Austria, Denmark, Finland and Luxembourg, and an individual entitlement in Belgium, France, Germany, Greece, Italy, Ireland, Portugal, Spain, the Netherlands and the UK. In Iceland, Norway and Sweden it is a mixed entitlement, part family and part individual – these countries are distin- guished by having a specific 'daddy leave', which is an entitlement for the father and which is lost if he fails to take it.

The duration of the leave and the compensation offered are the most important determinants of the decision to take leave, but whether the leave can be taken flexibly (in blocks of time, spread over the preschool years, and/or on a part-time basis), whether it is an individual entitlement for men and for women, and whether there is a right to return to the same job or

only a similar job, are also very important, with somewhat different implications for mothers and fathers. While job protection tends to be strong
for those taking parental leave, it is much weaker for those taking long
homecare leaves (almost always mothers), which can run on after parental
leave and which are also poorly compensated.

Take-up rates for parental leave are hard to come by outside the
Scandinavian countries. Because usage depends in particular on whether
the leave is paid and at what level (Moss and Deven, 2006), in the UK few
women or men make use of the short, unpaid parental leave. The UK is
also rather rigid in terms of when and how leave can be taken, compared
to virtually all other EU15 countries. Overall, the vast majority of leave
days in all countries are taken by women. It has become clear that fathers
will be more inclined to take leave if it is well remunerated (because families have more difficulty in doing without the earnings contributed by the
man, which are usually higher), flexible, and if there is a specific entitlement for the father. The English-speaking countries tend to provide very
little by way of well-compensated leave (usually defined in terms of two-
thirds replacement income) – nothing at all in the case of the US, whereas
Scandinavian countries provide around 12 months.

It is remarkably difficult to provide comparable statistics on different
forms of leave. Table 3.4 shows the results of various attempts; however
recent and continuing reform efforts in many countries mean that such
efforts date rather quickly. The first two columns rely on national reports.
It is particularly important to know how much leave is paid and at what
rate. The EU Compendium figures in column 3 aggregate maternity, paternity and parental leave and use a high replacement earnings test. Plantenga
et al. (2008) (column 4) were the first to try to compute a measure of what
they called 'effective' parental leave weighted by the level of payment.
Their figures aggregate maternity leave beyond 14 weeks and parental
leave. The final columns from the OECD's Family Database take a sterner
approach still, showing the number of weeks of leave that attract 100 per
cent of the average production worker's wage. Using these figures, Sweden
and France are most generous in respect of parental leave, followed by
Denmark and Austria. Finland is much less generous because of its long
but poorly remunerated homecare leave. In short, the differences between
countries in respect of statutory payments to those taking any kind of leave
relating to young children are enormous. In addition, in many countries
leaves are often enhanced by payments from employers to some categories
of workers.

Almost all countries have changed their statutory provisions since 2000,
with the fewest changes in the Nordic countries where parental leave
policies are long established. Some countries, particularly Germany, have

made major reforms (see Chapter 4), such that female labour market exit is no longer encouraged. However, within each country, the interplay of statutory leave rights with employers' extra-statutory provision, tax and benefit systems, labour market characteristics and childcare provision means that for any individual mother the statutory entitlement is quite likely to be exceptional. Employer-provided supplements to leaves often favour higher-earning mothers and are particularly important in the German-speaking countries, in Southern Europe (less so in Portugal), the Netherlands and the UK.

Gender equality and long leaves

There is particularly strong debate about the effects of long care leaves. Usually, these are taken after a period of maternity or parental leave that is well compensated, and may run for a further one or two years, but at a low level of payment. In face of the shift to an adult worker family model and employment-led social policies, long care leaves in particular often seem of doubtful benefit to policymakers, who have tended to pay more attention in recent years to promoting childcare services. In Germany, for example, when parental leave was introduced in 1986, the main policy outcome was to enable women to leave the labour market, particularly low-income, married mothers (Ostner, 2006). Recent policy effort in Germany has focused much more on the provision of childcare services. At the EU level, nothing has been done to strengthen parental leave since 1996 (although further reform was discussed in 2007). Rather, the 2002 Barcelona Council set targets for childcare. Yet, in the past, parental leave policies were conceptualised in most countries as a way for mothers above all to be able to choose to exit the labour market for a specified period to care for young children (Koopmans et al., 2005).

Long homecare leaves are the province of mothers. Hook (2006) has argued that while policies allow women to continue to be employed, unlike the provision of childcare they actually serve to decrease the amount of time that men spend on unpaid work. Thus long leaves can be seen as the epitome of 'reconciliation for women', and may serve to reinforce the gendered division of paid and unpaid work (see also Windebank, 2001; Stier and Lewin-Epstein, 2007). Bergmann (2009) has argued that because men take relatively little leave of any kind compared to women in all countries, the only policy solution is to commodify as much care work as possible and to promote equality in the labour market. Certainly, the right to return to their jobs is particularly important for mothers taking long leaves. Indeed, it is interesting to note that in a few countries, including Sweden, women exercising an entitlement to take leave are counted as employed.[6] In Finland, where the leave taken is often long, the labour

Table 3.4 Various estimates of 'effective' employment-protected statutory birth-related leaves* †

	Statutory leave rights, 2006–07		Leave well compensated financially		'Full-time equivalent' paid leave		
	Moss and Wall (2007)				OECD Family Database 2005–06 data (weeks)		
	Total post-natal leave (months)	Total with some pay (months)	EU Compendium (2007), 2005 data, months @ ²/₃+ of salary	Plantenga et al. (2008) early 2000s data payment-weighted 'parental' leave (weeks)	Maternity	Paternity	Parental
Austria	24	24	4	63	16	0.4	21.8
Belgium	9.5	9.5	3.5	18	11.53	2	2.4
Denmark	10.5	10.5	11.5	47	18	2	28.8
Finland	36‡	36‡	10	107	11.7	3	15.6
France	36	36	4	48	16	2	40.2
Germany	36	14	3	49	14	nil	11.4
Greece	9	2	4	13	17	0.4	nil
Ireland	14	4.5	5	13	14.4	0.4	nil
Italy	13.5	13.5	5	24	16.8	nil	3.6
Luxembourg	n.a.	n.a.	10	54	16	0.4	16.1
Netherlands	8.5	2.5	4	11	16	0.4	nil
Portugal	34	4	4	20	17	1	nil
Spain	36	3.5	4	50	16	0.4	nil
Sweden	c.18‡	c.18‡	16	78	12	9.2	40.8
UK	18	6	1.5	21	12	0.5	nil

Notes:

* Cols 1–3 aggregate maternity, paternity and parental leaves. Col. 4 excludes paternity leave, treats maternity leave as lasting 14 weeks (meaning that in countries with, say, 20 weeks maternity leave, six weeks are added to their figure for parental leave), and weights effective leave in relation to the country's 'minimum wage' levels, counting weeks paid at 66+ per cent of the national 'minimum wage' as full weeks, weeks paid at 33–66 per cent as 66 per cent of a week, and weeks paid at 0–33 per cent as 33 per cent of a week. Cols 5–7 show 'duration of leave in weeks' payment (as per cent of Average Production Wage (APW) earnings) received by the claimant'.

†Statutory provision in the US for those covered by the FMLA is for 24 weeks of unpaid leave, within any given 12 months (12 weeks each for the mother and father, non-transferable).

‡ In Finland and Sweden, paid parental leave is denominated in days. In Finland, 'homecare leave' with flat rate payment extends from the end of earnings-related paid leave until a child is three. Paid parental leave in Sweden totals 480 days between the parents (60 days reserved for each parent and 360 days to be shared) and can be taken until a child is eight years old. Mothers may use part of their parental leave pre-birth, or, on medical grounds, may additionally take up to 60 days maternity (or 'pregnancy') leave pre-birth, paid at 80 per cent of earnings.

Sources: Moss and Wall (2007), pp. 66-7; Plantenga et al. (2008), Appendix, Table A.1; CEC (Commission for the European Communities) (2007), *Indicators for Monitoring the Employment Guidelines including Indicators for Additional Employment Analysis*, 2007 Compendium, Brussels: DG Employment, Social Affairs and Equal Opportunities, Table 18.M3; OECD (2007c) *Family Database*. www.oecd.org/els/social/family/ database, Table PF 7.1.

market participation rates nevertheless indicate that mothers do exercise their right to return to the same job (see Table 2.1). However, this does not gainsay the effect that long leaves may have on pay and promotion, or indeed that they may be serving as an alternative to unemployment (particularly for low-skilled women), or as a preferred alternative to low-paid routine work in some countries.

Galtry and Callister's (2005) review of the evidence on leaves and female employment led them to conclude that short leaves of about six months are best for promoting gender equality, but that children's health and developmental interests require one-to-one care for the first year. Taking what it acknowledges to be 'a narrow labour market perspective', the OECD (2007: 21) has recommended that the optimal period of leave for mothers is 4–6 months. There is therefore the potential for conflict between children's and mothers' welfare: the OECD's minimum of four months does not allow the WHO's recommendation of six months' breastfeeding to be met, while even the longer period of six months does not meet the developmental needs of the child, unless fathers step in to care for the second half of the child's first year.

Most research findings have found that long leaves have an effect on mothers' pay, on the gender wage gap and on gender segregation (Ruhm, 1998; Evans, 2002; Nyberg, 2004), although Correll et al. (2007) have emphasised the overwhelming importance of workplace-based discrimination against mothers. Some studies have suggested that long leaves also have an impact on female labour participation rates. The example of Norway is interesting. Norwegian mothers increased their employment rates considerably later than mothers in the other Scandinavian countries (Leira, 1992). Then in 1998, the Norwegian government introduced a long homecare leave for parents who did not make use of a public childcare place. This has been shown to have reduced female labour market supply, particularly in respect of highly educated women (Naz, 2004; Schone, 2004). In Finland and in France, it tends to be lower-educated women who take long leaves. Naz (2004) explains this difference in terms of the comparatively low rate of unemployment in Norway, but it might also be related to the 'cultural variable': the longstanding attitudes and beliefs regarding mothers' employment and the long history of female full-time working in both Finland and France in contrast to Norway, which historically has looked more like the UK than other Scandinavian countries in its pattern of women's employment.

The OECD (2005, 2007) has suggested that long leaves have held back the growth of labour supply and advised that benefits and/or duration should be limited. The European Commission has also advocated shorter leaves (CEC, 2003). Estévez-Abe (2005) has suggested that taking a long leave signals lack of commitment and depresses women's employment in the private sector. Gornick and Meyers (2009) have also suggested that long leaves erode human capital, making it more difficult for women to re-enter employment at the same level, which makes full job protection a prerequisite for successful return to the labour market.

It is also important to consider the terms of debate surrounding long leaves. When long homecare leaves were considered in Sweden in 1994 they were depicted as a 'trap' for women, because the issue of gender equality was highlighted, as it has always been in regard to work and family policies. But in Finland a similar policy was successfully introduced in 1980 on the grounds that it would increase the 'freedom to choose' (Hiilamo and Kangas, 2006). As Bergmann (2004: 243) has commented:

> where one comes down in this matter [of leaves] depends on the value one puts on gender equality, what value one puts on validating and preserving women's specialisation in caring roles, one's beliefs about the quality of formal care versus non-familial care, and what social arrangements one believes constitute gender equality.

In respect of work and family policy, Finland appears to be one country where the parents of very young children have a genuine choice to work or care, because the right to a childcare place and to a long leave exist in parallel rather than sequentially as is the case in most countries. But the state of the labour market, in particular high levels of unemployment, has nevertheless served to constrain choices for mothers (Naz, 2004; Salmi, 2006).

Fathers and parental leave
Galtry and Callister (2005) recommended that to meet the demand for gender equality, and to achieve higher labour market participation and improvements in children's welfare, it would be best if the mother took six months' leave, followed by the father for a further six months. We have seen in Chapter 2 how important the issue of gender divisions of unpaid (and, relatedly, paid) work are at the household level. Brighouse and Olin Wright (2009) have advocated making leave taken by mothers dependent on an equal amount being taken by fathers (after the first month following the birth) in what they term a 'radical' policy to promote gender equality. But 'forcing' men to do unpaid work is politically extremely difficult; is likely to run counter to the preferences of some women as well as many men, and to different cultural practices; and is likely to violate the moral qualities of attentiveness, responsibility, competence and responsiveness that have been identified as part of the ethic of care (see above, p. 81). Fathers in certain minority ethnic groups play very little part in the care of their young

children (Dex and Ward, 2007). In Denmark, a two-week 'daddy quota' of leave introduced in 1998 was abolished by a right-of-centre government in 2002, on the grounds that it interfered in the private affairs of families (Borchorst, 2006). This was a dubious argument given the 'use it or lose it' nature of 'daddy leave': the measure does not 'force' men to take care leave. Any legislative attempt to do so would in all likelihood undermine the ethic of care. Providing the possibility of a 'genuine choice' to care is likely to be the only realistic progressive way forward politically.

Given that women's behaviour in respect of labour market participation has changed so much and men's behaviour in respect of unpaid work so little, state policies could help to reinforce the idea that change is necessary and desirable. However, gender equality per se has not been high on the work and family policy agenda outside Scandinavia, even though it is possible to make an economic case for policy to address the division of work at the household level – albeit more easily in male low-earner households – because the development of services on the Scandinavian model would prove very expensive (for example Boeri et al., 2005). Even in Scandinavia, there is considerable research evidence to suggest that fathers who take leave are subject to career penalties at worst or a degree of ostracism at best in many workplaces, especially in the private sector (Brandth and Kvande, 2001; Haas et al., 2002; Bygren and Duvander, 2006). It is only in some of the Scandinavian countries that there has been a concerted attempt to reserve a portion of parental leave for fathers. But the take-up of leave by men is still low compared to that by women: 20.6 per cent of parental leave days were taken by men in Sweden in 2006 – the highest, followed by 19 per cent of men in the Netherlands. Elsewhere in Europe, including Denmark, fewer than 5 per cent of days are taken by fathers. Nevertheless, in some countries a large percentage of men take some leave and there is strong evidence that the proportion increases if a 'daddy quota' is introduced. In Norway, the percentage of fathers taking leave rose from 4 to 90 per cent after the introduction of the quota of one month's leave in 1993. In Iceland, the figure rose to 80 per cent after the introduction of the three-month quota. However, in Sweden, while the introduction of one month's daddy leave resulted in a doubling of the parental leave days taken by fathers, no such dramatic effect followed the introduction of a second month in 2002 (Hobson et al., 2006). Daddy leaves are important in lending legislative sanction to fathers who would like to take leave and thus in also helping to make such behaviour normative.

But other factors, particularly compensation rates, are crucial. In Sweden very low-paid fathers and those who earn above the compensation ceiling are less likely to take leave (even though on the whole, highly educated fathers tend to have more access to, and to take more, leave days)

(Nyberg, 2004). The relatively high proportion of Dutch fathers taking leave is explained largely by the high rates of compensation (75 per cent) enjoyed by men who take leave in the public sector. Nevertheless, Ekberg (2004) has argued that while it is relatively easy to give men incentives to take parental leave, it is not clear whether it is worthwhile, either in terms of the effect of fathers taking on more unpaid work, or in terms of the child's welfare. He notes that when a month's leave was first reserved for fathers in Sweden, the total number of parental leave days taken fell by five, which is arguably detrimental from the point of view of the child. Kenworthy (2009) has also argued that because fathers tend not to take leave, child welfare must be allowed to trump gender equality, and the entitlement of fathers to leave should be limited. In addition, questions are often raised about how much care work or other domestic work men on leave actually do.

In terms of gender equality, de Henau et al. (2006) have argued that the best incentive for fathers is not a quota, but a higher replacement income – a position that receives some support from the Dutch data – but that no matter how leave policies are designed they will not prove very attractive to fathers and are hence likely to produce employment traps for mothers (see also Bergmann, 2009). This gloomy view is reinforced by UK data that find men still identifying mainly as 'breadwinners' (for example Warin et al., 1999), and by a Eurobarometer (2004) survey of 5688 men over 18 in the EU15 which found that only 4 per cent thought that parental leave is for men and women equally, and reported that while awareness of parental leave was reasonably high, 84 per cent said that they had not taken leave and were not thinking of taking it in the future.

Fathers may not want to take much by way of parental leave, but also many women may not want to share it with men; Ellingsaeter (2006) reported this to be the case for many Norwegian women. Thus, leave policies aimed at men cannot be the sole answer to issues of gender inequality in the division of unpaid work, although they do have an important role to play in legitimating changes in behaviour. Brighouse and Olin Wright (2009) have suggested that when a substantial percentage of fathers care for small children – 20 or possibly 40 per cent – it will become normative behaviour. Furthermore, if the state does nothing in this respect it is highly unlikely that employers will fill the gap, especially for low-paid, low-skilled mothers (OECD, 2001; Evans, 2002).

Working Time

More attention has been paid by governments since the late 1990s to what happens at the level of the firm, particularly the promotion of 'flexible patterns of working'. In many countries greater flexibility in terms of when employees work (and, to a much lesser extent, where they work) is higher up the agenda for policymakers, employers and employees. Flexible working takes many forms: part-time work and the ability to reduce working hours are the most common (see above Chapter 2), but shift working, overtime, weekend working, school term-time working, control over start and finish times, the possibility of 'banking' time, annualised hours, compressed hours, and working at home all fall within the various definitions of flexible working. Comparative data on flexible working are difficult to interpret, and the various forms of flexibility may or may not benefit family life, depending largely on the amount of control that is permitted the worker, the particular nature of the working pattern, and the extent to which the terms of any particular practice are 'dictated' by the employer.[7] It is of course possible for a worker to experience different forms of flexibility and different amounts of control over these. Short-term and fixed contracts, which tend to apply to female more than male workers, are not popular with employees and are generally regarded as employer-led flexibility. Fagan (2003) has also argued that overtime is 'negative flexibility' because it does not improve work–life balance, although male workers especially may welcome the possibility of extra hours that are more highly paid. Flexible working patterns are often negotiated between workers and employers at the level of the firm, formally in a country such as Germany with institutionalised arrangements for negotiations between employers and employees, or informally as is usually the case in the voluntarist systems of industrial relations in the English-speaking countries. However, at the EU level, the Commission has sought to give greater security to those working part-time and to regulate long working hours, and in the 2000s many Western European governments, including the UK, have used legislation to encourage flexible working.

Employee- rather than employer-led flexibility is usually promoted by those concerned about the promotion of work–family balance. Certainly, in the UK, flexible working has long been reported to be popular among parents (for example DTI, 2000), but this could be because historically the only mode of reconciliation has been via working hours and mothers' part-time work in particular, in the absence of state intervention on childcare services and leaves. But employee choice and control may not result in a balance acceptable to both men and women at the household level. Men and women may have different interests, thus those fathers who prioritise their careers may opt to increase their hours, while mothers may opt to decrease theirs, which may in turn be a source of either satisfaction or stress. Such matters are difficult to negotiate at the household level (Lewis, 2001a). Nevertheless, Crompton and Lyonette (2008) have shown (using

UK attitudinal data) that acceptance of the traditional male breadwinner model can also be a major source of stress, dissatisfaction and unhappiness for women.

Flexibility has also become a watchword of governments, often meaning the capacity of the workforce to move in and out of employment, to retrain, and increasingly to have 'portfolio' rather than standard careers. But in addition, flexibility indicates a desire to encourage employers to 'modernise', to explore 'new ways of working' and to 'work smart' in order to make the most of an increasingly diverse labour force (Messenger, 2004). Indeed, in some countries, a strong business case has been made for 'family-friendly working' (which may include the provision of childcare and parental leave, as well as flexibility), emphasising the extent to which work–family balance policies and programmes at state and workplace levels can exercise a positive influence on absenteeism, motivation, productivity, stress levels and the retention of key workers (for example Halpern, 2006 citing US data; Dex, 2003 using UK data). However, evidence that family-friendly working increases profitability is mixed (Bloom and van Reenen, 2006; OECD, 2007). The business case is stronger when female workers are difficult and expensive to replace and for larger companies, where it is easier to manage flexible working.

Employers often want types of flexible working that are not so popular with employees – particularly irregular long and/or atypical hours, for example at weekends and in the evenings – and which may also not meet the European Commission's concern to promote high-quality employment. Burchell et al. (2007) have reported that in the EU27, men in white-collar jobs tend to have more autonomy over tasks at work than do women, although in blue-collar jobs women tend to have more autonomy in this respect. Men also have more control over flexible schedules than do women. But even when employees have considerable control over how they work, it is a feature of work in the 'new economy' (Perrons et al., 2007) that workers appear to 'choose' to work longer (Brannen, 2005). Van Echtelt et al. (2006) have referred to this as the 'paradox of autonomy': more employees have more responsibility for deciding how they will meet production goals, and hence have more autonomy and more interesting work, but their job security is dependent on performance. Given that work often comes in 'lumps', even part-timers can end up working overtime. The notion of people becoming 'time lords' (EOC, 2007), and exercising ever greater control over the way they work seems rather far-fetched.

Hours of paid work are important because, as we have seen in Chapter 2, households must somehow balance out or allocate hours of paid and unpaid work between men and women. Usually, women end up working fewer paid hours and in many countries men, particularly the fathers of young children, end up working relatively long hours. When more than 45 hours per week are worked, medium to high levels of stress are reported, and these rise sharply when 55 or more hours per week are worked (OECD, 2007: Table 7.A1.1). On the other hand, in some countries many women working part-time find that they are not entitled to pro rata benefits and suffer a larger gender pay gap than full-time workers, both of which characterise the situation in the UK. The pay gap for part-timers is smallest in the Netherlands and Denmark. Long-hours working on the part of fathers curtails the options open to mothers in respect of balancing paid work and care work; long-hours working by both mothers and fathers is likely to result in strong feelings of 'time pressure'. Table 2.4 showed the differences in full-time and part-time working hours for mothers and fathers of children under 15 responding to the European Social Survey in 13 member states and highlighted the long hours (over 46) worked by more than 40 per cent of full-time fathers in Britain, Ireland and Spain and the relatively short hours worked by Dutch fathers. It also showed the long hours worked by full-time mothers in Southern Europe (where part-time work is relatively scarce), and the short part-time hours worked by mothers in the Netherlands, but also in Germany. Interestingly, in the 2005 European Working Conditions Survey, men reported more dissatisfaction with their work–life balance than women, especially when they worked long hours, which is more likely to be the case when they are fathers (Parent-Thirion et al., 2007).

The possibility of varying starting and finishing times is often particularly appealing to parents. But using the 2004 European Labour Force Survey, Hardarson (2007) concluded that high proportions of employees have fixed working hours (although the European Working Conditions Survey suggests the existence of rather more flexibility; Parent-Thirion et al., 2007), and that a slightly larger proportion of women than men in nearly all countries covered by the survey have fixed working hours (Greece and Luxembourg were exceptions and in Spain the proportion of men and women with fixed hours was the same). Indeed, non-parents, the highly skilled and those in managerial occupations are the most likely to be able to work flexibly. While Danish and French employees are more likely to be able to vary their starting or finishing times or their work schedule as a whole, in Germany (above all) and Finland, time-banking arrangements are more common. In Germany a substantial majority of companies (67 per cent) have instigated working time accounts (Fagan et al., 2006), which offer the right to accumulate time in order to care, pursue education or take early retirement (Hildebrandt, 2006). But Gottfried and O'Reilly (2002) have argued that such innovative policies tend to be aimed more at core male workers than the largely part-time German female workforce (see also Hardarson, 2007). The Netherlands has legislated a new life-course time-saving measure (see below pp. 131–2), which also tends to benefit men saving for early retirement, rather than men or women wanting to take parental leave.

Atypical work, or antisocial hours, can help parents to balance work and care, but can also put relationships at risk (Perry-Jenkins et al., 2007; Fredriksen-Goldsen and Scharlach, 2001): parents working shifts and taking turns to care for their children can be as ships passing in the night, and overtime rarely improves work–life balance (Fagan, 2003), although in low-wage countries, such as the UK, it may provide a crucial boost to the family economy. There is evidence to suggest that flexibility, particularly atypical working patterns and antisocial hours, is beneficial only when it is negotiated; in other words, when the employee has some control. There is also evidence from the UK and France to suggest that flexibility is only helpful for work–family balance when it is predictable (La Valle et al., 2002; Le Bihan and Martin, 2005; see also Eurofound, 2005); but shift work, evening and weekend work are often unpredictable (Van Bastelaer and Vaguer, 2004; OECD, 2004). The European Working Conditions Surveys for 2000 and 2005 actually showed that parents in full-time work with reasonable, flexible working times tended to have a poorer balance than those with fixed and/or predictable working times, which may be because flexibility often involves long hours at short notice (Parent-Thirion et al., 2007; Eurofound, 2007). Parent-Thirion et al. (2007: 74) concluded that: '[r]egularity may be a more important consideration for workers than flexibility when it comes to ensuring that their working hours fit in well with their non-work commitments'. Parents endeavouring to arrange formal childcare find sudden changes in shifts difficult to accommodate. Flexibility imposed by employers, especially at short notice, poses problems.

Table 3.5, using ESS data, shows when mothers and fathers report working atypical hours, in the form of evenings and nights, overtime at short notice and weekends. As with long hours, more fathers than mothers work atypically. The country rank orders are in many cases similar for men and women for the different types of atypical working, which suggest that these are related to the nature of the labour market. A high percentage engaging in one form of atypical working – and here we may include long-hours working (see Table 2.4) – is often offset by low figures in other categories. Thus Greece records high proportions working long hours and weekends, but relatively little by way of frequent evening working or short-notice overtime for mothers or fathers. France and Germany record the highest figures for overtime at short notice for fathers. What distinguishes Denmark is that it records close-to-average or low figures for all these forms of working (Finland and Sweden have large percentages of mothers and fathers working evenings or nights). What distinguishes Britain is the extent to which high numbers of fathers not only work long hours, but also work all sorts of atypical hours, a finding in line with OECD data for all UK men (OECD, 2004: Tables 1.8 and 1A2.4). The OECD data for women's atypical working suggest it is more widespread in Britain than do the ESS data for mothers in Table 3.5 (one possible explanation is methodological: that the ESS put the questions on atypical working only to those who said their main activity was paid work, to the possible exclusion of part-timers working shorter hours). The impact of atypical working may not be perceived as wholly negative in a country such as the UK, since it permits a high degree of shift parenting (La Valle et al., 2002) where parental care is highly valued, and where it is combined with a prevalence of short-hour working on the part of women. But it can also be argued that the large numbers of men working long hours, together with a high incidence of other forms of atypical work for men, make it difficult for fathers to do care work. Still, research has shown that when these conditions do not prevail, fathers do not necessarily increase their share of unpaid work, as per the high work–life conflict scores Crompton (2006) found for women in France (where the '35-hour' legislation was introduced in 1998 and abandoned in 2008), which she attributed to the very unequal domestic division of labour.

As matters stand, government regulation in this policy field has been limited but there are in any case issues as to how far and in what ways flexible working patterns can help to reconcile work and care, and further gender equality. Governments face a difficult task in walking the tightrope between employer and employee interests. The ways in which the EU Directives on working hours and part-time work have been implemented vary hugely. In the case of the UK, employees have retained the individual right to opt out from the 48-hour week, but trade unions have suggested that some employers exert pressure on employees to opt out (TUC, 2007). Similarly the implementation of the Directive on the terms and conditions of part-time employees was implemented in the UK in such a way as to exclude the large number (5 million out of 6 million) who do not have a direct full-time comparator from most of its provisions (Kilpatrick and Freedland, 2004; Himmelweit and Land, 2007).

All employees have gained the right as individuals to more flexible hours in Germany, Denmark and the Netherlands, and working parents have gained a 'right to request' in Austria, Greece, Finland, Portugal, Italy and the UK (Plantenga and Remery, 2005; Moss and Wall, 2007). In Germany, the legal entitlement to work part-time during parental leave was legislated as part of parental leave reform in 2000. Employees can usually only elect to change their working patterns at best once in any year and only after a

Table 3.5 'Atypical' working hours: parents with children aged 0–15*

%	Partnered 'mothers'			Partnered 'fathers'		
	Frequent evenings/nights	Frequent overtime at short notice	Frequent weekends	Frequent evenings/nights	Frequent overtime at short notice	Frequent weekends
Austria	16.4	19.4	29.5	12.4	15.3	26.2
Belgium	21.0	12.6	28.6	22.6	23.3	34.0
Denmark	17.8	13.9	29.0	23.4	18.4	30.5
Finland	32.2	11.6	28.1	32.1	26.6	33.9
France	16.6	15.6	29.3	26.9	36.1	29.9
GB	24.4	10.7	21.3	36.9	30.4	50.0
Germany	12.2	17.1	24.2	22.3	36.9	28.3
Greece	13.6	6.0	40.2	17.0	16.1	43.9
Ireland	20.2	3.9	26.5	32.1	27.1	46.2
Netherlands	26.9	9.7	24.0	26.0	17.6	32.3
Portugal	10.9	9.0	22.4	19.4	19.3	40.1
Spain	16.7	7.3	26.6	26.8	24.0	39.8
Sweden	28.6	13.7	26.8	30.8	18.3	27.2
Total	18.4	13.0	26.2	27.2	29.2	36.2
	N = 1739			N = 2254		

Notes:
* 'Mothers' and 'Fathers' are partnered adults with dependent child. 'Frequent evenings and nights' and 'frequent overtime at short notice = several times a week or every day; 'frequent weekends' = several times a month or every weekend. Question asked only of those who said their main activity was 'paid work'.

Source: Lewis et al. (2008), Table 5.

period of service that varies from six to 36 months between countries. In some countries (not the UK) the employee must be employed in a larger firm: in the Netherlands in an enterprise of ten or more employees, in Germany 15, and in Austria 20, yet women are often employed in smaller enterprises. While some of the legislative provisions thus look more encompassing in the UK than in many other countries, there is no effective right of appeal via a tribunal in the UK. In the cases where disputes in Germany and the Netherlands have reached the courts, which are few, there has been a tendency for decisions to go in favour of the employees in the matter of reducing hours, but in favour of employers in respect of the detailed scheduling of working hours (Burri, 2005). Table 3.6 sets out the differences in the legal rights to working time flexibility that apply in Germany, the Netherlands and the UK. Take-up of the right to work flexibly has been higher in the UK than in Germany (Hegewisch, 2005); however, this may be because in the UK previously informal arrangements have been formalised.

It has been strongly argued that flexible working hours should be universally available in order to make non-standard ways of working more generally acceptable (for example Hewlett, 2007), again, as a means to changing attitudes and behavioural norms. This is important, because governments differ in terms of who has been made eligible for the right to request different hours of work. In the UK and Italy, the right is confined to the parents of young children (and in the UK also to carers of adult dependants from 2007, with the possibility of further extension to the parents of older children), but it is available to all employees in the Netherlands and Germany. Whereas there is a good case in terms of promoting gender equality for limiting cash payments to carers rather than making them more generally available to fund other sorts of leave – for example for further education or early retirement, uses that would almost certainly be taken more by men while women continued to take care leaves – the case for universalising flexible working practices is stronger.

From the employers' point of view, a universalist approach avoids the possibility of resentment on the part of workers who are excluded from the legislation. From the point of view of employees, a universalist approach stands a better chance of changing the work culture. There is a considerable body of research showing the intractability of work cultures in relation to the issue of flexible working. Insistence on 'face-time' – the often long-hour presence of the worker in the workplace – and doubts as to the commitment of workers who ask for flexible work in order to care make it difficult to challenge the traditional (male) career path (Moen and Roehling, 2005; Den Dulk, 2001). Middle managers have been shown to be particularly important in these respects: even if a company has a policy of

Table 3.6   *Statutory rights to flexible working: Germany, the Netherlands and the UK*

	Germany*	Netherlands	UK
What legal provision?	Part-time and Fixed Term Employment Act, 2000	Working Time Adjustment Act, 2000	Employment Act 2002
Date operational	January 2001	July 2000	April 2003
All employers?	No: >15 employees	No: >10 employees	Yes
All employees?	Yes	Yes	No: parents with child under 6 (under 18 if disabled) and carers of adults since April 2007
Service requirement?	Yes: >6 months	Yes: >12 months	Yes: >6 months
How often?	Once every 2 years	Once every 2 years	Once per year
What can you ask for?	Increase/reduce hours and scheduling of new hours*	As Germany	Wide range of changes, especially reduced hours, schedule, location
Change to contract?	Permanent change to contract	Permanent change to contract	Permanent change to contract
Process of request?	In writing	In writing	In writing
Notice of request	3 months before proposed starting date	4 months before proposed starting date	Not specified
Anything else?	–	Subject to collective agreements, except part-time working	Must be justified on grounds of care. Employee must explain what effect if any on business, and suggest solution
Response: how quick?	Until one month before starting date	Until one month before starting date	Employer must arrange meeting with employee within 28 days and reply within two weeks of meeting

Table 3.6   (continued)

	Germany*	Netherlands	UK
Can employer reject?	For business or organisation reason, not necessarily 'serious'	For serious business reason, but not in case of hours reduction	Can be refused for a range of business reasons, listed in regulations
Can employee appeal?	Yes at first internally, then in the courts	Yes at first internally, then in the courts	Much more limited: procedural only
Penalty for employer?	No, appeal is for change of contract	No, appeal is for change of contract	Yes, damages of up to £270 per week for eight weeks

Note:
*German parents of young children may also spread their parental leave to work part-time.

Sources: Hegewisch (2005); Fagan et al. (2006).

encouraging flexible working, an unsympathetic middle manager can make it difficult for employees to pursue the 'right' to work flexibly (Blair-Loy and Wharton, 2002; Houston and Waumsley, 2003).

From a gender equality perspective, Hardarson's (2007) analysis of the European Labour Force Survey concluded that mothers have the least access of all to flexible working practices, defined in terms of being able to 'bank' working time or to have control over working schedules. The kind of flexibility that is on offer under the limited legislation that has been passed in some countries, and in some (usually bigger) firms, is crucial. A majority of women exercising their 'right' or 'right to request' flexible working seek to reduce their hours. While this is important for achieving work–family balance, in some countries – in the UK, but not nearly as much in the Netherlands where part-time work is less precarious – this poses problems for future careers, pay and pensions. Some Scandinavian researchers have begun to suggest that more legislative attention to the balance of working hours between men and women, rather than flexibility per se, is needed because long parental leave has tended to reinforce care work as women's work and to exacerbate the problem of a highly sexually segregated workforce. Thus Larsson et al. (2006) have proposed that the state should compensate a parent reducing his or her working hours at a wage replacement rate of 30 per cent, rising to 90 per cent if both parents choose to reduce their hours, which would encourage gender equality.

Such attention to the detail of possible policy intervention is crucial. A general hours reduction will not necessarily lead to greater gender equality, as has been shown in the case of France, although highly qualified working mothers expressed more satisfaction with the 35-hour legislation than did women with low qualifications, who experienced more employer-imposed patterns of flexibility (Méda and Orain, 2002). However, the availability of reduced working hours for parents may disadvantage them in the work-force, and like many such policy proposals, the Swedish one does nothing for lone parents. But it is interesting that this call for reform has emanated from Sweden, which has gone furthest in developing other forms of work–family balance policies.

CONCLUSION

Much of the American literature on work–life balance reads as though this is policy territory for the firm alone (for example Rapoport et al., 2002; Kossek and Lambert, 2005), however, Evans's (2002: S205) conclusion based on a wide-ranging review is worth quoting:

> The pattern suggests that if public policy crowds out efforts by firms, this happens only at very high levels of national provision. On the other hand, when national provision is comparatively low, there is little sign that firms will fill the gap.

In fact, there has been considerable convergence between Western European countries in terms of favouring state intervention on the matter of work and family reconciliation, and in the use of similar policy approaches, albeit that the nature and balance of instruments have differed considerably, something that the next chapter explores in more detail for a limited number of countries.

The range of policies on time, money and services that have been developed to address the issue of work and family balance are all necessary if there is to be a genuine choice to engage in paid and/or unpaid work, and as Chapter 6 suggests, a wider range still is probably needed. Countries have tended to put the emphasis on a particular dimension of the policy package, depending on policy goals which, as the next chapter shows, have also changed over time in some places. In the UK, where policy development in this field is recent, childcare services have received the most attention and the most financial investment, which fits with the twin policy goals of promoting the employment of mothers (demand-side subsidies via tax credits are in effect restricted to working parents) and promoting children's early learning. The Daycare Trust (2006) and the right-of-centre policy think-tank Policy Exchange (Hakim et al., 2008), in the UK, have pushed for a longer homecare leave payment, along the lines of many other Western European countries. In Finland, parents can choose between taking a cash payment for caring for a child under three or taking up a subsidised childcare place; in Norway, only by forgoing the childcare place does the parent become eligible for the homecare leave payment. As we have seen, it is women who tend to take both parental and long homecare leaves, which poses difficult issues for gender equality. Is there anything wrong with promoting part-time employment and care leaves given that it is not possible or even desirable to commodify all care work, and that many women in some countries appear to want these for all the reasons that were explored in the early part of this chapter? This brings us back to preferences and the extent to which they may be constrained or 'conditioned' – why it might be that lots of Dutch and German women 'want' to work part-time, but relatively few French women, for example. In Finland, where there is a rare example of a genuine choice between a formal childcare place or a care leave in respect of children under three (although less by way of part-time work opportunities), more women (but not men) seem to choose the long care leave; but then, as we have seen, this choice must be located in the context of higher unemployment rates for less-educated women and the fact that very large numbers also opt to return to full-time work later.

But there are broader considerations in respect of gender equality that have so far not penetrated policy debates outside Scandinavia and Sweden in particular. Increasingly it is assumed that individuals, male and female, will be able to be more 'self-provisioning' as autonomous worker citizens in the adult worker model family. In such a context choice can be problematic when people make the 'wrong' choices (see above p. 17). In the UK, women's position in the labour market is particularly unequal, much more so than in the Scandinavian countries, or in France or Belgium, as the raw data on gender pay gaps for full- and part-time workers indicate. In Scandinavia, welfare systems have long been dominated by employment-led social policies, supported by state policies to enable people (effectively women) to leave the labour market for cause, particularly in order to care for children. But some have begun to question whether this gender-differentiated, supported adult worker model family does not impose undue penalties on women in terms of a sexually segregated labour market (Smith, 2003).

The nature of the interactions between work and family balance policies and labour markets are complicated. Western welfare states now share the assumption that all adults should be in the labour market, which means that there are proportionately greater dangers attaching to policies that may serve either to weaken women's labour market attachment or to have a detrimental effect on their future pay and career advancement (see also Himmelweit and Land, 2007), without encouraging men to change their behaviour. This has strengthened the long-standing conviction of some American commentators in particular that the most helpful policy strategy is to strengthen women's position in the labour market (for example Bergmann, 2009). But writing off the issue of care work has little appeal and is not useful. In any case, employment-led work and family policies must consider the issue of care work in its own right if they are to be successful. There is a strong argument to be made that, from the perspective of gender equality, the key policy task has to be conceptualised in terms of challenging the standard male career as an ideal for women and for men, whether in terms of working hours or assuming responsibilities for care work. Real choices to work and to care require care services, time and money to care, and care-oriented workplace reform. Chapter 6 will suggest that they must also encompass policies committed to securing gender equality in the workplace. While too much should not be claimed for policy influence on behaviour in this field, such an approach reinforces the need for both care-centred policies, and much more attention to initiatives that may change work cultures and challenge the norm of the standard male career path.

The next chapter examines developments in work–family balance policies in four countries – France, Germany, the Netherlands and the UK – in more detail. A range of policies to address the issue of work–family balance has long been established in Scandinavia and in some Western European countries, especially France (and also Belgium), while elsewhere a focus on a particular policy – such as parental leave in Germany – has prevailed until recently. The structure of existing policy packages, which often favour one kind of policy more than another, exerts influence on the shape of reform initiatives. Nevertheless, the next chapter shows that the emergence of new policy goals can also have a considerable effect. In the UK, which started late – in 1997 – with a well-nigh clean slate in this policy area, there was an opportunity for the development of a coherent and comprehensive policy package – 'a continuum of work/family support' (OECD, 2007) – to which considerable importance has been attached if policies are to be effective (see also Hantrais, 2004). In terms of the linkages between childcare, care leaves and working time regulation in the UK there is coherence, but the most concentrated reform has been undertaken in the most long-standing policy area: maternity leave. Such a strategy posed the least political threat, but has done little to challenge gender inequalities.

NOTES

1. Esping-Andersen's methodology has been subject to intensive scrutiny; see for example Scruggs (2006).
2. The compulsory age for starting school ranges from age four in Ireland, to seven in Finland and Sweden, with the vast majority of children in the EU15 starting at age six. In the US, the starting age ranges from five to seven between states.
3. The data were not robust enough for other countries to distinguish formally between childcare used by parents of children above and below the age of three.
4. Strictly, the ESS questionnaire enquired about views of childcare provision 'in your present situation'. It is hard to believe that so many mothers, working or not, would have expressed themselves content with current levels of provision if a wish to change their 'present situation' had made them strongly dissatisfied.
5. The OECD has recently moved from using an 'average production worker wage' (APW) to using an 'average wage' (AW). The latter includes a wider range of workers than does the APW, but is not the same as a mean or median wage.
6. This is an important issue when labour market participation rates are considered comparatively, as we saw in Chapter 2.
7. It is noteworthy that surveys of employers can report higher levels of employee-led flexible working availability than do surveys of employees.

4. Patterns of development in work–family balance policies for parents in France, Germany, the Netherlands and the UK during the 2000s

Co-authored with Trudie Knijn, Claude Martin and Ilona Ostner*

A role for the state in reconciling family responsibilities and employment has long been admitted in all the countries considered in more detail in this chapter, except the UK. In these countries, as in most other Western European Union (EU) Member States, policies designed to permit the combination of paid and unpaid work in the form of services for childcare,[1] care leaves, and reduced and/or flexible working hours have been subject to debate and varying degrees of reform in the 2000s, and in most countries have assumed greater prominence. As we have seen, governments have promoted, and have been encouraged to promote, work and family policies as a means of addressing a wide range of challenges facing Western welfare states (for example, OECD, 2005, 2007). The main concern has been to raise employment rates and to encourage flexible working for men and women, particularly mothers. But this core goal has been joined to the need to tackle a number of other pressing issues: population ageing (by enabling women to earn and thereby improving the dependency ratio); falling fertility rates, particularly in Germany; child poverty, particularly in the UK; children's development, particularly in Germany after the shock of the Organisation for Economic Co-operation and Development (OECD)'s cross-national educational assessments and in the UK (OECD, 2001a; Evers et al., 2005); and managing increasingly diverse and pluralist workforces (Dex, 2003; OECD, 2005; Bronchain, 2003; Den Dulk, 2001).

In line with the core policy goal of increasing women's employment rates, there has been a shift away from policy assumptions based on the existence of a male breadwinner/female carer model family towards the promotion of an adult worker model family, especially in Germany, the Netherlands and the UK. More generally, Orloff (2006) has argued that this policy shift amounts to the 'end of maternalism'. Increasingly, the assumption is that all adults will be, or indeed are already, 'individualised' in the narrow economic sense. Work–family policies have thus increasingly been regarded as employment issues, as much as family policy issues, in all these countries.

In line with this overarching policy goal and the kind of debates over different forms of work–family policies that were discussed in the last chapter, we might expect to see the following trends in work and family policies at Member State level: (1) more attention to stimulating the pro-vision of childcare services; (2) the promotion of flexible working hours, which often entail reduced hours but which may nevertheless increase labour force participation and can also be linked to the modernisation of work cultures; and (3) substantial reform of childcare leaves, especially long homecare leaves. However, policy change at the level of member states, while sometimes radical, has been much more complicated than this.

CONTEXT

The four countries considered in this chapter[2] started the twenty-first century in different places in terms of patterns of female labour market participation and attitudes towards whether the mothers of young children should work, as well as in respect of existing policy packages. There are different degrees of tension in each of these countries regarding mothers' employment, the role of fathers in care work and the needs of children. The amount of policy continuity or change that has been experienced has much to do with established patterns of behaviour and attitudes, as well as existing instruments and as we have seen, recent case studies of childcare have made a convincing argument that there is an iterative relationship between attitudes and behaviour, and that policies can help to change both (Himmelweit, 2005; also Kremer, 2007). The rhetoric of 'choice' – in terms of choice for mothers or 'parents' to work or care, and choice of type and nature of provision – has increasingly become important for policy-makers seeking to negotiate these tensions in many countries (including Scandinavia: Ellingsaeter and Leira, 2006).

The four countries have had different traditions in terms of ways of combining work and family responsibilities, with (West) Germany,[3] the Netherlands and the UK having a stronger historical attachment to the male breadwinner model and to the support of adult women primarily as wives than France, where family policies have served to support women as both mothers and workers (Pedersen, 1993; Lewis, 1992). In France, it has long been accepted that the state should play a role in this policy field, while in the UK above all work–family reconciliation was in the main a private family responsibility until the late 1990s. Table 2.1 showed that women's employment increased in all the countries between 1994 and 2006, with a particularly large increase of 13 percentage points in the Netherlands. However, part-time employment is especially important in the Netherlands (which has the largest proportion of women working fewer than 20 hours) but also in Germany and the UK, although the proportion of women working part-time has fallen slightly since 1994 in the UK. The female employment rate in France is the lowest of the four countries, but it also has one of the lowest gender employment gaps in Western Europe because women are more likely to be working full-time.

Table 2.3 showed that in Germany, the Netherlands and the UK the presence of even one child has a marked effect (of ten percentage points or more) on women's employment rates, but in France, the employment rate only declines by four percentage points. However, a second child results in a 7–11 per cent decline in France, Germany and the UK, but only a 2 per cent decline in the Netherlands, probably because a large proportion of mothers are already working very short hours. A third child results in by far the largest decline in all four countries, but particularly in France, where there are relatively generous benefits and the possibility of long leave arrangements in respect of the third and subsequent children, and in the UK, where work–family reconciliation measures and financial support for families are still the weakest.

Table 2.8 showed considerable variation between countries in terms of the degree to which attitudes were traditional on issues to do with the gendered divisions of paid and unpaid work. Mothers with children aged 0–15 were most conservative in their answers to the proposition that a 'woman should be prepared to cut down on paid work for the sake of her family' in Germany and Britain, followed by France and the Netherlands. In response to 'men should have more right to a job than women when jobs are scarce', mothers were most conservative in France, followed by Germany, Britain and the Netherlands. Analysis of the 2002 International Social Survey Programme data (Ostner and Schmitt, 2007; Pfau-Effinger, 2006; Crompton, 2006), on attitudes towards the idea that a preschool child will suffer if the mother is employed, and on the importance of paid work for women's economic independence, has suggested further that the dissonance between behaviour and attitudes is greatest in France, setting up particularly strong tensions for policymakers to negotiate. The strongly gendered division of domestic labour in France (see above p. 59) flies in the face of the high percentages of mothers and fathers responding favourably to the idea that men and women should share domestic work. German policymakers have to face the problem (in West Germany) of both encouraging mothers' employment and countering a particularly low fertility rate in the face of traditional attitudes and, it has been suggested, the importance attached to self-realisation (see above p. 46). The UK achieved relatively high female labour market participation rates by the mid-1990s in the absence of state action in the work–family policy field; however this may have represented a kind of 'growth to limits': as much change as is possible to achieve in the absence of legislative support or of men doing more at home. While UK attitudes tend not to be as traditional as those in West Germany, a strong steer on the part of the government to increase the participation rate of the mothers of young children is also likely to be controversial. During the 1990s and early 2000s, the Netherlands pursued policies which have sought to expand part-time work for women via a 'combination scenario', involving participation in both paid and unpaid work for men as well as women, all of which appeared to fit well alongside the long-standing labour market behaviour and attitudes of Dutch women (see also Visser, 2002; van Wel and Knijn, 2006). Again, any attempt to engineer a major shift away from these policy goals would probably prove contentious.

The next part of the chapter attempts to map the nature of policy development to promote childcare services, time to care in the form of leaves, and flexible or reduced working hours for each country in relation to political assumptions regarding individualisation and an adult worker model family, and debates about choice. The aim is to look at policymaking in these three policy fields in the context of labour market behaviour and attitudes in particular, examining the gendered implications. This chapter also pays more attention than was possible in the previous chapters to the extent and nature of continuity and change over time in: (1) policy goals; and (2) policy instruments, in terms of how far existing instruments have been reformed and how far there has been change in the balance between the main types of instruments across countries.

None of the four countries has given priority to the goal of gender equality, although as we shall see, it reached prominence in the Netherlands and in Germany for a short period around the turn of the century. Indeed, there has been a tendency to stress the importance of enabling 'parental choice'. Developments in work–family balance policies have therefore been instrumental, serving for the most part the goals of employment policies and, in Germany, also the goal of raising fertility. An appreciation of the nature of policy goals in each country is essential to reaching a clearer understanding of the choice of policy instruments. Thus, for example, legislation to regulate working time flexibility has much to do with the much larger goal of modernising working practices. In respect of childcare services and leaves, it might be expected that there would be more attention to the former as an unequivocal means of increasing mothers' employment, and that this would additionally entail a switch away from cash benefits to provide time to care, to the provision of services. But cash subventions give governments more leeway in terms of providing incentives to different kinds of provision and providers and, it is argued, to individuals to change their behaviour. In addition, cash payments make it easier for governments to respond to the 'choice' agenda. However, they may carry with them policy implications that may in the end be at variance with what is needed to increase labour market participation, particularly of women. This chapter aims to show for this more limited number of countries the extent to which continuity and change in goals and policy instruments relate to labour market behaviour and attitudes, and to the constraints of the particular welfare mix.

POLICY CHANGE IN FRANCE, THE UK, GERMANY AND THE NETHERLANDS

France

French policy in the work–family field, alone of all four countries, has been driven since the mid-1990s by the issue of unemployment above all. Childcare coverage in formal settings for children of three years and over has been very high and free at the point of access for decades; 32 per cent of two-year-olds also have places in preschools. However the rate of increase in the provision of places in crèches for the under-threes slowed dramatically from the creation of an average of 5000 new places per year between 1985 and 1996, to 1500 between 1996 and 1999, and 530 between 1999 and 2005 (Périvier, 2003; Bailleau, 2007). In contrast, there has been a substantial increase in public expenditure on cash benefits that allow parents either to hire an informal carer or to care for their children themselves.

In 1986 a benefit for working parents hiring a domestic worker to care for a child at home – the *allocation de garde d'enfant a domicile* (AGED) – was introduced, followed in 1991 by the *aide pour l'emploi d'une assistant maternelle agréée* (AFEAMA), which provided additional financial support to families employing a registered childminder (Martin et al., 1998; Fagnani, 1998). Both measures were part of the effort to increase the number of *emplois de proximité*. Taxpayer parents could roll up these benefits with the tax credits provided for childcare. In the case of the AGED, the tax credit benefited the better-off. Between 1994 and 2000, public expenditure on the AGED increased 54 per cent, and on the AFEAMA 177 per cent (Leprince and Martin, 2003). In 2004, the AGED and AFEAMA were replaced by the *prestation d'accueil du jeune enfant* (PAJE), which includes a universal basic allowance until the child is three, and a *complément de libre choix du mode de garde* (CMG – 'supplement for the freedom of choice in childcare arrangements') for the parents of a child under six who want to work. Those choosing a registered childminder do best.

In respect of policies addressing caring and working time, France has also had the possibility of a three-year, flat-rate parental leave since 1985 – the *allocation parentale d'education* (APE). Eligibility has been per family rather than per individual parent and was confined in 1985 to parents with three or more children; in 1994, it was extended to those with two children. However, the introduction of flexibility into this leave has not been a priority, although a 'parent' (effectively a mother – only 4 per cent of leave days are taken by fathers) can take leave part-time. The leave was introduced as an employment policy intended to reduce the level of unemployment by promoting female inactivity (Morel, 2007). Young, unemployed and low-paid mothers were the main recipients and tended to experience problems re-entering the workforce (Algava and Bressé, 2005; Piketty, 2005). Between 1994 and 2001, public expenditure on this benefit increased by 213 per cent. In 2004, in parallel with reform of the AGED and AFEAMA and as part of the PAJE reform, the benefit was renamed the *complément de libre choix d'activité* (CLCA – 'supplement for the freedom of choice to work or not'). It enables parents to work part-time, or to stop working, to take care of their children. The CLCA (340 euros per month) is paid for six months after maternity leave in respect of the first child, and for subsequent children until the youngest child reaches three. Since July 2006, a new allowance – *the complément optionnel de libre choix d'activité* (COLCA: 'optional supplement for the freedom of choice to work or not') has been available to parents with three or more children. It pays up to 230 euros per month more than the CLCA for one year only, varying with the parents' income, age of the child and type of childcare used. Thus the rate of increase in public expenditure on allowances and leaves has been much higher than on crèches and institutional care.

Finally, in respect of working time as opposed to time to care, France introduced a statutory 35-hour week for all workers, which lasted from 1998 to 2008 and has been shown to have had a positive impact on family organisation for a majority of parents with school-age children, albeit less so for parents who work non-standard hours and have little control over them (Fagnani and Letablier, 2004; Le Bihan and Martin, 2005). Indeed, 81 per cent of French mothers working full-time with children aged under 11 have reported difficulties in achieving work–life balance because of alternating working times, compared to 42 per cent of other women workers (Eurofound, 2005). French parents already had a right to reduce working hours and to work part-time, although this is taken up mainly in the public sector.

Thus French policy development in the work–family field shows striking continuities in terms of the state support given to women as both mothers and workers (Lewis, 1992), regardless of the political party in power. However, while French social policy has traditionally been familialist in its orientation and concerned with redistribution between families with and without children (Pedersen, 1993), this has been changing since the mid-1980s. Indeed the main policy goal in the recent development of reconciliation policies during the 2000s has been employment creation, which in the context of high unemployment and the particular work–family policy mix in France, is as likely to promote the exit of mothers of young children (especially those who are low-paid), as their employment. Nevertheless, France has a long history of high female labour participation rates (even though this rate is now the lowest of the four countries), and a high proportion of women working full-time. While the recent changes to the legislation affecting childcare and time to care have been couched in gender-neutral terms, the use of the term *'libre choix'* ('free choice') signals continued support for women as workers and mothers, even though a large proportion of new public expenditure has gone into measures that give incentives to mothers to stay at home, just as the balance of new expenditure on childcare for the under-threes has favoured home-based rather than institutional care with the aim of increasing the number of jobs. France has not encouraged more flexible (including part-time) work on the part of women, and part-time female employment rates have not increased. Nor has it introduced measures specifically designed to encourage men to care: the only new measure – the '35-hours' legislation, which in practice limited working hours over the year – has not resulted in a significant change in men's contribution to domestic work and French men take no higher proportion of parental leave than German, Dutch or British men (Eurobarometer, 2004). The continued reliance on state intervention and continuity of policy instruments in France is striking, nevertheless the shift in policy goals away from work–family policies as part of family policy and towards employment creation has resulted in a shift in the balance of support towards cash subventions to parents.

Germany

Germany has exhibited much more change than France in terms of policy goals and instruments. A long and relatively generous parental leave was introduced in 1986. According to Plantenga et al.'s (2008) index of parental leave, weighted by the level of payment, Germany and France had the longest 'effective' leave of all four countries at 49 and 48 weeks respectively prior to the 2007 reforms in Germany (compared with 21 weeks for the UK, and 11 weeks for the Netherlands) (see Table 3.4). Generous leave, together with generous financial support for children, was designed to support child-rearing by mothers at home. It was not until 1996 that an entitlement to a childcare place was introduced for children over three and more attention was paid to the development of early childhood education and increasing access to full-time care (Evers et al., 2005).

The reforms of the first Red–Green Coalition focused on parental leave and on working time, using the language of choice between employment and care, but at this point – 2000–2001 – with the explicit intention of promoting more equal opportunities between men and women to engage in both employment and care work. In 2000, parental leave was individualised and both parents were permitted to take leave at the same time. A parent on leave could work for longer on a part-time basis – up to 30 hours. However, if the parent returned to work after only 12 months, the amount received in benefit was one-third higher, changing the balance of incentives in favour of employment for mothers, who continued to take the vast majority of leave. In 2001, a universal entitlement was given to reduce working time (see Table 3.6). The Christian Democrat Party continued to see this new measure in terms of its commitment to a traditional division of household labour and wanted it confined to parents with children under 12, but the universal measure was designed to serve the goals both of promoting work–family balance and, more importantly, of increasing employment: the calculation was that 1 million part-time jobs would be created. Take-up has been relatively low, whether because of the deterrent effects of high levels of unemployment, lack of support from employers and/or because working-time accounts – which offer the possibility of 'banking' time – are becoming more common at the level of the firm, at least among white-collar employees (Leitner, 2005; Klammer and Letablier, 2007).

In 2001, the failure to extend the equal opportunities legislation of 1994 to the private sector resulted in a shift to a more voluntarist approach to securing workplace-based change in respect of flexible working. At the same time, much greater attention was being paid to the Lisbon targets for female employment, to the problem of low fertility, and to children's early learning: for example in Chancellor Schroeder's Agenda 2010 document, which resulted in a more instrumentalist approach to work and family policy (Joos, 2002; Leitner et al., 2008). This shift in goals has been strengthened by the Grand Coalition government that came to power in 2005. The 2004 Daycare Expansion Act (TAG) had already focused attention on greater institutional provision for the under-threes, and in

2006 the goal of making affordable childcare available to 33 per cent of under-threes was set in accordance with the EU's Barcelona Council target. Federal subsidies for under-threes were significantly increased in 2007 to ensure the target for provision is met, but debate continues about cost-sharing between the municipalities, the *Länder* and the federal government. In 2007, parental leave was cut to 14 months (to include a two-month 'daddy leave' on the Scandinavian model in the case of couple families), but the previous means-tested, small, flat-rate benefit was also replaced by an unconditional wage replacement of 67 per cent (up to a ceiling of 1800 euros per month). However, some collective agreements continue to offer additional leave with varying amounts of payment (Klammer and Letablier, 2007).

Thus, the German case has exhibited considerable change in policy goals, which has resulted in reform to existing policy instruments and the introduction of new instruments. Germany has shifted away from positive familialism and support for a traditional gendered division of labour, towards greater de-familialisation and incentives for women's employment (Leitner, 2003; Leitner et al., 2008). It has become increasingly reluctant to offer families cash for the care of children (even though it does so in respect of carers for elderly people), preferring to pay for childcare services, which it does by a mix of local and central public funding to day care centres and childminders, rather than by providing cash subventions to voluntary and/ or private sector providers or to parents (as in the UK, the Netherlands and increasingly in France). However, there is an ongoing debate on vouchers, which illustrates the extent to which German policymaking elites are also questioning standards of parenting: the vouchers would be confined to the purchase of institutional childcare (Knijn and Ostner, 2008).

In the early 2000s, the rhetoric of choice was, unlike France and the UK, but like the Netherlands at the turn of the century, linked to an explicit attempt to promote the 'real choice' of mothers and fathers to work and care, marking a departure from the illusory choice offered by the earlier system of parental leave which effectively promoted female labour market exit. But since 2002, work–family reform has been much more instrumentalist, with a commitment to equal parental employment – less so to equal parenting – and hence to the development of institutional childcare, shorter parental leave and flexible working. While a Scandinavian-style 'daddy leave' of two months was included in the new policy package, employers still expect long working hours from fathers (as in the UK), despite the existence of a right to reduce working hours for all parents (Hegewisch, 2005). The 2006 Report on the Family, issued by the Federal Ministry for the Family, also made reference to more pluralism in family forms and greater individualisation, thereby explicitly justifying the move away from assumptions that presume the existence of a married, two-parent family and a traditional gendered pattern of behaviour on the part of the adults within it, toward the more individualised set of assumptions associated with an adult worker family model (BMFSFJ, 2006; Bertram et al., 2006). Yet attitudinal data show that people continue to favour the care of small children at home by their mothers. Indeed, the German government has made the most radical series of changes in terms of policy goals of all four countries, taking steps to promote the adult worker model family, accompanied by significant reform of, and changes in, policy instruments.

The UK

The UK has had the least by way of a track record in the work and family policy arena. While limited childcare services had been available for 'at risk' children, it is not inappropriate to think of policies in all the main work–family policy areas as being initiated at the end of the 1990s, after the election of the New Labour government in 1997. Policy attention focused first on the provision of childcare, using cash subsidies to providers and to working parents: between 1998 and 2005, the average subvention for parents' childcare payments had doubled and overall spending had risen more than 16 times, with further expansion planned (Brewer et al., 2005). The policy goals were clearly those of promoting mothers' employment and children's early learning; the free part-time care provided to preschool children was governed by an early-years curriculum and was provided in the first instance to children in poor neighbourhoods. Policy documents also showed a clear appreciation of the extent to which the traditional male breadwinner family had been eroded and of processes of individualisation (for example DTI, 2000: para. 2.5–6; HMT and DTI, 2003: para. 2.2). By 2004, free part-time nursery care was being offered to all over-threes, but an obligation on local authorities to provide childcare did not come into operation until 2008, thus the UK was the last of the four countries to give an entitlement to a childcare place, and then only to parents in work or training. Provision for under-threes is mainly in the hands of parents, grandparents and childminders. Indeed, in keeping with the strong tradition in the UK of non-involvement by the state in the private sphere of the family, the policy documents stressed from the beginning the importance of gender-neutral, 'parental' choice of how to combine work and family, and as to the type of childcare (DTI, 2000: para. 1.7; HMT and DTI, 2003: para. 5.31).

Leave policies were developed incrementally alongside childcare services from 1999 and were aimed mainly at mothers; very little has been done in respect of fathers. Thus the rhetoric of choice had little to do with enabling 'real choice' as it did in Germany and the Netherlands around 2000, or with supporting women as mothers and as workers as in France, but rather had more to do with the need to present policy change in such a way as to take account of the gap between policy goals regarding mothers' employment on the one hand, and behaviour on the other. Parental leave was implemented in minimal compliance with the EU Directive in 1999. Instead, the UK focused on providing long and much better-paid maternity leave, which has been increased from 14 weeks to nine months, with plans to extend it to 12 months in 2010. It is already the longest in the EU (Deven and Moss, 2002). Maternity pay has been doubled. The 2006 Work and Family Act makes it possible for the mother to transfer the last six months of maternity leave to the father if she returns to work, but the rate of compensation for fathers is low.

The Government's policy documents noted that mothers in the UK wanted longer paid maternity leaves (DTI, 2000), and by the early 2000s ambivalence about encouraging the mothers of very young children into the labour market was being freely expressed in the press. In addition, longer maternity leave chimed with evidence emanating from the US about the need for one-to-one care in the first year of the child's life (for example, Gregg and Waldfogel, 2005), and was easier for employers to accept in a country with no history of parental leave and where employers feared the prospect of having to top-up the benefits of fathers on leave. However, on working hours, the UK government moved from a voluntarist to a statutory policy in respect of the right to request flexibility, introducing legislation in 2003, whereas the German government moved in the reverse direction, away from further legislation on flexible working. Take-up of the right to request flexible working patterns has been mainly by women asking for part-time hours and has been higher than in Germany, although Fagan et al. (2006) have suggested that in part this may be a story of formalising what was already informal practice.

The UK government has had primarily an 'employment' agenda in promoting work–family policies, and like Germany after 2002, it has wanted to promote mothers' employment. However, in face of labour market behaviour that is not dissimilar to that of German women (albeit that attitudes in the UK tend to be less traditional) it has been more cautious in terms of policy instruments and the presentation of policy goals: promoting childcare services, but also improving leaves for mothers and flexible working – effectively also for mothers – under the banner of enhancing 'parental choice'. Flexible working has also been promoted as part of the modernisation of working practices that will benefit employers as well as parents. The rhetoric of choice has been deployed mainly in order to address criticism of the employment-led policy goal for mothers that dominated policy in the late 1990s, although the cash payments to parents for childcare services have also been extolled as a means for parents to choose the type of childcare that suits them best. Yet, it is not possible to use the money to pay grandparents, who remain the most prevalent source of care in the UK, while the pattern of financing formal childcare services has perpetuated the existing mixed economy model, in which the private sector dominates.

Acceptance of a role for the state in the work–family policy area marked a major change in the UK and the policy package that has developed since 1997 is coherent in terms of the range of instruments used and significant in terms of the amount of public investment. New instruments, like the right to request flexible working, have been relatively cautious in terms of their scope; major change has been confined to existing policies, particularly maternity leave.

The Netherlands

The Netherlands has also seemingly made a large shift in the assumptions underlying work–family policy goals and has introduced – in 2006 – a major new policy instrument in the form of a life-course savings scheme, which rests implicitly, but firmly, on the idea of an individualised adult worker model family. While it is too early either to comment on the outcomes of this new measure or to know how far it may signal the favoured policy path of the future, it raises some interesting issues regarding individualisation, choice and the role of cash as opposed to services in structuring work–family policy instruments.

The development of the Dutch one-and-a-half-earner model family was a clear outcome of agreement between social partners and people, male and female, in response to the economic crisis of the 1970s, and differed from both the British unregulated model of long working hours for men, balanced by short working hours for women, and the German more tightly enforced assumptions regarding the desirability of the male breadwinner model. The Netherlands started to develop formal childcare provision at the end of the 1980s via subsidies to providers of childcare: by 2004 these amounted to 650 million euros. However, short-hour part-time working by women meant that informal care by parents predominated. In addition and in contrast to the other countries, a relatively large number of employers (72 per cent in 2004) co-financed childcare for their employees in return for a 30 per cent tax reduction per childcare place (Kok et al., 2005).

As in Germany and the UK, the Netherlands introduced a right to request a change in working hours in the early 2000s: in the Dutch case, all employees have been able to request either a reduction to part-time or an increase to full-time hours since 2001 and take-up has been the highest of the three countries. At the beginning of the 2000s, as in Germany, the Netherlands couched some of its major work–family legislation in the context of achieving greater equality between men and women, setting out the 'Combination Scenario', whereby both men and women would engage in paid work and unpaid work, as its main policy goal (Commissie Toekomstscenario's Herverdeling Onbetaalde Arbeid, 1997; SZW, 1997, 1999, 2000). Even though the parental leave measure introduced in the 2001 Work and Care Act offered only unpaid leave, the public sector offered paid leave at 75 per cent compensation to its employees, and take-up of leave among fathers has been the highest in the four countries (19 per cent of fathers took leave in 2005; Portegijs et al., 2006). This has been attributed to the high levels of compensation in the public sector and the fact that leave is an individual entitlement and can be taken flexibly. As Brandth and Kvande (2001) have shown for Norway, the cultural variable is very important in influencing fathers' behaviour, and Dutch men are more likely to work shorter hours than men in the other countries (see Table 2.4) as well as to take parental leave.

However, despite similar patterns of female employment to Germany and the UK, public expenditure in the work–family policy field has fallen, which is unusual in the EU15. According to Plantenga et al.'s (2008) weighted index of parental leave, Dutch provision was the lowest of the four countries at 11 weeks, because it is largely unpaid in the private sector (see Table 3.4). In respect of childcare provision, there has been very little public provision for, or concern about, the position of children under three. Public subsidies for childcare fell from 53 per cent in 1990 to 14 per cent in 2002. The shortfall has been picked up by employers, who paid 11 per cent of childcare costs in 1990 and 72 per cent by 2005. The 2005 Childcare Act provided subsidies only to parents and tax concessions to employers, on the assumption that the employer will pay at least one-third of the cost. The issue of quality control and early learning – regulated by the municipalities – has not been at the forefront of political debate. Indeed, while the existence of a childcare market is usually associated with the UK, the reforms in the Netherlands in the mid-2000s have promoted a purer market model.

This pattern of favouring cash over services and thereby seeking to maximise the choice of the individual worker/consumer has been reinforced by the Life Course Savings Scheme (LCSS), introduced in 2006, which replaced the 2001 Work and Care Act and may be used to fund periods of unpaid leave, such as parental leave or early retirement. Parental leave is still unpaid by the state; however the scheme permits employees to take additional paid leave via their LCSS entitlements. Male and female workers can save 12 per cent of their wages per year up to 210 per cent of their last earned salary in order to take time out of the labour market. The money is treated as deferred income and is only taxed on withdrawal (Delsen and Smits, 2007; Koopmans et al., 2005; Knijn, 2004). Take-up was lower than expected in 2006 (5.5 per cent rather than the predicted 20 per cent; CBS Statline, 2007) and is likely to remain low, a reason for its architect, the Christian Democratic economist Lans Bovenberg, to declare the scheme a failure one and a half years after its introduction (Bovenberg and Conneman, 2007). The low-paid are highly unlikely to be able to save 12 per cent of their wages per year and those working part-time will prob-ably not join the scheme. In addition, it is unlikely that sufficient savings can be accumulated quickly enough to finance a period of parental leave; (male) savings for early retirement (which runs counter to the desire to lengthen working lives) are a more realistic prospect. The LCSS represents the clearest example of a policy based on the assumption that men and women can be treated the same: as individualised workers, choosing when to move in and out of an increasingly flexible labour market.

In the 2000s the Dutch government has promoted longer part-time working for women, but continues to support the one-and-a-half-bread-winner model family as the main means of reconciling work and family responsibility in the Netherlands, providing substantial protection for part-time workers, which has been of a higher standard than in the UK and somewhat better than in Germany (Vlasblom and Schippers, 2006). Furthermore, unlike the other three countries, the state has not radically extended its financial commitment to this policy area, rather, more costs have been passed to employers, especially for funding childcare provision. However, the Netherlands has rebalanced its mix of policy instruments and has shifted much more than other countries towards highly individualised cash benefits for childcare as well as to support different kinds of exit from the labour market. This is in line with the desire of most Western govern-ments to facilitate life-course transitions in and out of the labour market over a longer working life (Schmid, 1998; Supiot, 2001; Bovenberg, 2005). But it also implicitly assumes a more individualised and economically independent adult worker model family, which raises the possibility of sig-nificant gender inequalities if the use of individualised cash-based policies like the LCSS were to be extended.

CONTINUITY AND CHANGE IN POLICY GOALS AND INSTRUMENTS

The dominant policy goal of employment-led social policy, has character-ised thinking about social policies at the EU level and in member states since the late 1990s, and has been underpinned by assumptions about the trend to greater individualisation and the political concern in many countries to promote choice. Thus it may be expected that there would be a greater emphasis on increasing women's employment rates, particularly of mothers, which proved to be the case in all four countries. In Germany, discussion of fertility in relation to reconciliation policies has been strong since 2003, and in Germany and the UK, but not the Netherlands, there was more focus on the need to promote children's early learning. Above all, therefore, it might be expected that policy instruments such as childcare services and flexible working hours that unequivocally favour employment would also be favoured, along with reform of the often lengthy care leaves that have long existed for a considerable time in France and Germany. However, policy developments have not been this simple. The actual patterns of development can be related to existing (and differing) patterns of labour market behaviour and attitudes towards parental involvement in work and care.

While all four countries accept and have promoted the goal of an adult worker model family, this manifests itself differently. In the Netherlands, where attitudinal data suggest that there is the least tension around the issue of mothers' work, it seems that there is most acceptance of the adult worker model as a fait accompli. However, women's hours of work are the shortest and Dutch Governments effectively supported a 'combination scenario' that resulted in the one-and-a-half breadwinner model family, which has been promoted from the 1990s to the present. Nevertheless, policy in this country has gone furthest in the direction of individualising provision and hence treating all adults as if they are indeed already fully individualised, economically autonomous workers. In France, there has also been continuity in policy goals in respect of women's employment, despite the major shift in approaching reconciliation policies as employment rather than family policies. This shift has tended to be implicit rather than explicit, but it has had implications for the reform of existing policy instruments. The French focus on the goal of reducing unemployment has not been explicitly gendered, indeed France has continued explicitly to support the idea that women should be able to 'choose' to be primarily mothers or workers. However, these policy changes have produced greater inequality between mothers.

Germany and the UK have articulated the policy goal of employment in respect of women most clearly. In Germany, the shift from reconciliation policies as family policies within the context of the male breadwinner model, to employment policies within the context of the adult worker model family, has been the most dramatic. The promotion of women's employment was seen in the early 2000s as a means of promoting gender equality, but later was linked more instrumentally to the desire to make it easier for women to have more children as well as to work. In the UK there has been a more explicit focus on mothers' employment (especially lone mothers)[4] in association with the goal of tackling child poverty. But in the UK, where state intervention in the work–family policy field is so recent, there has been a much greater effort to use the language of enabling 'parental choice' in order to avoid the oft-voiced criticism in the British press of a 'nanny state' that seeks to dictate the kind of arrangements that parents make. In Germany, policy goals have been articulated in a much more openly instrumentalist fashion. Given the more conservative attitudinal data for Germany, this amounts to the state seeking to provide a more radical lead in a contested policy area.

In France, unlike the Netherlands, continuity in policy goals has also resulted in continuity of policy instruments, albeit with reform and rebalancing in favour of cash benefits to encourage the employment of women as carers in the home or as childminders (mainly in urban areas), or to permit long leaves especially for low-paid, young women, for whom the leave is often an alternative to unemployment. Nor has France introduced any new instruments specifically aimed at work–family reconciliation; the goal of the 35-hours legislation was focused on employment creation, even though there were also (largely positive) outcomes for work–family balance, albeit mainly for the well-off working in the public sector.

In the UK, as might be expected given that work–family policy is a new area for state intervention, almost all the instruments were new: childcare provision with an emphasis on early learning, the right to request flexible working patterns, as well as very limited parental, paternity and adoption leaves. Nevertheless, despite its preoccupation with encouraging women's employment, the UK has radically lengthened the duration of, and improved the pay for, the existing policy of maternity leave. This is best explained by employers' familiarity with this policy and opposition to the new instrument of parental leave, together with the need for government to address the evidence that mothers wanted longer leaves. Both the UK and Germany have also given much more attention to funding childcare services than in the past. Indeed, German academic commentators have stressed the shift in Germany from cash to services, which seems to be at odds with the changing balance in the work–family policy field in other countries. However, this interpretation at the national level refers to the shift away from public funding for the raising of children – in 2001, 46 per cent of the total costs of children were met by the state (Spieß and Bach, 2002; Bleses and Seeleib Kaiser, 2004) – whereas this chapter focuses on the balance between different kinds of work–family reconciliation policies.

In regard to the latter, Germany now provides a relatively high level of wage replacement for those taking parental leave, which rewards success in the labour market, privileging better-off mothers. As a result of the more recent reforms, the balance between the different kinds of policies is now much more in line with the Western and Northern European norm. This cannot be said of the Netherlands, where there has been a retreat from state spending on childcare services, albeit with the aim of promoting more provision on the part of employers. But the balance of provision is now very much in favour of cash, whether for childcare providers or for the individual to save for extra leaves.

Thus, all countries have seen some reform of existing instruments and some change in the balance of policy instruments. It might have been expected that parental leave would be reformed to provide more incentives to those who take it (mainly mothers) to return to work earlier; this has certainly been the case in Germany, but reform has not been clear-cut in this regard in either France or the Netherlands, while in the UK, maternity leave has been significantly lengthened, albeit from a relatively low base. There has been more focus on the provision of childcare services in all countries, but this has not necessarily involved an increase in state provision, particularly in the Netherlands and the UK, where private companies are the main providers, with state subsidies made either directly or through the tax system. Neither has it necessarily meant a shift from cash to services: in all countries except Germany cash subsidies have increasingly been given to parents to buy childcare. All countries have also introduced new instruments since 2000, particularly in respect of working hours, with the UK seeing the introduction of the widest range of new policy instruments in terms of leaves, services and working hours.

POLICY DEVELOPMENT AND GENDER IN RELATION TO ATTITUDES AND BEHAVIOUR

Chapter 2 suggested that existing labour market behaviour and attitudes are important to the formation of policy goals and instruments in what is acknowledged to be a very contested policy area, involving in particular strongly held notions of 'the proper thing to do' (Finch and Mason, 1993) for the mothers of young children. This argument holds up best for the UK case, where successive Labour governments have sought to promote the adult worker model family and mothers' employment, but have used the idea of parental choice in a gender-neutral fashion together with a major extension of maternity leave – popular with mothers and acceptable to employers – to address negative perceptions of state intervention in family

arrangements and to ensure the possibility of parental (almost certainly maternal) care in the first year of life. However, in Germany, where the government faced some of the most traditional attitudes (among West Germans), policy goals have become more explicitly determined to secure behavioural change on the part of women in particular. In Germany, work–family policy is part of a much wider reform effort that is far from finished, and which is designed to 'modernise' the welfare state in the face of new social risks.

In France, there has been a less visible change in policy instruments in the work–family field, albeit that reconciliation policies are now part of the growing focus on (un)employment. The French case shows that employment-driven policy goals need not lead directly to the promotion of mothers' employment. Policy debates have remained focused on instruments that enable mothers to choose 'freely' how to combine work and care (Centre d'Analyse Stratégique, 2007; Pécresse, 2007), with little by way of specific policy initiatives to address the gap between attitudes and behaviour regarding the role of fathers in particular. Nor is work–family reconciliation per se any longer at the forefront of Dutch policy goals since the election of a right-of-centre government. While policy goals continue to assume a one-and-a-half-earner family model, in the late 2000s the government moved away from active promotion of a 'combination scenario' for men as well as women in respect of paid and unpaid work, towards a set of policy assumptions regarding the existence of a model of individualised provision and responsibility. Germany has also moved away from advocating reconciliation policies explicitly as a means of promoting gender equality and encouraging fathers to do more care work. The promotion of genuine choice to work or care for mothers and fathers was confined to a few years around the turn of the century in both Germany and the Netherlands.

There is therefore the potential for dissonance between the behavioural and attitudinal reality, and the necessarily unequal gendered outcomes from policies that seem to assume a degree of economic individualisation that does not exist. Work–family balance policies are about combining paid and unpaid work, and therefore have implications for the gendered divisions of that work. Employment-led social policy goals have increasingly dominated this policy field in the four countries, with low fertility rates playing an additionally important role more recently in Germany. The growing acceptance of the adult worker model family represents what governments want to see by way of labour market participation. An individualised model of this kind is also easier for governments to build upon in societies in which intimate relationships are increasingly fluid, and where norms regarding adult behaviour and contributions to families are becoming harder to identify as populations become more diverse. The main policy focus at EU and Member State level is on how to ensure a measure of 'flexicurity', that will enable adults to move in and out of the workforce for socially and politically acceptable reasons – whether educational, care-related or to do voluntary work – at different points in their (longer) working lives. This larger perspective provides an additionally important means of understanding why there has been no simple switch from cash to services in the development of policy instruments in the work–family field. While consideration of care-centred policy requires a mix of care leaves, care services and reform of working hours, both to address the additional burden of care work that can be expected in ageing societies and to promote the achievement of gender equality (for example Gornick and Meyers, 2003; Lewis, 2006), the current focus on the need to promote employment and on the individual's employment biography is more susceptible to cash-based solutions, and in this regard the Dutch LCSS reform may be a harbinger of things to come. However, such a policy approach assumes that men and women are similarly situated in the labour market, which they are not in respect of wages, working hours or even access to flexible working patterns. It is also problematic for policy to equate care work and early retirement which may well be used for leisure (Knijn, 2004; Knegt, 2005; Anxo and Boulin, 2006; Lewis and Campbell, 2008). Indeed, patterns of development in work–family balance policies may become increasingly antagonistic to the kind of fully individualised, flexible and longer working lives that policymakers want to see if the policy focus continues to be strongly on the employment side of the work–family policy equation, and to assume the existence of steady progress towards gender-equal patterns of individualisation. They may also be at odds with the desire to promote fertility; for much research has suggested the importance – in most countries – for policy to remove the obstacles that impede the documented desire of a majority of people in Europe for more children than they actually have (Fahey and Speder, 2004). Childcare services have been identified as being of particular importance in this regard, but also family benefits and measures to promote the role of men in unpaid work. Both the balance of policy instruments and their precise nature matter.

NOTES

*   An earlier, shorter version of this chapter was published in *Social Politics*, (2008), **15** (3), 261–86.
1.   Provision for elder care (as opposed to pension provision) has featured strongly on the political agenda only in Germany, which introduced statutory social care insurance in 1995.

2. The case of Germany is particularly problematic. The discussion and commentary on the nature of policy development and change is filtered through the West German perspective.
3. The data that follow are for the united Germany, but the polarisation between East and West in respect of women's labour market behaviour in particular, and attitudes, must be remembered.
4. In 2007, the UK government announced its intention of extending this to a work obligation for lone mothers with children over 12 years of age in 2008 and for those with children over seven in 2010 (DWP, 2007). The labour market participation rates of this group have also been the focus of attention in the Netherlands and France (Knijn et al., 2007).

PART II

5. Policy development in the UK, 1997–2007

The patterns of development of paid and unpaid work of women and men have been somewhat different in the UK from those of most other Western European countries. Women's employment rates increased rapidly during the 1980s, and had reached the Lisbon target of 60 per cent by the early 1990s, but then slowed. Further increases in women's employment have been concentrated among mothers with dependent children (Walling, 2005; Simon and Whiting, 2007; Berthoud, 2007). The expansion of women's paid work in the UK occurred in the absence of statutory programmes to reconcile work and family responsibilities. As in some other continental European countries, notably the Netherlands and Germany, mothers' employment has tended to be part-time, although in those two countries, particularly the Netherlands, more generous employment conditions have been afforded part-timers. In addition, UK fathers work some of the longest hours in the EU15, longer than German fathers and much longer than Dutch fathers (see Table 2.4).

Thus the picture for the UK is very far from one of full individualisation in respect of the labour market or of 'equal sharing' of paid or unpaid work between men and women at the household level. Nevertheless, despite long working hours, fathers have contributed increasingly to childcare, something made possible not least by growing 'flexibility' and shift work. As ever, it is difficult to know what people 'want' or 'would like', especially given the entrenched pattern of a one-and-a-half-breadwinner model family and the expectations regarding the domestic division of labour that accompany it. However, successive Labour governments in the UK have, since 1997, made 'balancing work and family' an explicit area of policy-making for the first time, although, as the last chapter indicated, the most extensive changes were made in the longest-established policy: maternity leave. The promotion of gender equality has not been an explicit goal of government policy.

This chapter sets out first what has been happening in terms of behaviour and attitudes since 1997: at the very time that policy began to address the issue of work–family balance, the increase in partnered, but not lone, mothers' employment rates slowed, as did the rate of increase in more liberal attitudes towards the kind of contributions men and women make to households. The main part of the chapter then explores the development of each dimension of work–family balance policies – childcare, leaves to care and the promotion of flexible working patterns[1] – in more detail, highlighting the tensions between different policy goals, particularly in respect of childcare, and the conflict between policy actors, particularly regarding flexible working. As I argued at the beginning of this book, it is not possible to draw causal relationships between the changing context of behaviour and attitudes on the one hand and policy development on the other. But it does seem that increased recognition in the early 2000s of the reported desire of mothers in the UK to care for their young children as well as to work made an impact on the emerging balance between the different policy dimensions. Certainly, the emphasis in the UK has been primarily on 'reconciliation for women', which has substantial implications for the pursuit of gender equality.

CONTEXT[2]

Table 5.1 uses Labour Force Survey (LFS) data to show the changes in employment rates and in hours of employment for men and women since 1997. The figures refer to men and women aged 20–59. The employment rate of teenagers is generally low and the mean age of women at childbirth has continued to rise, reaching 29 in 2006, very nearly a year older than in 1996 (*Population Trends*, 2008): paid work and the unpaid work of care are thus increasingly concentrated in the middle years of life. The employment rate for all women rose by almost five percentage points between 1997 and 2007, but among mothers, the increase for lone mothers was much more significant than for partnered mothers, albeit that it remains well below the government's target of 70 per cent (these figures include mothers who are taking statutory leave to care for their young children). The gap between the employment rates of partnered mothers and of lone mothers with younger children has shrunk, particularly for those with children aged 5–9, and even more so for those with children aged 10–15. The employment rate for all men increased just over four percentage points and almost three percentage points for fathers, with the increase for fathers with preschool children being very slightly higher than for fathers with children aged 5–15.

In terms of hours of work, Table 5.1 shows that the proportion of all women and of all mothers, partnered and unpartnered, working short (under 16) part-time hours has decreased significantly. Partnered and lone mothers with older children have been more likely to increase their hours to full-time (defined in this table as more than 30), and those with preschool children have been more likely to increase their hours to long part-time. The proportion of lone mothers working under 16 hours and hence falling under the tax credit threshold has fallen considerably below that for partnered mothers. The proportion of men and of fathers working between 30 and 44 hours has increased significantly, but the percentages working long (more than 45) hours has fallen, especially for those with preschool children. However, there was some sign that the steady fall in men's working hours was stalling at the end of 2007. So, while the increase in mothers' employment rate has slowed, their hours of work have tended to increase, while fathers are less likely to work excessively long hours.

Nevertheless, it is still the norm for women to work part-time. While levels of women's satisfaction with part-time work are high, because it is concentrated in low-paid occupations and remains less well regulated in the UK than in the Netherlands or Germany, it is still a major cause of women's low pay. The gender pay gap is more than twice as wide for part-time as for full-time women workers, and the pay gap between full-time and part-time women has widened (EOC, 2005; Manning and Petrongolo, 2005, 2008; Grimshaw and Rubery, 2007; Gregory and Connolly, 2008). The proportion of women working part-time falls between ten and 20 years after the first birth (Paull, 2008), but almost a quarter of women with no dependent children worked part-time in 2005/6 (Simon and Whiting, 2007). Part-time work is heavily concentrated among white mothers; black Caribbean lone mothers and black African partnered mothers are much more likely to work full-time.

At the household level, fathers tend to work longer hours and women to shorten their hours dramatically at the birth of the first child. However, while there is evidence of a 'rebalancing' in the distribution of total paid working hours at the birth of a child and at the point of school entry, it seems that men's long hours stem from a trend of rising hours that precedes the birth of the first child (Paull, 2008; see also Dermott, 2006). Furthermore, there are also strong trends towards 'work-rich' and 'work-poor' households. The proportion of couples where the man is the sole breadwinner has fallen dramatically (see Table 2.6). But as Berthoud (2007) has pointed out using the General Household Survey, it is mothers who have increased their employment rates: most mothers have a partner, and most partnered men have a job, so the change in mothers' labour market behaviour has led to an increase in two-earner families. Simon and Whiting's (2007) analysis of the 2005/6 Family Resources Survey data has shown that 33 per cent of partnered men, with and without children, who work full-time have full-time female partners, 41 per cent have part-time partners, and 24 per cent inactive partners. But 62 per cent of men who were inactive were likely to have a partner who is also inactive. Thus,

*Table 5.1 Employment rates and usual hours worked in the UK, 1997 and 2007**

A. Women and 'mothers'

| | % employed | | Of whom, % of employed working particular hours | | | | | |
| | | | 1–15 | | 16–29 | | >30 | |
	1997	2007	1997	2007	1997	2007	1997	2007
All women	68.5	73.3	14.4	10.1	23.5	25.3	61.3	62.7
N	27640	21412						
Mothers in couples								
All	66.9	71.5	22.5	16.5	34.6	36.2	42.3	45.4
N	9209	7217						
With youngest child aged								
0–4	57.6	62.8	24.9	18.8	35.3	39.4	39.3	40.0
5–9	71.2	75.6	26.0	18.0	36.4	36.8	37.2	43.4
10–15	77.6	79.9	16.7	12.7	32.3	32.0	50.2	53.3
Lone Mothers								
All	42.2	57.6	19.6	7.4	35.2	39.8	42.2	50.5
N	1581	1792						
With youngest child aged								
0–4	29.2	40.7	20.8	7.7	39.8	47.9	38.9	42.9
5–9	46.6	60.1	22.1	7.9	36.6	43.3	39.8	46.2
10–15	58.1	68.1	16.1	7.0	30.1	33.6	53.0	57.1

B. Men and 'fathers'

All men	82.3	86.4	4.5	4.9	45.7	52.0	48.3	40.2
N	30 983	22 584						
All fathers	88.1	90.9	3.3	4.3	41.8	50.0	53.8	43.1
N	12 191	9 330						
With youngest child aged								
0–4	88.6	91.8	3.4	4.3	41.8	51.7	53.5	41.6
5–15	87.7	90.2	3.1	4.3	41.8	48.5	54.0	44.3

Notes:
*All figures are for age group 20–59 for the March–May quarter in 1997 and the April–June quarter in 2007. Percentage in employment includes the self-employed (about 8 per cent of women and 18 per cent of men in 2007).
'Mothers' and 'fathers' are identified at family unit level as all adult men or women who are head or partner of the head of a family unit in which there are dependent children; therefore it includes step-parents (the figure for fathers includes lone fathers, a tiny proportion). Lone mothers are defined as not married and not cohabiting. Coupled is defined as married and cohabiting.
The table shows 'usual' working hours in respondents' main jobs. 'Usual' working hours is a measure that includes usual hours of overtime but is less affected by public holidays, sickness and other absences from work than 'actual hours' and is not limited to a particular reference period.

Sources: ONS (Office for National Statistics) (1997), *Labour Force Survey 1997*, London: ONS; and ONS (2007), *Labour Force Survey 2007*, London: ONS. I am grateful to Ludovica Gambaro for her calculations.

while the one-and-a-half-earner model is the single most prevalent model in the UK, men's longer hours of work have not necessarily impeded an increase in women's working hours. But 'work-rich' households are likely to experience more difficulty balancing work and family responsibilities, and if one or both partners work long hours there are likely to be 'negative job-to-home spillover' effects (White et al., 2003). The reasons for women with unemployed partners not to work are complicated and include the operation of the household-based social assistance system. The relatively high proportion of workless households in the UK are also disadvantaged in work–family balance policies, particularly in respect of help in accessing childcare, which, as we shall see, is geared to those in employment.

As Table 3.5 showed, the UK also has high proportions of men and women working 'atypical' hours, which may be a source of stress, but may also make it easier for couple families to cope with their responsibilities for paid and unpaid work. Using 2000 UK time-use data and a definition of atypical working as work falling outside the hours of 0800–1900 Monday to Friday, Barnes et al. (2005) concluded that atypical working had in fact become the norm. Indeed, a majority of households have at least one atypical worker (Butt et al., 2007). Atypical working is likely to result in greater reliance on informal childcare, either by kin or by partners, including fathers. Warren's (2003) study of British Household Panel data showed that childcare was largely shared by 40 per cent of working-class mothers and fathers, who were the most likely to have split or opposite shifts, and by only 28 per cent of middle-class mothers and fathers. Calderwood et al.'s (2005) analysis of the Millenium Cohort Survey data showed that fathers were most likely to work shifts and to undertake childcare while the mother was at work in households with male full-time and female part-time workers. Thus mothers' part-time work, combined with fathers' atypical hours and the relatively high cost of formal childcare, have resulted in a high degree of parental caregiving.

It has been argued that fathers have been 'forced' by circumstances to do more childcare in the UK than in a country like France where there is much more by way of state support for formal childcare (Windebank, 2001), but Calderwood et al. (2005) showed that women still bore most of the responsibility for children and for housework (see also Warren, 2003). Fathers responding to the British Social Attitudes Survey in 2004 were more likely to identify problems in fulfilling family responsibilities than in finding time to do domestic chores, which suggests that their work–family balance concerns have more to do with childcare than with doing housework (Bell and Bryson, 2005; see also Gatrell, 2005). Crompton and Lyonette (2008) have shown that men are most likely to do unpaid work if they have a female partner who works full-time and is also a high earner. Part-time work for

women is thus best characterised as a 'modified male breadwinner model',
with men continuing to do rather little domestic work.

In respect of attitudes, Crompton et al.'s (2003; and Crompton and
Lyonette, 2008) analyses of the British Social Attitudes Survey have shown
that attitudes have closely paralleled changes in female labour market
behaviour (see also Crompton, 2006). Table 5.2 shows responses to two of
the basic questions asking about attitudes towards women's and mothers'
employment over time. Women's attitudes have been consistently less
traditional than those of men. The proportion of men with traditional attitudes about the male breadwinner model family fell from around a third in
1989 to around a sixth in 2006, but with rather less signs of change between
2002 and 2006 – when the increase in mothers' employment rate also slowed
– than previously. Attitudes towards the effects of the employment of
mothers with preschool children on children's welfare have been much more
ambivalent, with very little change in men's attitudes since 1994. Indeed,
Wall's (2007) analysis of the International Social Survey Programme data
for 2002 revealed a very broad range of attitudes regarding the different
possibilities for combining paid and unpaid work between men and women
in the UK, with only 17 per cent of respondents supporting an equal dual
earner/carer model. While only 10 per cent supported the strong, traditional
male breadwinner model family, a full 36 per cent supported some form of
this, with a further 15 per cent favouring only part-time or no paid work
for mothers (and some sharing of unpaid work), and 11 per cent paid work
for mothers (but no sharing of unpaid work). The variety of combinations
of attitudes regarding paid and unpaid work at the household level that
have emerged with the erosion of the male breadwinner model has failed to
provide policymakers with a 'clear steer'.

From this brief review of the data on behaviour and attitudes regarding
paid and unpaid work in the UK, it seems that policymakers face a society
that is far from individualised, and where there may be reservations about
progress towards further individualisation. The male breadwinner model
family has largely disappeared, but the emergence of, typically, the male
full-time and female part-time model, together with widespread atypical working, has made it possible to achieve high levels of female labour
force participation without, first, large-scale state intervention to reconcile
work and family responsibilities; or second, fundamental change in either
the gendered division of unpaid work, or men's commitment to unbroken
careers and often long hours of paid work.

The evidence regarding behaviour and attitudes in the UK is not easy to
interpret. Hakim (2000) has argued strongly that there remains a minority
of 'home-oriented' women and also that there is only a minority of women
committed to careers. However, this does not gainsay the possibility that

Table 5.2   Attitudes to women's employment, by sex, 1989–2006

% agree	1989		1994		2002		2006	
	Men	Women	Men	Women	Men	Women	Men	Women
'A man's job is to earn money; a woman's job is to look after the home and family'	32	26	26	21	20	15	17	15
'A preschool child is likely to suffer if his or her mother works'	53	42	42	34	42	31	41	29
Base	587	720	448	536	852	1108	834	1011

Source: Crompton and Lyonette (2008), Table 3.1.

a large majority of women – including those working part-time as well as those working full-time – may well be committed to pursuing both paid work and care work. There is considerable evidence to suggest that women may prioritise care at a particular time of their lives, particularly when their children are small, but have the intention of resuming work at some point in the future. Kent's (2007) analysis of women who reported themselves to be 'inactive' in the LFS showed that 45.1 per cent said that they were looking after home and family, and that 45.8 per cent of these think they will definitely work in the future. It may be that the involuntarily 'inactive' pool of female labour is now rather small, although there may still be some room to increase women's hours of work, especially after children go to school, if more support is offered. But, as in most Western European countries (see Chapter 3), the survey evidence shows a preference among women for long part-time working hours, although a 41–48-hour week tends to be seen as more acceptable for fathers (LaValle et al., 2002; see also Houston and Waumsley, 2003).

The Women's Budget Group (2005) concluded that maximising paid work for women is important for tackling child poverty and for securing women's economic independence, but that it is not always necessarily in the best interests of mothers or children at a particular point in time, which means in turn that support should be offered to mothers electing to stay at home for a period of time. This begs the question of what kind of support should be offered to whom for care work and for how long, and also what should be done to enable women's paid work. Since 1997, the UK government has, like other European states, prioritised above all the goal of increasing women's labour market participation as a means to economic growth and to tackling child poverty. But, partly in recognition of the conflicting evidence regarding attitudes and behaviour, it has also sought to enable 'parental choice'. This has effectively been conceptualised mainly in terms of women's choice to work or care.

LABOUR'S APPROACH TO WORK AND FAMILY BALANCE POLICIES

Before 1997, the UK lagged behind the rest of Western Europe on policies to help combine employment and family care responsibilities. Indeed successive governments eschewed the development of explicit family policies (Hantrais, 2004). Thus UK governments offered only very limited childcare services, historically aimed at 'children at risk' (Randall, 2000), and statutory maternity leave that was neither very long nor well remunerated. Since the election of the Labour government in 1997, the issue of 'work and family' has received considerable attention from several government departments, particularly the Treasury (HMT), Trade and Industry (DTI; from 2007 BERR) and Education and Employment (DfEE; from 2001 DfES, and from 2007 DCSF), but also the Home Office in 1997–99 and Work and Pensions (DWP).[3] Public expenditure has increased sharply, with the development of childcare services and care leaves (as well as other forms of compensation for care work, for example via the pension system). The government has also introduced a statutory right to request flexible working hours. Thus, over a ten-year period from 1997, an identifiable and coherent work–family balance policy package has emerged in the UK, albeit that it differs in significant respects from work–family balance (WFB) policy packages in other Western European Union (EU) Member States (see Chapter 4).

Apart from a late move to start helping parents with childcare via vouchers, intended to promote a pure market system of provision,[4] and a commitment to extend nursery education to four-year-olds, government policy until 1997 was almost entirely limited to sponsoring and funding research, and to pointing out to employers the business advantages that might accrue to them from adopting family-friendly policies. In New Labour's first term, policy initiatives in the WFB field were in the main inherited from longstanding Labour commitments (such as the promotion of nursery education), or were prompted by the commitment to sign up to the European Social Chapter (which entailed an obligation to introduce parental leave), or, as in the matter of providing preschool education for four-year-olds, were shared with the previous Conservative administration. The Home Office's Green Paper *Supporting Families*, issued in 1998, was the first explicit government document on family policy. It stressed the need to 'support' families financially and professionally (Home Office, 1998). However, it was not until New Labour's second term in office that all three dimensions of the WFB policy package were implemented, with further increases in public expenditure during the third term.

From 1997, the phrase 'family-friendly' was often used to characterise government as well as employers' policies, alongside the phrase 'balancing work and family'. The latter tended to predominate by 2000, when 'family-friendly' was largely dropped in favour of 'work–life balance' (WLB), particularly in relation to Labour's third major policy initiative in the field (after the extension of childcare services and care leaves): the introduction of the right to request flexible working patterns. However, throughout the period 1997–2006, policy documents have continued to refer to the importance of 'balancing work and family life' and while work–life balance policies carry the implication that they will be available to anyone – male and female – wishing to 'balance' a range of activities

outside work with employment, Labour has kept the promotion of a
balance between paid and unpaid work to the fore, and for mothers much
more than fathers.

There have been very few explicit references to gender equality in the
government's policy documents. Rare exceptions are to be found in the
1999 Pre-Budget Report (HMT, 1999: Box 5.2), where the emphasis was
mainly on gender equality in the labour market, and a later Treasury and
DTI discussion document (HMT and DTI, 2003: para. 3.7), where the
context was the importance of work–family balance policies to support
the participation of men in unpaid work, which may in turn permit greater
female labour market participation. However there is clear evidence that
the significance of family and labour market change has been understood,
in particular the erosion of the male breadwinner family model. This point
was elaborated by the Chancellor in his 1998 Budget speech:

> The starting point in 1998 is exactly the same as stated by Beveridge in 1944:
> 'That nothing should be done to remove from parents the responsibility of
> maintaining their children and that it is in the national interest to help parents
> discharge that responsibility properly.' But we implement these objectives in a
> changed economy where parents try to strike the right balance between paid
> work and family responsibilities. In that new context we must do more to
> encourage family-friendly employment that will help children and their parents.
> (HC, 1998: col. 1107)

The reference to both the changing economy and the impact of the changes
in the contributions made by men and women to the household since
World War II, particularly in terms of reliance on two incomes, was picked
up in 2000 by the Department for Education and Employment (DfEE) and
the DTI (DfEE, 2000; DTI, 2000: 2.5–6). It was again highlighted in the
Budget speech of 2002 (HC, 2002). This contrasted with the continuing
attachment exhibited by many Conservative MPs to the traditional, male
breadwinner/female carer family model.[5] But one of Labour's main policy
aims, in common with EU-level policy and many other Member States, has
focused exclusively on mothers and on increasing their employment. In the
UK, it has been the relatively low level of lone mothers' employment (see
Table 5.1) that has been the main focus of attention. Labour has argued
that women's skills and knowledge must contribute to the economy and
that WFB policies should be seen as part of a 'modern social agenda' that
will improve standards at work and enable women to participate in the
labour market (HMT, 2002). The other main policy aim has concerned
children: emphasising the extent to which higher employment rates for
mothers will help to address the problem of child poverty, which Labour
vowed to halve by 2010, and how early-years education in particular will

increase children's educational attainment and improve their employment prospects.

Thus, in large measure, WFB policies have been instrumental, especially in their early conceptualisation, in serving the ends of employment policy, whether in respect of mothers or in respect of children as future 'worker citizens' (Lister, 2003). However, the Treasury has been at pains to stress the self-reinforcing linkages between economic and social policy concerns. Labour began by stressing above all that WFB policies were a necessary part of adapting to new economic circumstances and would benefit business. In fact the WFB policy documents started from the position of wider, more long-term economic needs, rather than the shorter time horizons of business, although the interests of the latter appeared to predominate for a short period between 2000 and 2001 (particularly in respect of the debates around the introduction of the right to request flexible working). Indeed, the Department of Trade and Industry (DTI) continued to emphasise the importance of the business case until well into New Labour's second term of government. However, in respect of the goals of childcare provision, flexible working arrangements, and the balance between childcare services and leaves to care (which as we saw in Chapter 3 has been the subject of concern in terms of their effect on mothers' employment), government policy has become more rather than less concerned to put the welfare of family members, particularly children, at the heart of its agenda. By 2003, when major reforms were introduced in all three areas of work–family balance policies, the link between economic interests on the one hand and the interests of family members on the other had been turned on its head, and WFB policies were presented by both the Treasury and the DTI as being about family welfare in the first instance, and broader economic and business issues second (HMT and DTI, 2003). The message became: 'what is good for families is good for the economy': 'To be successful, the needs of children and families cannot be traded against the demands of the labour market, but must be advanced together' (HMT et al., 2004: para. 2.4; see also DTI, 2005: para. 1.25), and policies focused on providing longer leaves for mothers to care for children as well as on more formal childcare and more flexible working patterns. But whether the design of the policy instruments is such that welfare ends can be fully achieved is another matter.

In any case, in the UK it remains difficult for governments to justify intervention in this policy field in respect of adults. The charge that a 'nanny state' is seeking to interfere in the way in which men and women organise their work and family lives at the level of the household is never far away. Thus, despite the fundamentally gendered nature of work and family balance issues and policies, the UK policy documents invariably refer to gender-neutral 'parents'. They have insisted, more strongly as time has passed, that parents must be enabled to make their own 'choices', with no apparent recognition of the very different structural positions of mothers and fathers in most two-parent families. In fact, policymakers have had the behaviour of mothers more firmly in mind than that of fathers, which is problematic given that genuine choice for mothers also depends on what fathers are able (and willing) to do. There is also opportunity for tensions to arise between the interests of children – as defined by policy developments in the childcare arena – and parents: for instance, if the parents prefer informal unregistered care to early-years education, or if mothers do not want to accept or cannot fit the emerging expectation that they will care at home for the child in its first year and then return to work. In 2000, Margaret Hodge told the Select Committee on Education and Employment that: 'we are not about in any way forcing mothers into work. What we are about is ensuring that those mothers who need to or choose to work . . . are given appropriate support in the childcare infrastructure . . . it is all about providing choice, it is not about forcing anyone into work' (HC, 2001, Q 499). However, as we have already seen, both policy logics and the nature of the policy instruments attempt to and may succeed in influencing behaviour in respect of how paid and unpaid work are combined.

Since 1997, a coherent WFB policy package has emerged in the UK, which in common with other Western European member states tends to encourage care at home during the first year and virtually universal (albeit part-time) formal provision from the age of three, but is significantly different in respect of the way it treats fathers. The UK also differs from other Western European countries in terms of how much it manages to deliver, particularly in terms of affordable and high-quality childcare places. Indeed childcare provision, on which most money has been spent, is particularly fragmented.

CHILDCARE PROVISION

In 1997, the UK was near the very bottom of the EU childcare provision league tables. The vast majority of non-parental childcare was provided either informally or by childminders. Free institutional provision tended to be reserved for 'children at risk' and was otherwise expensive (Randall, 2000; Land and Lewis, 1998). Planned public expenditure on childcare thus required a major shift in thinking in regard to what Kremer (2007) has called '*ideals*' of care': away from the assumption that mother or mother-substitute care is normal (and best) for preschool children, and towards formal care, increasingly delivered by professionally trained staff. The extent to which this was as a result of a considered assessment of children's best interests, or had more to do with the desire to raise mothers' employment rates, is a matter of debate; as we have seen, policy goals shifted somewhat over the decade from 1997. In respect of welfare outcomes, the fact that Labour did not attempt to change the mixed economy of public, private and voluntary provision, which has long characterised social care more generally in the UK, had a significant, negative impact.

Labour's first major policy initiative in the WFB field was the publication of a National Childcare Strategy in 1998 (DfEE,1998) and investment in childcare services has continued to be a major commitment in New Labour's second and third terms in office, with further expansion planned to 2010 (HMT et al., 2004). The 1998 strategy document set out an ambitious plan for funding 'early-years learning' for both three- and four-year-olds. In addition, the new Sure Start programme was set up, targeting disadvantaged areas, with the aim of bringing all services for children – care, health and education – under one roof. As a result, there has been a rapid expansion of places from one for every eight children under five,[6] to one for every four children by 2007 (Balls, 2007), with further increases planned to 2010. Nevertheless, public expenditure on childcare and early-years education remains slightly lower than the Organisation for Economic Co-operation and Development (OECD) average of 0.7 per cent of GDP.

The 1998 childcare strategy made clear the double dividend that Labour hoped to reap: an increase in women's employment and a better start for children, particularly for those in disadvantaged areas (DfEE, 1998). Much of the financial investment in WFB policy has been channelled into childcare with the explicit aim of encouraging women, especially lone mothers, to enter the labour market, but also to address the issues of child poverty and development by increasing family income and giving children a better start by providing good-quality 'early-years learning' (Lewis, 2003; Penn and Randall, 2005). But, because childcare has historically been considered to be a private responsibility and because there is still considerable debate about the desirability of formal childcare, Labour has increasingly sought to emphasise the importance of 'parental choice' of type of childcare. In the 2004 Ten Year Strategy for Childcare, promoting parental choice took first place; however, it was also recognised that parents needed to be able to make '*real* choices between attractive and viable alternatives' (HMT et al., 2004: para. 2.52, emphasis added.)

More (academic) commentary and criticism has focused on childcare services than on other WFB policies: in relation to reliance on the private sector for provision, problems of sustainability, the governance of childcare at the local level, the amount of choice parents actually have between different kinds of formal care, the continued high cost of childcare, the degree of success in targeting poor children, the continued doubts about the quality of childcare, and the attention paid to early learning rather than more holistic approaches to childcare (for example Lewis, 2003; Moss, 2006; Penn, 2007; see also HMT et al., 2005). From the point of view of gender equality, the recognition accorded the need to promote childcare services has been welcomed, but the instrumentalism inherent in the firm link between higher targets for mothers' employment, especially for lone mothers, and eligibility for cash transfers to help with childcare costs, has been a concern (Himmelweit and Land, 2007). The social investment model used to justify the development of childcare provision has made it particularly necessary to make the case for increased public expenditure on grounds of economic efficiency. Thus PricewaterhouseCoopers (2003) was commissioned to report on value for money in this respect, and concluded that the benefits generated by 'enabling more parents to work and boosting the long-term productivity of children' would indeed exceed the costs of additional childcare provision. But at the same time, the report drew attention to the difficulties of making such a prediction: a single percentage point variation in the effect on mothers' employment rates would increase the costs of the expansion in provision by £20 billion.

Regarding the second main goal to give children a better start, by the mid-2000s academic findings on the effects of early-years provision on children were also clearer and were cited by ministers and in policy documents, particularly the research of the large-scale Effective Pre-school and Primary Education (EPPE) project following 3000 children in the UK. This concluded that high-quality and longer-duration preschool attendance gives children a better start in school at age five, and, so long as the care is good quality, this advantage is still perceptible at age ten (Sylva et al., 2007; Sylva et al., 2004). There is also consensus in the literature on both sides of the Atlantic that infants benefit from one-to-one care, but there is considerable debate on the behavioural and cognitive effects of formal childcare provision on children aged between one and three.

Even though the UK government started in 1997 with almost a clean slate in respect of childcare provision, policy development has nevertheless tended to perpetuate the long-standing historical division between early-years education, which was the responsibility of the Department of Education, and childcare, which fell under the Department of Health. The system that has been developed since 1997 remains complicated, fragmented and lacking in coherence. Early-years learning has developed differently from childcare, despite efforts to bring more unity in their administration. The main goal in the case of the former has centred on children's development, and in the case of the latter on enabling mothers'

employment. Education has become a free, universal (part-time) entitlement for three- and four-year-olds, while care is subsidised on the supply
side mainly in disadvantaged neighbourhoods and also on the demand
side via tax credits for lower-income parents. Both forms of provision are
characterised by a mixed economy of private, voluntary and public sector
providers. The 2004 Ten Year Strategy for Childcare acknowledged that
'local delivery has been complex, with a number of separate initiatives and
funding streams' (HMT et al., 2004). Indeed, the government admitted
early on that it chose incrementally to support the piecemeal development
of childcare provision (HC, 2001a: Q84). There have been moves towards
some greater consolidation since the mid-2000s: the 2006 Childcare Act,
the first ever such piece of legislation in the UK, has given clear responsibilities to Local Authorities for securing a supply of childcare and there
are signs of more coherence in respect of the development of a universal
programme of Children's Centres (previously confined mainly to Sure
Start disadvantaged areas). But there is still a childcare market, which is
what leads to the complicated mixture of funding streams and types of provision and hence problems of sustainability, which in turn pose problems
for parents and children using childcare.

Early-Years Education

In 1999 all four-year-olds were given an entitlement to 12.5 hours per week
early-years education for 33 weeks per year, followed in 2004 by a similar
provision for three-year-olds. An early-years curriculum was introduced
in 2000. In 2006 the number of weeks was increased to 38, and the number
of hours offered is due to increase to 15 by 2010. Free part-time places are
also under consideration for two-year-olds. Beginning in 2007, 20 pilot
areas offered 15 hours' education a week and on a flexible basis: over
three days rather than five. However, Bryson et al.'s (2006) survey of 8000
parents' use of childcare in 2004 showed that the lack of flexible provision
of childcare generally was a major concern for 43 per cent of parents, which
is not surprising given the prevalence of 'atypical working'. From 2008 the
new Early Years Foundation Stage has permitted children to go at their
own pace to meet learning goals, with no fixed curriculum. Expenditure on
under-fives education rose dramatically from £116 million in 1997–08 to
£2402 million in 1999–2000, and by 2005–06 it was £3990 million (DCSF,
2007).

Table 5.3 shows the pattern of development since 2003. The vast majority of four-year-olds attend either nursery schools, or nursery or 'reception' (infant) classes in primary schools. While there has been a fall in the
numbers of children attending reception classes, as a proportion of the

population of four-year-olds, attendance has increased slightly. This is important because of the issue of quality. EPPE's findings show that only high-quality childcare settings result in good and longer-lasting outcomes for children (see above, p. 155). Reception classes have a much less favourable staff–child ratio than nursery schools or classes; the size of reception classes in England in 2007 averaged 24.8 (House of Commons Written Answers, 20/2/07, col. 670W). A report on the structure of primary school education in England compared to other continental European countries and New Zealand commented on the comparatively early entry of English children into formal education, with seemingly little positive impact on later attainment (Riggall and Sharp, 2008).

Provision for three-year-olds is much more mixed. The private sector has always been the largest provider for these children, and has increased in importance over time. Take-up among children aged three is somewhat lower than among four-year-olds and survey data show that it is mainly children from low-income families and workless households who are not receiving free early-years education. Early-years education is free, but 2004 survey evidence shows that some providers have been charging a substantial number of parents a 'top-up' fee, which would pose particular difficulties for low-income families (Butt et al., 2007).

Daycare

A three- or four-year-old child who receives early-years education for two and a half hours each day is likely also to need childcare for some part of the day. Care may be provided in the same place, or the child may have to be taken elsewhere. Bryson et al.'s (2006) survey of parents showed that 42 per cent used more than one childcare provider, particularly for children aged three or four. Younger children may also use some form of childcare. A survey of childcare providers in 2006 reported that 20 per cent of children in full day care were under two, and a further 24 per cent were two years old (Kinnaird et al., 2007).

Table 5.4 shows the pattern of provision since 2003. The amount of care provided by childminders (who must be registered and who may take a maximum of six children) remained stable during the period 2003–07. However, this form of care – historically the most used by parents – had declined sharply between 1998 and 2001, with the introduction of early-years education and the rapid expansion of privately provided daycare centres (Lewis, 2003). Full day care has seen an enormous expansion, although it should be remembered that the number of children attending is likely to be lower than the increase in the number of places, because two children may occupy a single place by attending part-time. Market

Table 5.3   Three- and four-year-olds benefiting from some free early education, 2003 and 2007* (data refers to January in each year)

| | Number of children '000s | | | | | | % of population | | | | | |
| | All | | 3-year-olds | | 4-year-olds | | All | | 3-year-olds | | 4-year-olds | |
	2003	2007	2003	2007	2003	2007	2003	2007	2003	2007	2003	2007
'Private' sector												
Private and voluntary providers	365.1	420.7	264.5	323.7	100.6	97.0	31	37	46	55	17	17
Independent schools	40.5	37.9	16.1	17.5	24.4	20.4	3	3	3	3	4	4
Public ('maintained') sector												
Nursery/primary schools	690.9	663.8	218.7	221.4	472.2	442.4	59	58	38	38	80	79
Of which:												
Nursery schools/nursery classes in primary schools	331.3	318.9	216.2	220.0	115.1	98.9	28	28	37	37	19	18
Infant classes in primary schools	359.5	344.9	2.5	2.4	357.0	343.5	31	30	–	–	60	61

Special schools	4.4	3.7	1.9	1.6	2.5	2.0	–	–	–	–	–	–
All	1,100.9	1,126.1	501.2	564.2	599.7	561.8	94	98	87	96	101	100

Notes:

* A funded early education place consists of a minimum of 12.5 hours early education for 38 weeks of the year for all three- and four-year-olds. Percentages are of all children of relevant age. Take-up is likely to be lower than shown, because some children are double-counted if they attend more than one provider and figures for three-year-olds include some two-year-olds.

'Infant classes' include reception and other classes not designated as 'nursery classes'. 'Special schools' includes hospital schools. Rounding may cause discrepancies in totals.

Source: National Statistics (2007), Table 1.

159

Table 5.4   Childcare provision, children 0–7, England*

	Providers		Places		
	March 2003	Sept 2007	March 2003	Sept 2007	Change
Childminders	68 200	67 443	300 900	308 700	+7 800 (2.6%)
Full daycare	9 600	14 069	381 600	612 500	+230 900 (60.5%)
Sessional daycare	11 600	8 783	280 800	218 100	−62 700 (−22.3%)
Out of school care	8 000	10 801	285 400	372 600	+87 200 (30.6%)
All	99 300	103 906	1 281 300	1 560 400	+279 100 (21.8%)

Note: * All provision is outside the child's home. 'Full day care' means availability for more than four hours continuously; 'Sessional' means less than four hours continuous; 'Out of School' is for at least two hours in any day outside school hours.

Source: Ofsted (2003) *Registered Childcare Providers and Places in England*, Quarterly Statistics, March. Manchester: Ofsted, Table 1; Ofsted (2007a), *Registered Childcare Providers and Places in England*, Quarterly Statistics, September. Manchester: Ofsted, p. 4.

research carried out by Laing & Buisson (2007) has reported that the daycare market is seven times the size it was at the end of the 1980s, with evidence since the mid-2000s of increasing market share and consolidation on the part of large corporate providers (Butt et al., 2007; Penn, 2007). The private, voluntary and independent sector accounted for 89 per cent of full day care providers in 2006, with a fall of 12 percentage points in the proportion of private providers and a 16 percentage point rise in the proportion of voluntary providers (Kinnaird et al., 2007). This is largely because of the development of Neighbourhood Nurseries and Children's Centres, which are more likely to be run by the voluntary sector (HC, 2007). The number of sessional day care providers and places has shrunk, but it is possible that some of these providers have turned themselves into full daycare centres. Out-of-school provision for older children has also increased and will do so further: the policy aim is for all parents with children aged 5–11 to be able to access school-based childcare on weekdays between 0800 and 1800 hours, and for all secondary schools to be open these same hours on weekdays by 2010. As per the possibility of greater flexibility in taking up early-years education (on three days rather than five), so longer hours of care for older children is seen as crucial to the success of the employment and flexible working agendas. However, private daycare providers tend to restrict their operations to the core hours of 0900–1600 hours because it is too expensive to open for longer, which does not enhance parents' choices. In addition, despite childcare during school holiday periods having been identified as a particular concern for parents (La Valle et al., 2002), the proportion of daycare providers offering holiday care has remained unchanged since 2004 (Kazimirski et al., 2008).

There has been and is a wide range of public, voluntary and, above all, private provision under the heading of 'daycare', which attracts significant, but extremely piecemeal and often short-term, supply-side public expenditure. Government supply-side funding has been particularly important for stimulating provision in disadvantaged areas, ensuring that about 30 per cent of full daycare providers are in the 30 per cent most deprived areas. Supply-side funding has also supported the development of Children's Centres via Sure Start programmes since 2003, and the Neighbourhood Nurseries initiative, launched in 2001 and funded to 2005. In addition, a relatively few Early Excellence Centres were funded by government from 1997 to act as beacons of good practice throughout England. These programmes pioneered the integration of early years education and care. Targeting disadvantaged areas made sense in respect of both main policy drivers: increasing mothers' employment (and thus also tackling child poverty), and ensuring better educational outcomes for children. But the fact that as many as 40 per cent of poor children live outside the areas designated as disadvantaged (HC, 2003) led to the government's broader commitment to 'progressive universalism' being extended to childcare. Thus, the 2004 Ten Year Strategy for childcare announced that Children's Centres would become universal by 2010. Public expenditure on Sure Start has risen from £53 million in 1998–09 to a planned £3268 million in 2007–08 (DCSF, 2007), a large part of the increase being the funding of Children's Centres. Questions have been raised about whether making such centres universal will involve a cut in funding per centre and a dilution of state support for the disadvantaged (HC, 2007). However, the 2006 Practice Guidance made it clear that centres will have different functions in different areas: in the better-off neighbourhoods, they will be mainly information centres and are not expected to provide childcare.

The government has intervened in the childcare market to ensure provision in disadvantaged areas. Ed Balls (then a Treasury minister) acknowledged the potential for conflict between market means and welfare ends in a 2005 speech to the Daycare Trust:

> There is a market in childcare in our country with parents paying for care from the private sector, as well as the voluntary and public sectors. But this is not by any means a well-functioning market and, as the Government's agreed ten year strategy sets out clearly, there are real constraints on the ability of market

mechanisms alone to deliver for parents the kind of reliable and quality care at affordable prices that we need. (Balls, 2005)

Nevertheless, the 2006 Childcare Act embedded the mixed economy of childcare in primary legislation: Section 8.3 states that from 2008 an English local authority may not provide childcare unless the authority is satisfied that no other person will provide, or that there is a problem with what is being provided. The same piece of legislation gave local authorities the responsibility of making and managing the childcare market, so that any working parent or parent in training for work can exercise their new entitlement to a childcare place. Prior to 2008, early-years partnerships involving local government, the voluntary sector and the private sector had carried the responsibility of developing provision (Lewis, 2003; Penn and Randall, 2005).

The shift towards making the availability of places a responsibility of local government represented a major effort to coordinate the childcare market, but the market is far from easy to make or manage. Sustainability of provision poses particular difficulties. A 2004 National Audit Office Report showed that of the 626 000 childcare places created between 1998 and spring 2003, 301 000 had closed (NAO, 2004). Closure rates for providers were particularly high in 2004/5, and the proportion of full day care providers making a profit or surplus fell by 14 percentage points between 2003 and 2006 (Kinnaird et al., 2007). The National Audit Office (NAO, 2006) raised doubts the sustainability of children's centres in poor neighbourhoods; certainly, the evaluation of the neighbourhood nurseries initiative concluded that nurseries in disadvantaged areas would need continuing subsidy unless they were able to attract high fee-paying parents (Smith et al., 2007). But the many supply-side funding streams initiated by government since 1998 have been time-limited. Without a long-term commitment to such funding it is difficult to see how provision can be sustained, especially in poor areas. This view is confirmed by Christie + Co., who provide market advice to childcare providers, and who concluded in the summer of 2007 that 'many subsidised nurseries will not be viable business opportunities once revenue funds have expired' (Christie + Co., 2007). In addition, by 2006, 77 per cent of day care centres reported vacancies (Butt et al., 2007), which may be in large part because the employment rate of mothers slowed (Table 5.1), although their hours of work have increased. Nevertheless, parents often report lack of availability of care (Bryson et al., 2006; Kazimirski et al., 2008; Hoxhallari et al., 2007); childcare markets are profoundly local.

The 2004 Ten Year Strategy for Childcare identified the affordability and quality of childcare, as well as availability, as major issues (sustainability was acknowledged, but weakly) (HMT et al., 2004: para. 5.35). All these issues remain problematic,[7] largely because of the complicated and fragmented system that is the UK childcare market (Penn, 2007). Regarding affordability, childcare providers charge high fees. Since 2005, the government has given more encouragement to employer-supported childcare, by allowing parents to claim tax and national insurance relief on £50 per week of their childcare payments (raised to £55 in 2006). This has proved popular, covering as many as 36 per cent of employees by mid-2006 (Kazimirski et al., 2006). But demand-side funding via tax credits has been the most important part of the effort to make market-based childcare affordable for working parents. The childcare tax credit was linked to the working tax credit (WTC), rather than to the child tax credit, which is a means-tested benefit paid to all families with children under 16. The WTC is available to lone parents working 16 hours or more a week and to couple parents where both work 16 hours a week or where only one works 16 hours and the other is incapable of work. Thus demand-side subsidies have been firmly attached to working parents and, in the case of couple households, to dual-earner households, in line with the desire to promote mothers' employment. In fact, the childcare tax credit benefits recipients who are in the middle of the income distribution the most (Brewer et al., 2005). Workless parents, with whom 15.3 per cent of children live (NAO, 2007), are not eligible for WTC or the childcare element. But despite tying the demand-side financing of childcare firmly to mothers' employment, formal childcare is used by non-working mothers: the 2005 Families and Children Survey showed median spending per week on childcare in term-time by non-working lone mothers with children under 16 to be slightly less than a third of spending by working lone mothers, and spending by non-working mothers in couple families to be just over 50 per cent of working partnered mothers (Hoxhallari et al., 2007).

Spending on the childcare element of WTC has increased enormously: it stood at £880 million in 2004/5 with projections of a rise to £1 billion in 2007/8. From 2005, the childcare element of WTC has paid 80 per cent of childcare costs up to a maximum of £175 a week for one child and £300 for two or more. However, childcare costs for parents are high (the average figures given vary considerably according to their source, for example according to the Daycare Trust the average costs of a full-time day care place for a child under two in 2007 was £152 per week, but £138 according to the market research of Laing and Buisson).

PricewaterhouseCoopers (2006) reported that parents pay 77 per cent of the costs of day care provided by the private sector. This is crucial because when such a large proportion of childcare costs fall to parents, they are more likely to choose on the basis of cost than quality (Melhuish, 2004).

In London, where average costs are particularly high, a new programme – the Childcare Affordability Programme – was set up in 2005 to provide a subsidy of £30 a place to tax credit recipients in order to bring the actual cost of a place more in line with the £175 paid for by the childcare tax credit. But this means that a parent must know about and apply for two different kinds of funding. In fact, just under a quarter of the total number of WTC claimants – a somewhat greater proportion of lone parents than couple-parents – also get the childcare element (HMRC, 2007). Lone mothers often have older children and work fewer than 16 hours, and a substantial number of couple parents are in single-earner families: neither group qualifies for the childcare element of WTC. A 2004 survey of parents reported that 11 per cent found childcare to be unaffordable, and 24 per cent found it difficult or very difficult to pay (Bryson et al., 2006). These figures were lower than in the previous (2001–02) survey, probably reflecting the rise in demand-side subsidies and the extension of free early-years education to three-year-olds. However, while the latest survey of parents' take-up of childcare using 2007 data showed a further slight fall in the percentage finding childcare to be unaffordable, the take-up of early-years education and of other formal childcare has not risen since 2004 (Kazimirski et al., 2008). In practice, parents usually buy relatively small amounts of childcare: the median weekly expenditure of a working lone parent on childcare (during term-time) in 2005 was £31, and of a couple (with a working mother) £30 (Hoxhallari et al., 2007).

The issue of quality is also crucial in a country where childcare has historically been both high-cost and relatively poor quality. Quality is, as West (2006) noted, an elusive concept. Parents seem to attach more importance to a warm and caring atmosphere and a good physical environment than to low staff–child ratios, and to unstructured play as well as to education (Butt et al., 2007). But the main concern of government has focused on the outcome measure of the child's 'school-readiness'. In respect of this goal, the EPPE project made clear the importance of high-quality early-years education and care; state-maintained nursery schools have consistently come out best on government measures of quality largely because their staff have higher levels of qualification. Ofsted, the official body that has inspected early-years education and care providers since 2001, reported that settings achieving a good or outstanding inspection score fell from 61 per cent in 2005–06 to 57 per cent in 2006–07 (Ofsted, 2007). The most striking fall in quality was registered by childminders, but the inspection body reported that a large number of new and inexperienced providers were inspected (providers are inspected every three years). The state-maintained sector provides the highest quality of provision overall, with the voluntary sector showing the largest gains since the 1990s (Mathers et al., 2007).

Compared to the Scandinavian countries in particular, the UK child-care workforce has long been low-paid and poorly qualified. This helps to account for the high turnover rate: 17 per cent of workers in full daycare centres changed jobs within the sector or left the sector in 2004 (above the average small business rate of 14 per cent), although by 2006 the figure had fallen to 13 per cent. Pay has increased since 2003, but remains lower than for workers in elder care and, on average, amounts to just under two-thirds of that for primary school teachers. The Early Years Foundation Stage, implemented from the end of 2008, demands that managers must hold a level 3 qualification and 50 per cent of all other staff level 2,[8] but in their 2006 survey of providers, Kinnaird et al. (2007) reported that 70 per cent of staff across all settings had already achieved level 2; the Daycare Trust (2006) has charged that the targets for staff qualifications have been set too low. Indeed, media reports have continued to expose low standards of staffing.[9] By 2010, the aim is to have a 'graduate leader' (someone with a level 6 qualification) in all Children's Centres, but the presence of a graduate leader will enable the provider to operate with the much higher staff–child ratio of 1:13; where there is no graduate employee the ratio has been set at 1:8. Government funding was provided between 2006 and 2008 via the Transformation Fund (£250 million) for staff training and a £40 million Graduate Leader Fund was introduced in 2008, but these funding streams are, as usual, short term. Labour costs are a major part of the ongoing costs borne by providers and in the context of a childcare market it is difficult to improve skills rapidly.

Parents have increased their use of childcare substantially since the 1980s, when mothers' employment rates started to expand rapidly (Land and Lewis, 1998), but there are signs since the mid-2000s that demand has tailed off, with higher vacancy rates among full day care providers. Despite the huge increase in public expenditure on childcare, the majority of care used by parents remains informal rather than formal. The 2007 survey of parents' use of childcare reported that 65 per cent of parents used informal care during the past year, compared with 54 per cent using formal care, although when asked about the previous week, the two figures were almost the same (40 and 39 per cent respectively) (Kazimirski et al., 2008; see also Hoxhallari et al., 2007). Chapter 3 (see Table 3.2) showed the extent to which grandparent care in particular remains very important in the vast majority of EU15 countries, the UK included. While the chances of having a maternal grandmother under 70 years of age have risen since the early 1980s, she is less likely to be living nearby (Gray, 2005). In two-parent families, the choice of informal care by grandparents is followed by care by partners, reflecting in part the prevalence of split shifts. Skinner and Finch (2006) have concluded that if the government's target of a 70 per cent employment rate for lone parents by 2010 is to be met, then state subsidies should be extended to informal care, but it is not possible to regulate the quality of this form of care. Thus the goals of increasing mothers' employment and children's school readiness come into conflict. In poor neighbourhoods, parents have not increased their use of formal care in large numbers, despite the government's focus on ensuring provision in these areas. Parents in disadvantaged areas have remained difficult to reach. The evaluation of the Neighbourhood Nursery Initiative (NNI), which was concentrated on poor neighbourhoods during the early 2000s, showed that only one in ten of parents with preschoolers in 'NNI-rich' areas used one of the nurseries (Smith et al., 2007). Low-income parents are least likely to use formal childcare provision (Butt et al., 2007) and there are also low levels of attendance among certain ethnic minority groups, particularly Pakistanis and Bangladeshis (Bryson et al., 2005; Dex and Ward, 2007).

The development of childcare provision in the UK since 1997 has been dramatic and has not been easy for government to justify in a country where historically childcare has been considered a private responsibility. But the expansion has been driven by a number of different factors that are not necessarily compatible and has taken place in a fragmented and complicated system. There is still a distinction between early-years education and care in terms of practice as well as eligibility and access, despite legislation effecting integration in 2008. From the first, early-years education centred more on the child and reflected the policy goal of investing in children to enable greater school readiness and earning power as adults, with considerable supply-side spending going to disadvantaged areas and transfers to lower-income parents to support the extension of part-time education to three-year-olds. This provision is an entitlement for the child, it is universal and free (albeit that some providers have charged parents 'top-up' fees). The development of daycare, which is needed by many parents to supplement the limited hours of free education, as well as for younger children, has had more to do with promoting mothers' employment. From 2008 there is an obligation on local authorities to ensure sufficiency of supply, but only for parents who are working or in training. The demand-side funding is also tied to parental employment. While childcare centres are promised to be universally accessible by 2010, they will not provide childcare in the better-off areas and there is no firm principle that day care should also be child-centred, as there is in the Scandinavian countries. Furthermore, the development of childcare has been market-based, and by the mid-2000s was beginning to show similar characteristics to those developed by the social care market for elder care a decade before (Lewis and Glennerster, 1996). It is widely assumed that the existence of multiple providers increases choice to parents (Le Grand, 2003), but in the crucial area of flexibility this is not necessarily so, as shrinking profit. margins result in shorter opening hours. In addition, not withstanding the huge increase in public expenditure, childcare remains expensive for parents. This is important not least because childcare costs often tend to be set against the mother's, rather than the household's income, with the result that the calculation becomes the extent to which the woman's wage covers the cost of formal care. The fact that more parents use informal than formal childcare – whether because of costs and what must often be the need to combine informal with formal care; continuing doubts about the quality of formal care; or out of genuine choice – is not recognised in terms of state subsidies.

The development of formal childcare provision remains to some extent contentious in the UK. Conservative politicians continue to voice strong doubts about its desirability for children under three (HC, 2006: Qs 11–17), characterising provision in terms of 'rows of mothers at work and rows of tiny children in uniform state-run nurseries' (Osborne, 2006): in fact, provision is mainly in the hands of the private sector and is hardly uniform. But childcare in the UK is far from institutionally embedded. The way in which it has been developed as a mixed economy means that there are large issues about how sustainable provision will prove to be in the medium and long term. Labour has been at pains to stress the importance of 'parental choice' first and foremost, but the way in which provision has developed can be held to have limited parents' real choice. Ministers have been most concerned about choice in the sense of the right of mothers (not necessarily fathers) to stay at home, but the nature of the childcare offer in terms of its availability, affordability and quality also serves to structure choice, as does the development of other parts of the work and family balance policy package.

CHILDCARE LEAVES

Leave policies have been developed incrementally alongside the investment in childcare and the development of the right to request flexible working hours. These policies have again been aimed mostly at mothers, notwithstanding the strong desire of successive Labour administrations to increase female labour market participation. Indeed, the UK now has the longest maternity leave entitlement of any EU member state (there are other member states with much longer 'homecare' leaves, see Chapter 3). In making the case for radically extending paid maternity leave, the policy documents cited the relevant research on both the health and developmental aspects of child welfare (HMT et al., 2004: 2.25–6; DTI, 2005:

2.1). Nevertheless, until 2003, the main emphasis in Labour's policy for childcare was firmly on institutional provision; acknowledgement of the importance of one-to-one care in the first year came later, and with it a renewed commitment to improving maternity leave.

There is considerable evidence that in the UK working mothers wanted and welcomed longer paid maternity leaves (DTI, 2000; Maternity Alliance, 2000) and there has also been some evidence of continuing unease about employing mothers of young children on the part of Conservative politicians and the press. Whereas leave policies in continental Europe have increasingly made explicit efforts to enable the choices of fathers, these kinds of initiatives have been much weaker in the UK. Rather, maternity leave provision has been improved in terms of both duration and payment in order to meet the needs of the child for care in its first year, in the expectation that mothers will return to work soon thereafter. While there is evidence that long – two- to three-year – homecare leaves are damaging to women's pay and career prospects (see Chapter 3), shorter, paid maternity leaves are likely to make it easier for women to maintain their position in the workforce. Many commentators have advocated a six-month maternity leave as ideal for both the child's welfare (this being the period recommended for breastfeeding) and the mother's job prospects, but the UK has gone beyond this, with little incentive for fathers to play a greater role.

The first new initiative on childcare leaves was the transposition of the EU's 1996 Directive on parental leave (creating a leave that was gender-neutral – maternity leave had long existed in the UK, as is commonly the case in Western European countries, but not in the US). While parental leave had long been a feature of most continental European work–family balance policies and in some countries had become one of the main means of encouraging men to do more care work, Labour adopted a position of 'minimal compliance' with this piece of legislation. Parental leave totalling 13 weeks per child under six was made available to each parent, if they had worked for their employers for one year. The leave is not paid (although 40 per cent of parents taking leave get some pay from their employers) and must be taken in blocks of one week up to a maximum of four weeks a year. The government fully anticipated that take-up of this leave would be low: at 3–12 per cent (DTI, 2001a). The second Work–Life Balance Survey (commissioned by the DTI) reported that only 22 per cent of respondents were aware of parental leave (Stevens et al., 2004), although fathers in the UK are not very different from fathers in France, Germany and the Netherlands in terms of the (low) percentage taking leave (see Chapter 4).

Female Labour MPs discussed the possibilities for paid parental leave at length in the Social Security Select Committee, which costed both flat-rate and earnings-related payments (HC, 1999). But the Government opted for unpaid leave and refused to reopen the question of payment in its next major policy document (DTI, 2000: 4.27–4.32). In the first year of operation, 3 per cent of parents, mainly fathers, had exercised the right to parental leave. By spring 2002, about 10 per cent of employed mothers and fathers with children under 18 months old had taken parental leave (Hudson et al., 2004), and by 2005, mothers were typically adding a week of (unpaid) parental leave onto their maternity leave (Smeaton and Marsh, 2006).

While the approach to parental leave was minimalist, a proposal for (low-compensated) paternity and adoption leave was announced in 2000 (DTI, 2000) and implemented in April 2003, alongside longer, more gener-ously paid maternity leave. The vast majority of fathers (over 90 per cent) take some leave around the birth of a child, but a substantial proportion – as much as a quarter – have been shown to rely on annual leave rather than paternity or parental leave (Thompson et al., 2005). The decision to extend maternity provision and provide a short, two-week paternity leave, paid at the level of flat-rate statutory maternity pay (see Box 5.1), represents a UK-specific approach to the statutory provision of leave.

The nature and entitlements to different kinds of maternity leave and pay are complicated in the UK (see Box 5.1).While the earnings-related statutory maternity pay period has not been changed and remains fixed at six weeks, maternity leave paid at a flat rate was extended to 18 weeks in 1999 and to 26 weeks in 2003, with a further extension to nine months in April 2007, and is set to reach a year by 2010. Contractual rights to return to work were also improved: from 2007, those taking 26 weeks' leave carried the right to return to the same job up to one year after childbirth. Jacqui Smith, then Deputy Minister for Women and Equality, defended a longer maternity leave with the right to return to the same job as a means of protecting mothers against 'downshifting' and of promoting women's position in the labour market (HC, 2005). However mothers taking a longer leave were given only the right to return to a similar job. Between 2002 and 2005, the average length of maternity leave rose from four to six months (Smeaton and Marsh, 2006). Above all, financial considerations determine the length of time mothers remain on leave (Callender et al., 1997; Hudson et al., 2004; Smeaton and Marsh, 2006). Maternity pay for women with one year's continuous service has been vastly improved, with flat-rate statutory maternity pay slightly more than doubling between 1997 and 2008, and the numbers claiming it rising more than threefold. In 2000, maternity allowance, paid to those who have not worked for the same employer continuously for one year, became non-contributory, depending only on a recent employment record and earnings of more than £30 per week. These changes have benefited low-paid mothers in particular and the

---

BOX. 5.1   LEAVES: GLOSSARY OF TERMS

Additional Maternity Leave (AML): Statutory leave available when OML finishes until 29 weeks in 1997 and 52 weeks from April 2003. It carries a right to return to the same or a similar job.

Additional Paternity Leave (APL): Leave transferred from the mother to the father (or her partner) after the twentieth week after the birth, expected to be introduced in 2010.

Additional Paternity Pay (APP): Flat-rate pay for fathers during APL from 2010.

Maternity Allowance (MA): Statutory pay for leave periods for those employed but not covered by SMP, now paid at the same flat rate as SMP (or 90 per cent of earnings, whichever is the lower), paid by the government Benefits Agency.

Occupational Maternity Pay (OMP): Maternity pay funded as well as paid by the employer under individual or collectively-agreed employment contracts.

Ordinary Maternity Leave (OML): Statutory leave of up to 14 weeks in 1997 and up to 26 weeks since 2003 which carries the right to return to the same job.

Statutory Maternity Pay (SMP): Payment requiring a service record with the same employer. Paid for up to 18 weeks in 1997 (39 weeks by 2007) by employers (refunded by the government), the first six weeks at 90 per cent of earnings (no ceiling) and then at a flat rate.

Statutory Paternity Leave (SPL): Two weeks to be taken within eight weeks of the birth.

Statutory Paternity Pay (SPP): Pay during SPL at same flat rate as SMP (and MA).

---

numbers claiming maternity allowance more than doubled between 2002 and 2005. However, employers' extra-statutory provision of paid leave has continued to benefit a substantial proportion of mainly higher-paid women, while it remains the case that a minority of mothers cannot claim any maternity pay;-10 per cent of the mothers in Smeaton and Marsh's (2006) sample reported that they had received no pay.

    Opting for a very long maternity leave and minimalist arrangements for fathers does little to improve gender equality in terms of promoting a change in the division of unpaid care work in households. But

addressing fathers as carers as well as breadwinners became more of
an issue in the 2000s, as fathers' groups campaigned more stridently
for access to their children at the point of family breakdown, and as a
series of reports on fathers in relation to the issue of work and family
balance were published (Hatten et al., 2002; Reeves, 2002; O'Brien and
Shemilt, 2003). Accumulating research evidence in the UK and the US
suggested 'father involvement' to be important for children's development. For example, the analysis of Millenium Cohort Survey evidence
for 2000 and 2003 showed that having a father with low educational
achievement, little or no employment, who did not take paternity leave
and who did not share childcare responsibilities, increased the likelihood
that a three-year-old child would have developmental problems (Dex
and Ward, 2007).

In 2004, Labour proposed to address the issue of fathers and leave by
making some part of maternity leave transferable to fathers (HMT et al.,
2004). The Women's Budget Group (WBG, 2005) pointed out the incon-
gruity of calling a leave for fathers 'transferable maternity leave'. The 2006
Work and Families Act provided that the first six months of what will
become a 12-month maternity leave by 2010 will be available only to the
mother. But if she then chooses to go back to work, the father may (from
the twenty-first week after the birth) take the rest of her leave – renamed
'additional paternity leave' – drawing low, flat-rate statutory paternity pay.
Thus the father has no individual entitlement to leave, but must rely on a
transfer from the mother. But, unlike mothers, fathers will retain the right
to return to the same job throughout whatever period of transferred leave
they take.

The cross-national evidence on what parental leave should look like if
fathers are to take it is clear: it must be paid at a high rate of compensation, be an individual entitlement and be flexible (for example by making
possible shorter and longer blocks of leave either full- or part-time) (Deven
and Moss, 2002; Nyberg, 2004). UK provision meets none of these criteria.
Furthermore, other analysts have concluded that state initiatives on parental leave to encourage fathers to take care of young children are crucial
to changing workplace cultures (Brandth and Kvande, 2001; Hobson et
al., 2006), something that Labour has frequently reiterated as one of its
main aims (for example DTI, 2001a: 1.7). However, the government's own
Regulatory Impact Assessment of additional paternity leave made it clear
that it did not expect take-up of the new leave to be large (DTI, 2005a:
Table E2; see also Kilkey, 2005).

Many different issues can be seen to inform the UK's unique approach.
One of the most significant is the expense of replacing male wages.
Certainly, employers regarded the concept of parental leave with great

suspicion and the Confederation of British Industry (CBI)'s response to
the 2005 proposals to transfer part of the mother's entitlement to maternity
leave to fathers was fear that employers would be pressed to top up fathers'
pay as an occupational benefit (CBI, 2005). By the end of 2005, the CBI's
position on the proposed leave extensions had hardened to outright opposition (HC, 2006a: col. 865). But there may also be a broader reluctance
to regulate men's working hours (see below, pp. 177–8). Certainly, this fits
with the long-standing voluntarist pattern of industrial relations in the UK
(Fagan and Lallement, 2000), which is far away from the role both unions
and employers' organisations are used to playing in continental Europe.
Employers are familiar with maternity leave and were more likely to agree
to extending it. Maternity leave was thus more acceptable territory for
intervention than paternity leave, because of the expectation that women
will do the care work, and because the government proposed an additional
sweetener in the form of a simplified administrative framework (DTI,
2001b). Nevertheless, business representatives expressed concern about
the pace of reform (HC, 2005: Appendix 2) and small business remained
opposed (HC, 2005: Appendix 9).

It may also be that both fathers and mothers in the UK are not so keen
on the idea of fathers taking more leave. While a telephone survey commissioned by the Equal Opportunities Commission of 1200 fathers with a
baby aged 3–15 months reported that 70 per cent of the fathers wanted to
be more involved (Thompson et al., 2005), there has also been evidence to
suggest that a significant proportion of fathers continue to identify themselves first and foremost as breadwinners, particularly among some groups
of the population: Asian fathers tend to be particularly traditional in
their approach to gender roles (Warin et al., 1999; Henwood and Procter,
2003; Smeaton, 2006; Dex and Ward, 2007), although there may also be
particular need for many of these fathers to work long hours. Issues to do
with fathers' identity, skills and confidence as carers may also play a part –
although Thompson et al. (2005) reported that 79 per cent of their sample
of fathers were happy to stay at home with their children alone – as well
as issues to do with the temperament of the child. Taken together, these
factors may have as much or more effect on fathers' involvement with their
young children as the availability of policies facilitating leave from work.
However, survey data have confirmed existing evidence from continental
Europe that financial compensation while on leave, together with the flexibility that is permitted when taking leave, are considered important by
fathers.

With regard to mothers, in a telephone survey of 920 female partners of
the 1200 fathers (Yaxley et al., 2005), the women were asked how they felt
about one month of their maternity leave being allocated to the father on

a 'use it or lose it' basis. In other words, mothers were asked about giving up part of their own leave rather than about an individual leave entitlement for fathers; 59 per cent were opposed to the idea, and 37 per cent thought that it was important for babies to be with their mothers. Dex and Ward (2007) have suggested that the presumption that mothers and not fathers are responsible for the care of children is increasingly at odds with the expectations of men and women that they will be both working and caring. However, it seems that a significant proportion of fathers still identify mainly as breadwinners, and mothers as carers. The latest survey in the Policy Studies Institute's maternity rights and benefits series showed that the main reason mothers stay at home is because they want to care for their very young children themselves. The proportion of all mothers (including both those who worked during their pregnancies and those who did not) saying that this was indeed the case rose between 2002 and 2005 from 61 to 79 per cent (Smeaton and Marsh, 2006). The main reason given for returning to work was financial.

The proportion of mothers who worked during pregnancy and returned to work within 17 months of the birth remained steady between 2002 and 2005 at about 80 per cent (around a quarter of mothers were not in work during pregnancy). Lone mothers are somewhat less likely to return, but those who do, return sooner. Only a third of those without maternity pay returned to work (Smeaton and Marsh, 2006). There was however a five percentage point fall over the same period (to 68 per cent) in the proportion of those returning after 11 months, which was probably due to the extension of maternity leave. This percentage is remarkably similar to that for the earlier 1996 survey (67 per cent) (Callender et al., 1997). Nevertheless, the mothers returning to work in 2005 reported fewer obstacles than did those surveyed in 2002, with more opportunity in particular to reduce their hours of work (see below, p. 185).

Whereas 40 per cent of the mothers surveyed worked part-time hours when they returned to work in 2002, the figure for the 2005 returners was nearly 80 per cent (Smeaton and Marsh, 2006), even though the aggregate employment rates for UK women show a recent decline in part-time work (see Table 2.1). But the proportion of those returning to work who changed their employer halved between 2002 and 2005 from 41 to 20 per cent, which Smeaton and Marsh (2006) associated with the 2003 legislation giving the right to request flexible working patterns (see below, p. 183 et seq.). But the extension of the right to return to the same job, also in 2003, was probably also significant here. As Adserà (2004) has argued, mothers' employment stability may be achieved via increased flexibility and easier entry and exit to the labour market, or via better statutory provision. Employment stability is important because changing employers when returning to work after childbirth has been shown to result in 'downgrading' (Gregory and Connolly, 2008).

However, 5 per cent of Smeaton and Marsh's 2005 sample returned to work only temporarily. Dex and Ward's (2007) findings from the Millenium Cohort Study showed that 77 per cent of mothers who were employed during pregnancy and again when the child reached 9–10 months remained in continuous employment until the child reached three years, but 29 per cent had experienced intermittent spells of employment. Highly qualified mothers are much more likely to return to work than low-skilled mothers, although the gap narrowed somewhat between 1996 and 2002 (Hudson et al., 2004). Mothers with no skills are the least likely to return to work. Among the 20 per cent of the mothers in the 2005 maternity rights and benefits survey who did not return to work at all, the cost of childcare was cited as a major factor by 20 per cent and unsuitable working hours by 17 per cent.

The future well-being of mothers in a welfare system that assumes adult labour market participation and an ever greater capacity for self-provision must necessarily rest on their capacity to establish and maintain their status as workers (and increasingly as near full-time workers). But mothers have historically tended to reconcile their work and family responsibilities by cutting their working hours and a large number of mothers continue to express the desire to stay at home with small children. Policy design is thus difficult, especially when the variable needs of the child are also considered. As a result of their extensive review of the literature, Galtry and Callister (2005) concluded that the best compromise may be a six-month leave for the mother followed by a six-month leave for the father (see Chapter 3). The 2006 legislation allows a transfer of the second six months of the 12 months' maternity leave to the father, which in theory makes it look as though the UK has arrived at such a compromise. However, because leave is very poorly paid, there is little chance that men will take it. In all likelihood leave will remain the province of mothers, with consequent effects for gender equality in both paid and unpaid work.

FLEXIBLE WORKING

As many commentators have pointed out, flexibility may serve employers more than employees (for example Rubery et al., 2005), for example when employees are given no option but to work long and/or antisocial hours, or to take short-term contracts. Labour has put a lot of effort into promoting flexible working, insisting from the first that flexibility must be accompanied by 'fairness' (DTI, 1998). Most emphasis has been placed on increasing the availability of the option to work some form of flexible hours. Much of the government's effort has been exhortatory, especially in the late 1990s and early 2000s. But in 2003, 'light-touch' statutory regulation was also introduced. While public spending on flexible working has been small compared to childcare in particular, it has occupied an important place in the UK work and family balance policy package. This is because it has linked directly to government's desire for a more flexible labour force and to promote more 'modern' working practices. The promotion of flexible working was also a response to evidence that employees attach importance to workplace-based solutions, especially to their ability to vary their working hours, most often by reducing them or working flexitime. When employees were asked to identify the one main arrangement that employers could provide that would help them to achieve 'work–life balance' the most popular response was 'flexible hours', particularly among parents with children under six (Hooker et al., 2007). In a country where people have historically dealt with work and family balance problems by adopting a pattern of full-time work for men and part-time work for women, and where legislative intervention to secure time to care has been largely confined to maternity leave, it is not surprising that working hours and patterns of working – for example in term-time only (something that is particularly attractive to lone parents; Hogarth et al., 2001) – should be a major focus of attention. Then again, parents – and mothers in particular – may opt for flexible working if at all possible either because they prefer to look after their children themselves, or because they cannot afford childcare (Barnes et al., 2005).

As a policy issue, flexible working in the UK context has been as or more complicated a balancing act than the provision of childcare services and leaves: first, in terms of government's own policy goals, particularly the overarching tension between the pull of economic concerns as opposed to those about family welfare; and second, in terms of the interests of different groups, with employers' concerns bulking much larger in respect of this dimension of work and family balance policies. In regard to gender equality, the issue remains – as with time to care and the provision of leaves – whether flexible working is mainly intended for mothers. The answer in terms of the policy approach is complicated. The term 'work–life balance' was introduced in policy documents mainly in relation to the promotion of flexible working, with the firm indication that it was intended to include everyone and to reach beyond issues of family responsibilities and caring. The use of the term 'work–life balance', rather than 'family-friendly' or 'work–home' or 'work–family balance', became usual in the UK in 2000. A discussion document issued that year said:

> Some people talk of making jobs 'family-friendly'. We do indeed want to help employees who have family responsibilities. But we also want to see benefits for other people in work and for employers. So we are using the term 'work–life balance'. Good practice in work–life balance benefits *everyone*. (DfEE, 2000: para. 1.3)

A definition of 'life' was offered by the Department for Education and Employment in 2000:

> [Employees'] reasons . . . will vary. They may have children or they may be caring for disabled, sick or elderly dependants. They may want time to update their skills or to acquire new skills and qualifications, so as to be more employable in the long term. They may want to become involved in their local community, attend cultural or religious celebrations or pursue other interests and hobbies. (DfEE, 2002a: 7)

This seems to indicate that the government intended the term 'work–life' balance as shorthand for a multidimensional 'life outside work' in the broad sense, including leisure (Warren, 2004 and Perrons, 2000). But hobbies, unlike care work, need have no moral or social justification.

The problem with gender-neutral policy formulations, as we have seen with parental leave, is that in practice they are taken disproportionately by women and may therefore be held to reinforce the gendered division of labour. Survey evidence on the take-up of both workplace-based flexible working policies, and the 2003 legislation allowing a 'right to request' flexible working, shows that these provisions are also taken up more by mothers than fathers (Stevens et al., 2004; Bell and Bryson, 2005). 'Family responsibilities' are the main reason that mothers have sought to vary their working hours in particular. To treat a request for flexible working patterns to engage in a cultural activity, for example, as being on a par with a request from someone with care obligations for a disabled child may be problematic.

However, a survey of employees in 2003 showed that a large majority (78 per cent) felt that 'everyone' should be able to balance 'work and home' lives in the way they wanted to, with 57 per cent disagreeing with the notion that this was not the responsibility of employers, and 95 per cent believing that people work better if they are allowed so to do (Stevens et al., 2004). It is impossible to know how 'home' was being conceptualised in this instance. Furthermore, extending the possibility of flexible working to all may serve to make it a normative practice and to erode a set of expectations essentially derived from the male career model. Indeed, the argument over the implementation of flexible working practices is more finely balanced in this regard than that over parental leave, where there is considerable evidence regarding the adverse impact of long leaves on mother's careers.

Work–life balance for everyone may be additionally convenient from the policymaker's perspective because it plays into the wish to maximise individual choices and avoids any implication of state interference in the distribution of paid working hours within households. There may also be, as we shall see, difficult issues for employers if provision is made for only one group of employees.

Nevertheless, the 2003 light-touch legislation was firmly grounded in work–family balance concerns, giving a right to request flexible working hours to parents with children under six (and disabled children under 18). This was extended in 2007 to carers of certain dependent adults, with the promise in 2008 to extend it to the parents of older children. Government has tended to confine its arguments regarding the benefits of flexible working patterns for all to its exhortatory approach to employers. Indeed, there is evidence to suggest that the main target group for the legislation giving a 'right to request' flexible working was mothers rather than fathers, as part and parcel of the policy goal of developing measures that will encourage greater female labour market participation. After all, when part-time work regulations were introduced in 2000 (in accordance with the EU's 1997 Part Time Work Directive 98/23, which Labour implemented when it adopted the Social Chapter) they benefited mainly women insofar as women who returned to work within 12 months were permitted to switch to part-time hours. The EU Directive was intended to stop the less favourable treatment of part-timers in regard to hourly pay and access to benefits, but as Kilpatrick and Freedland (2004) have pointed out, the UK regulations eschewed reference to the fundamental rights of part-timers and, lacking a full-time comparator, the vast majority were excluded (Himmelweit and Land, 2007). The main policy driver was the desire to enable mothers' employment.

Furthermore, little has been done specifically to tackle the issue of long working hours among men working full-time, which as we have seen, tend above all to characterise the experience of partnered men with dependent children (Hogarth et al., 2001). In fact, when Margaret Hodge, then Minister of Employment and Equal Opportunities, announced the findings of the DfEE's baseline study on work–life balance practices (Hogarth et al. 2001), she stressed that men as well as women wanted to balance their work and home lives. Labour's 1997 election manifesto had emphasised its commitment to 'fairness at work' and included 'the rights of employees not to be forced to work more than 48 hours a week' (Labour Party, 1997: p. 21). However, the individual opt-out to the EU's 1993 Working Time Directive (93/104/EC), negotiated by the Conservative government in order to permit individuals to work longer than a 48-hour week, has not been reversed (a 2003 telephone survey of 1509 employees found that 70 per cent of those who usually worked 48 or more hours a week had not in fact signed an agreement to opt out; Stevens et al., 2004). Indeed, while at the EU level the debate about working time moved from a narrow health and safety focus to one of work and family reconciliation (CEC, 2003), in the UK the reverse happened, with the government stating that 'the Working Time Directive, which has a health and safety basis, is an inappropriate vehicle for dealing with work/family balance issues' (DTI, 2004: 1). The DTI argued that working time was a matter of (gender-neutral) individual choice at the household level: 'one [parent] may temporarily work longer to maintain the family income when the other decides to withdraw from the labour market or work reduced hours in order to spend time caring for their children' (DTI, 2004: 2.1). Thus long male working hours were not a problem for Labour and the individual opt-out remained in place. Rather, the government has sought to promote flexible working patterns, first by exhortation and then by light-touch legislation for (gender-neutral) parents of young children, but in practice mainly mothers.

Exhortation

Labour launched an exhortatory, high-profile campaign in favour of flexible working in 2000. The strongest reason for government to promote the idea of work–life balance policies seems to have been linked to its long-standing and more general desire to 'modernise' workplace cultures, clearly signalled as a major government aim by the then Prime Minister, Tony Blair, in his Foreword to the DTI's 1998 *Fairness at Work* document, and reiterated thereafter (for example DTI, 2000: para. 4.12). The adoption of the term 'work–life balance' had much to do with the perceived need to convince employers of the importance of this policy field in dealing with an increasingly 'diverse' workforce (DfEE, 2000: 3) and of moving away from employer-led flexibility to practices that were more 'fair' to the employee: 'Work–life balance isn't only about families and childcare. Nor is it about working less. It's about *working smart* . . . it's a necessity for everyone' (DTI et al., 2001: 4, emphasis added). The government's commitment to minimal state intervention when introducing new policies in the hope of promoting 'cultural change' in the work–family balance field has remained intact, and was stressed particularly strongly by the major policy document on work–life balance published at the height of its effort to make the business case for WFB (DTI, 2000: para. 4.12). Accommodating the diverse talents of individuals had long been presented in the American literature as essential for businesses in a competitive global market (Thomas, 1990). Work–life balance for all could be, and was, presented as a response to the needs of the individual rather than promoting the welfare of any particular group.

In an effort to convince employers of the case for work–life balance, the Department of Trade and Industry commissioned research on the 'business case' for flexible working. These reports showed businesses with WLB policies to experience less turnover and absenteeism, and greater retention, commitment, loyalty, ease of recruitment and productivity (Bevan et al., 1999; Hogarth et al., 2001; Woodland et al., 2003), and were frequently cited in an effort to redefine employers' perceptions of their interests. They were supported by independent academic evidence showing much the same (Dex and Scheibl, 1999). The message that work–life balance policies need not be feared as impossibly costly by employers, and that they could make a positive contribution to the workplace, continued to be an important theme in both independent and government-commissioned research: Dex and Smith's (2002) analysis of the 1998 Workplace Employee Relations Survey (WERS[10]; see Cully et al., 1999) found that 75 per cent of employers thought that there were no or only minimal costs attaching to such policies; Bell and Bryson's (2005) analysis of the relevant questions in the British Social Attitudes survey showed that flexible working programmes contributed to job satisfaction (rather more, in fact, than they did to help people achieve a work–life balance); while Whitehouse et al.'s (2007) examination of firms in both the 1998 and 2004 WERS concluded that workplaces in which provision had increased over this period were more likely to be identified by managers as having improved financial performance relative to others in the field. While this does not prove a positive relationship, it serves to counter the idea of a negative effect.

A Ministerial Advisory Committee on Work–Life Balance was set up in 2000, with members from business, the trade unions, employer organisations and the voluntary sector, and a £10.5 million Work–Life Balance Challenge Fund was made available to support employers in developing policies. But it is very difficult to demonstrate the success or failure of government's exhortations. There are well-established government-sponsored workplace surveys that either include or focus on the issues of work–life balance provision: WERS data for 1998 and 2004, as well the Work–Life Balance Studies (WLBS) (of employers and employees) for 2000, 2003 and 2006. But data are by no means comparable between the different series, or even between different reports in the same series, and their interpretation is difficult. In any case, it is not possible to establish any causal relationship between government exhortation, or indeed legislation – both of which might at the least be held to further legitimise flexible working arrangements – and developments at the level of the firm. Nevertheless, there is agreement that the trend in workplace provision has been upwards.

A comparison of firms that appeared in both the 1998 and 2004 WERS surveys has concluded that there was a marked, though not uniform increase in both the incidence and comprehensiveness of provision in the majority (Whitehouse et al., 2007). But 20 per cent of firms actually had less provision in 2004 than in 1998. The largest increase in provision was found in workplaces which had little in 1998. Large employers and workplaces with a predominantly female workforce had the most provision, indeed there were signs of widening disparities in access to workplace-based policies between male- and female-dominated firms. Whitehouse et al. (2007) also found that in workplaces reliant on part-time employees, the level of access to other forms of flexible working arrangements was lower. The 2007 WLB employer survey reported that the availability of part-time work had become near universal, while that of reduced hours had increased from 40 per cent in 2004 to 74 per cent, and flexitime from 22 to 55 per cent (Hayward et al., 2007). However, the biggest increases in particular types of flexibility occurred between the first and second WLBS, that is, between 2000 and 2003, the highpoint of the government's exhortatory policy and the point at which it also introduced legislation. The pool of employees wanting flexible working arrangements has remained largely static, and the WLBS reported falling unmet demand.

These reports focus in the main on formal work–life balance provisions, what Bell and Bryson (2005) have called 'fixed' arrangements. But informal arrangements have also been important, especially in small and medium-sized enterprises, which tend to employ a lot of women workers. Dex and Scheibl (2001) suggested that many surveys missed 'family-friendly' arrangements in these firms because they were informal and Bell and Bryson (2005) also found the level of informal provision to be relatively high compared to some of the 'fixed arrangements'. Forth et al.'s (2006) analysis of practices in small and medium-sized enterprises in the 2004 WERS data showed that in these smaller workplaces, managers were actually less likely to say that flexible working arrangements were available than were the employees, which was probably due to the existence of informal practices.

Managers were shown in the earlier work on work–life balance to be important gatekeepers to flexible working arrangements (for example Dex and Scheibl, 2001), but by the mid-2000s, their attitudes were shown to be much less significant (Whitehouse et al., 2007), which may be an indication of the extent to which at least the idea of flexible working arrangements had become acceptable. In addition, the WERS data showed that the differences between public sector and private sector employers diminished over time, a view supported by Bell and Bryson's (2005) analysis of data from the British Social Attitudes Surveys of 1994 and 2004, although the public sector is still likely to offer a greater variety of work–life policies (Nadeem and Metcalf, 2007).

While the general picture of work–life balance policies at the level of the firm has thus been one of general improvement in terms of availability, there remains the crucial issue of who has actually taken up flexible working practices. The Work–Life Balance Surveys showed that availability of flexible working arrangements increased much more than take-up in the 2000s (Table 5.5). The 2007 WLB employer survey found that where they were available, flexible working arrangements were offered to all employees in 60 per cent of enterprises (Hayward et al., 2007). But both Bell and Bryson's (2005) analysis of the relevant British Social Attitudes questions and Kersley et al.'s (2006) analysis of the 2004 WERS data showed that in terms of availability, the key factor characterising those employees likely to report the existence of flexible working arrangements was being female. This might be because women have become more flexible, or are likely to work in jobs where flexibility is more feasible, or because they need to make it their business to know more about the possibilities of working flexibly. In terms of take-up, mothers are the most likely to use the arrangements on offer (Bell and Bryson, 2005; see also Stevens et al., 2004); mothers' use of flexible working practices has been consistently higher than that of fathers, except for shift work (O'Brien and Shemilt, 2003). Interestingly, given the provisions of the legislation passed in 2003 (see below, p. 183 et seq.), parents with children under six were not more likely to take up the option of working flexibly. Men were more likely to express concern about whether flexible working was feasible in the jobs they were doing and to worry about the effect that working flexibly might have on their careers (Stevens et al., 2004). Nevertheless take-up among men has increased. However, Bell and Bryson (2005) found that the largest proportional increase in reported availability took place among men without children. They concluded that: 'the availability of and use of flexible working options among men are not occurring as a result of change in parenting roles or the nature of fathering, but rather in response to a more general shift towards the diversification of working patterns for all employees' (Bell and Bryson, 2005: 44), thus adding weight to the case for promoting a work–life balance strategy. However, a telephone survey of 1200 fathers with a baby aged 3–15 months showed a 20 per cent increase in new fathers actually making some change in their patterns of work or working hours (Thompson et al., 2005).

The increase in the availability of various forms of flexible working became more common over the decade to 2007, with the largest increase taking place when the DTI campaign was at its height and in the run-up to passing the right to request legislation. Furthermore, despite the fact that as might be expected, availability and take-up of flexible working was highest among women and mothers, the greatest rate of increase in availability

Table 5.5 *Flexible working practices, 2000, 2003 and 2006† (%)*

	WLB1, 2000		WLB2, 2003		WLB3, 2006	
	Availability*	Take-up	Availability	Take-up	Availability	Take-up
Part-time working	49	24	67	28	69	27
Reduced hours**	56	n/a	62	13	54	12
Flexitime	32	24	48	26	53	27
Job-share	46	4	41	6	47	6
Term-time working	22	14	32	15	37	13
Compressed***	25	6	30	11	35	9
Annualised hours	17	2	20	6	24	8
Regular homeworking	n/a	–	20	11	23	10
One or more	–	–	85	–	90	–
No flexible available	–	–	15	–	10	–
Not worked flexibly****	–	–	–	49	–	44
Currently working flex*****	–	–	–	51	–	56
N: Unweighted base	7561		2003		2081	

Notes:
† The figures in this table report the survey results from the Work–Life Balance (WLB) Surveys conducted in 2000, 2003 (before introduction of 'right to request' legislation) and 2006. Take-up percentage is 'amongst all employees' in workplaces at any time in last year for WLB2 and WLB3 but 'all employees' for WLB1.
*Includes those answering 'depends/probably'; **for a limited period; ***compressed working week; **** Not worked flexibly in last 12 months; *****currently working flexibly or has done in last 12 months.

Source: Hooker et al. (2007), pp. 61–5.

182

was for men who were not parents. Thus, at the level of the workplace, work–life balance for 'everyone' seems to have characterised the pattern of policy development at the level of the firm. While it is impossible to say how far the government's exhortatory policy effected real change, the importance of cultural change (and also of the role legislation can play in securing it) is broadly supported by the academic literature (for example den Dulk, 2001; Haas et al., 2002; Blair-Loy and Wharton, 2002; Lewis, 1997). However, the government's exhortatory policy did not survive the mid-2000s. In 2005, the DTI passed responsibility for its website on work–life balance over to a government-funded service, Business Link, and much of the energy went out of the campaign.

Legislation

State intervention to regulate the hours of workers, especially male workers, has been an extremely sensitive issue for both employers and trade unions in the UK from the early twentieth century. Labour backed off from ending the individual opt-out to working more than 48 hours (see above, p. 171), and there was every expectation of opposition from employers' organisations to state intervention in respect of working patterns. The Confederation of British Industry (CBI) and the Institute of Directors (IoD) favoured a voluntarist approach. As the IoD put it early on in respect of parental leave, it was 'very comfortable with family-friendly policies in the workplace', provided that these were voluntary (HC, 1999: para. 16). But in 2001 Sir George Bain (who had already successfully piloted through the National Minimum Wage legislation) was appointed to chair the Work and Parents Taskforce to 'consider how employers and working parents' could be 'encouraged to adopt a constructive dialogue' on working patterns (DTI, 2000a, Executive Summary, para. 1). The Taskforce secured the support of employers and unions for a 'light-touch' legislative duty on employers to consider requests for flexible working patterns from parents of children under six, which the government accepted, and legislation followed in 2003. In 2007 the right to request flexible working was extended to carers of certain adults, and at the end of 2007 Labour set up an independent review into extending the right again, to parents of older children (Walsh, 2008), accepting its recommendation that the right to request be extended to the parents of all dependent children. Parents and carers who have worked continuously for the same employers for 26 weeks may ask to change their working patterns. Only one application may be made in a 12-month period, with no right to revert to the previous working pattern.
 The British 'right to request' legislation constituted an individual right to approach the employer, whereas similar rights in other European countries

were embedded in collective bargaining structures (see Table 3.6). The hardening of the government's opposition to removing the individual opt-out from the EC Directive on working hours was also defended in terms of individual choice. A Memorandum to the House of Commons' European Scrutiny Committee by Gerry Sutcliffe, the then DTI Minister responsible (HC, 2004), referred to the desire to avoid 'requiring' collective agreements on working hours. The insistence on 'parental choice' and the right of a parent to decide on the kind of work–family trade-offs he or she wishes to make chimed with New Labour's defence of individual rather than collective rights in the workplace, as well as with the gender-neutral approach to work–family balance policies in general.

The Work and Parents Taskforce stressed that while government was committed 'to introducing something special for parents of young children' (DTI, 2001a: para. 1.5), employers and individuals 'fear that treating working parents of young children as a priority is likely to cause resentment within an organisation' (DTI, 2001a: para. 2.17). The literature review on work–life balance commissioned by the DTI and published in 2003 argued, first, that if a right to request confined to parents was divisive then it made sense to extend it to all; and second, that because work–life balance was about 'working smart' it should not be seen only as something for those with family responsibilities (Wise, 2003). Evidence to the Education and Employment Select Committee from the Confederation of British Industry highlighted employers' concern about the problem of differentiating between the rights of different groups of employees to access WLB programmes: 'If . . . one has an elder care problem, one a childcare problem, how do I prioritise the two?' (HC, 2001b: Q.44; see also CBI, 2001: 5). However, survey evidence suggests that the fears of a backlash of this kind were largely unfounded. The baseline study of work–life balance practices showed that 43 per cent of employers feared an unfavourable reaction from those excluded from the programmes, but that only 25 per cent of employees felt similarly (Hogarth et al., 2001). Employers continued to favour a more inclusive strategy, and yet at the same time remained concerned about any extension of the legislation.

The TUC (2005), as well as the Women's Budget Group (2005), the Equal Opportunities Commission (EOC, 2005a) and the Select Committee on Business, Enterprise and Regulatory Reform, also called for the right to request flexible working patterns to be extended to everyone: as the TUC put it in evidence to the Employment Select Committee, 'it does not make logical sense to restrict these [benefits of flexible working] only to working parents' (HC, 2001b: Q.15). The BERR Select Committee agreed that restricting the right to request to parents and carers ignored the 'wider changes in work' (which result in more people changing career, having portmanteau careers, or working shorter hours at some point in their careers), thus condemning flexible working to a 'perceived if not actual' ghetto as a woman's problem (HC, 2008, para. 58). Certainly, surveys of employees have shown very little opposition to extending the right to flexible working patterns to all (Holmes et al., 2007; Jones et al., 2007). Barnes et al.'s (2005) study of atypical work made a plea for extension of legislation to grandparents, given the continued importance of informal childcare.

The individual right to request flexible working patterns is a new policy instrument and a radical departure for the UK. The measure is weak relative to legislation in many continental European countries – Gregory and Connolly (2008) have termed it 'anaemic' – with no right to appeal to a tribunal, but take-up levels have been high, for example in comparison with Germany (Hegewisch, 2005; see Chapter 4).The WLB Surveys of employees in 2003 and 2006 reported that the proportion saying that they had used the legislation to ask for a change in their working arrangements had held steady at about 17 per cent (Stevens et al., 2004; Hooker et al., 2007). The most common requests were to reduce hours (including the request to work part-time), or to change hours and the number of days worked. The highest number of requests came from women for part-time hours. Women were at least twice as likely as men to request a change in working patterns. The differences reported by the WLB Surveys are much higher than those reported by the 2004 and 2005 Flexible Working Surveys (FWS) of employees, which have monitored the impact of legislation. The FWS found that the most important reason for women making a request was to do with childcare needs, but that men were almost as likely to cite the desire for more free time as childcare as a reason for making their requests (Palmer, 2004; Holt and Grainger, 2005). Both sets of surveys reported that around 80 per cent of requests were fully or partially agreed to, with those made by women more likely to be successful. But it was also the case that part-time workers were more likely than full-time workers to meet with success, so the gender difference could be in part a function of the different nature of part-time and full-time jobs.

Labour felt that it had to proceed with caution in new WFB policy initiatives, especially with new programmes like the right to request that affected employers directly. The decision to move from exhortation to legislation was a bold one in the context of the voluntarist tradition of UK industrial relations, and was part of an explicit drive to 'modernise' work cultures. It was easier to make extensive changes to established programmes, especially maternity leave, which was less threatening to employers. The right to request legislation was implemented with little opposition in 2003. However, in the course of 2005, the fragility of the consensus with employers was exposed. Labour went a step too far on the very issue that employers had found most familiar and easy to accept: maternity rights. The CBI insisted that the government must take over responsibility for administering the new maternity leave provisions, and when it refused, the CBI opposed the extensions to the right to request flexible working patterns that were proposed in the 2005 Work and Families Bill. In a press release issued in 2005, the CBI stated that while employers had accepted the 2003 legislation, 'there are limits to the number of requests that can be accommodated', adding that the proportion of its members reporting that the right to request was having a negative impact on business had grown from 11 to 26 per cent (CBI, 2005). In 2007, the CBI expressed additional concern over any further extension to the parents of older children. The 2006 WLB Survey of employers also reported that 67 per cent of managers agreed that it was not easy trying to accommodate employees with different patterns of working, and that employers' perceptions of the effects of the legislation had become more negative (Hayward et al., 2007). Yet the Chartered Institute of Personnel and Development was, like the Trades Union Congress, still keen on extending the right to request to everyone (Emmott, 2007), arguing that it would be easier to accommodate requests once there was a critical mass of people with flexible working patterns.

While Labour has progressively sought to extend the right to request, it has not included non-carers. The legislative approach to flexible working has remained a work–family balance policy, even though at the level of the firm, various types of flexibility are often offered to all workers. This is important not least because at the EU level, relatively little attention has been paid to the need for the inclusion of measures to promote work–family balance as part of the 'flexicurity' strategy (CEC, 2007). The survey evidence has shown the idea of flexible working patterns to be a popular work–family balance policy in the UK. This may be because historically variation in working hours has been the main way in which women have sought to balance their work and family responsibilities. The policy also fits with the evidence suggesting that mothers of preschool children rely heavily on informal care, including care by partners, and indeed that many prefer to take care of their small children themselves as much as possible.

Flexible working may be of particular value because it does address workplace cultures, challenging the idea of standard, often long working days and the need to put in 'face-time' during certain hours (Rapoport et al., 2002). To the extent that the survey evidence on workplace practices shows that flexible working patterns have become more common, traditional male work norms may be changing. Nevertheless, it is mothers who made the most use of flexible working, using both policies implemented by firms and the new legislation.

CONCLUSION

UK policymaking in the field of work–family balance has had multiple policy goals, even within a single dimension of the policy package. Thus, while policies to promote early-years learning aimed mainly to further child development, childcare policies were tied firmly to paid work and focused on securing the greater labour force participation of mothers. Similarly, the promotion of flexible working patterns had much to do with the government's desire to modernise work cultures (for everyone), as well as to promote balance between work and home responsibilities, and to enable employment, particularly by mothers. In fact, in the UK as well as in other Western European countries, including Scandinavia, the largest increases in mothers' employment occurred before the implementation of reconciliation policies, although there may nevertheless be a iterative relationship between policies and behaviour. This does seem to have been the case for lone mothers, whose employment rates have increased sharply since 1997, and whose behaviour has been shown to be particularly responsive to policy changes (for example Kiernan et al., 1998).

Labour began by investing heavily in childcare, which was an obvious fit with its commitment to increasing mothers' employment. But by the early 2000s, it was addressing family welfare issues more explicitly, particularly the need of children for one-to-one care during the child's first year, as well as the already established emphasis on the importance of early learning. Nevertheless, the decision to expand the substance of work–family balance policies in 2000 to encompass leaves and flexible working seems to have been taken at a time when the presentation of the case for these policies rested largely on the benefits for business rather than the family, which suggests that the priority accorded the business case in 2000–01 was designed in large part to win over employers, the most powerful interest group likely to oppose these initiatives. Labour approached innovative legislation cautiously. In the case of parental leave and flexible working, it favoured minimalist provision designed to set minimum standards. However, the intention in the case of flexible working was that it would provide a catalyst for cultural change and the modernisation of working practices in the private sector. Some of the largest changes were made in the policy field that was most familiar to employers: maternity leave and pay. The most social expenditure went to childcare, which was very underdeveloped in the UK. But while there was huge potential for creating a coherent, accessible, available and affordable childcare system, this did not happen. Multiple goals and a continuing commitment to delivery via a mixed economy of care have resulted in the perpetuation of a fragmented system that is also expensive for parents.

The claim for policy coherence thus rests on the construction of the policy package, rather than on particular dimensions of it or on its delivery. The explicit commitment to a work–family balance policy package was a new departure in the UK, born of both family change and welfare state change, which Labour sought to push along a path similar to that favoured in EU-level documents and by other Member States, even though other countries occupied very different starting places and used different policy instruments. But there were also underlying continuities in regard to the different policy dimensions: the decision to expand the familiar maternity leave rather than develop a more continental European leave system, and the continued commitment to a mixed economy of childcare. Indeed, it is difficult to sum up the work–family balance policy balance sheet in the UK after ten years of policy development. Reports by the European Commission always placed the UK alongside or below the Southern European countries in this policy field before 1997. This is no longer so; policy has been developed quickly in the face of long-standing political opposition to intervention in the private sphere of the family and by the opposition of employers to intervention affecting the workplace. But the chosen policy instruments have not delivered as much as might have been hoped, or indeed possible. While multiple goals have characterised policy development in other countries too, other Western and Northern European countries have developed much less complicated and fragmented systems, which are also more sustainable and more firmly socially, politically and institutionally embedded. In a report on the early-years workforce, the left-leaning think-tank, ippr, concluded that: 'it is hard to see how a world-class, transformational early years sector, with a high quality, fairly paid workforce, can be delivered on existing levels of spending through the current market model' (Cooke and Lawton, 2008: 7).

Gender equality has not been an explicit policy goal; indeed the whole package of policies in the work–family field in the UK has been explicitly gender-neutral and has placed a premium on individual choice and on 'parents' deciding what is best for them and their children. Nevertheless, the WFB package has been focused largely on mothers, and while it has been tied to a strong employment agenda for mothers, the generous extensions to maternity leave and pay, together with the new legitimacy accorded reduced working hours by the 'right to request' legislation, have also reinforced the importance attached to mothers' work as carers. This raises the issue as to whether 'supported' female earning, underpinned by childcare leaves as well as services and by a degree of legislative protection for part-time work, is preferable to the 'unsupported' model of the US. The answer is not as straightforward as it might appear: there is a high degree of sexual segregation in the labour market in Scandinavia, where the 'supported' model is most developed and often involves rather long child-care leaves, usually taken by women. Nevertheless, there is little support in UK attitudinal or behavioural data for an 'equality-as-sameness' model along the lines of the US. As we have seen, there is considerable evidence to suggest that many mothers want to be able to look after their small children, either by not working for a period of time or by working part-time, although the constraints imposed by the shortcomings of childcare provision is also a factor. Returning to the labour market within 18 months after childbirth, but very often part-time and sometimes only on a temporary basis, has become much more common. The right-of-centre think-tank Policy Exchange has proposed a universal long homecare leave (to run until the child is three) which is payable to the 'main carer' – effectively the mother – in order to promote 'choice' (Hakim et al., 2008). However, without a parallel entitlement to a childcare place or assurances regarding job protection and pension provision, such a proposal likely becomes another salvo in the debate over the proper role of mothers, rather than addressing the relationship between paid and unpaid work for men and women.

Indeed, UK work–family policy has had relatively little to say about fathers. Yet, sharing care work at the household level poses particularly difficult issues, for there is a tension between the individual's real freedom to choose and gender equality. Men have steadily increased the time they spend caring for children (although not the time they devote to housework), but the option to follow Scandinavia in setting a 'daddy leave' quota or in setting legislative limits on the often long hours worked by British fathers was not taken by the UK government. In large part, this is because economic objectives have been prioritised for men more than for women. For men, paid work is assumed to take precedence over unpaid work. But in the UK context in particular, it is fundamentally important above all to rethink the existing male career path as the norm and also to promote care work on the part of fathers if gender equality is to be promoted.

It is possible to suggest that arguments for work–life balance for all, rather than work–family balance for parents and carers, have a better chance of including men and changing their behaviour. In this view, if the need for 'balance' is mainstreamed, it will have greater purchase. Mainstreaming carries the idea that policies for gender equality are no longer confined to an equal opportunities 'ghetto', but are integrated across all fields of policymaking (Rees, 1998). Arguments for the 'right to request' flexible working for everyone emphasised inclusivity, making it easier to include men and in so doing to pose a challenge to the standard, male career path. But the issue of inclusivity became a strategy to deal with 'diversity' in the workplace more than gender equality. This may in turn lead to downplaying gender issues, and yet the divisions of paid and unpaid work are profoundly gendered and are structured by gender inequalities. Recognition of the necessity for and value of care work at particular times over the life-course requires more innovative policy approaches to ensure that the costs of doing care work, particularly in terms of income and pensions foregone, do not lie where they tend to fall – mainly on women. In addition, while mothers may well want to reduce their hours and to work part-time, there is no reason to suppose that they are happy to be penalised as heavily for doing so as they are in the UK, particularly in terms of pay.

The idea of promoting a 'life-course perspective' (HMT, 2005; see also Anxo et al., 2006) by making provision for the movements that adult workers make in and out of the labour force as a result of care responsibilities, retraining and portfolio careers may effectively mainstream the kind of career path that has hitherto been more the province of women than men. But recent developments in Dutch policy discussed in Chapter 4 show there is a danger that (inadequate) compensation for care may be largely confined to women, and the possibility of saving for early retirement or compensation for lifelong learning to men. The assumptions regarding increasing individualisation in terms of economic independence that have become the crucial underpinnings of social policies of all kinds mean that policies to enable women to maintain their attachment to the labour market are very important (see also Himmelweit and Land, 2007).

NOTES

1. Some of the data and policies discussed in this chapter apply only to England and Wales.
2. This chapter does not include discussion of fertility, which has not been a major policy issue in the UK. The fertility rate remains relatively high (in European terms).
3. UK government departments change their names with bewildering frequency. DfEE: Department for Education and Employment; DfES: Department for Education and Skills; DCSF: Department for Children, Schools and Families; BERR: Department for Business, Enterprise and Regulatory Reform.
4. Land and Lewis (1998) and Sparkes and West (1998) trace the way in which the Conservatives' childcare voucher policy failed to promote a 'pure' childcare market.
5. See for example, Leigh, House of Commons, Debates, 9/7/96, c. 265 and Paice, c. 275; Brady, 5/11/99, c. 627.
6. The age at which children in the UK enter school, which is younger than in almost all other Western European member states, where it is commonly six and sometimes seven.
7. West's (2006) analysis in this respect still holds.
8. Level two is equivalent to more than five GCSEs at grades A*-C, one A level, or GNVQ intermediate; level three is equivalent to 2+ A levels, or GNVQ Advanced, National Diplomas.
9. BBC 1 (2008) *Whistleblower*, broadcast 5 March 2008.
10. This national survey is sponsored by the DTI (now BERR); the Advisory, Conciliation and Arbitration Service; the Economic and Social Science Research Council; and the Policy Studies Institute.

6. Concluding reflections on gender equality and work–family balance policies

Work and family balance policies have taken a larger place on the political agenda in most EU15 member states since the late 1990s. Structural, social and economic changes in families and labour markets have made work and family issues more prominent. The changing contributions that women in particular make to families, which have involved many more mothers earning, have resulted in more time pressure, especially, many would suggest, in respect of the unpaid work of care. It can be argued that governments have increasingly recognised a set of 'new social risks' arising from these changes, particularly in terms of making additional provision via cash benefits or services for childcare. For example, explicit recognition of the erosion of the traditional male breadwinner model family that was the basis of the early twentieth century welfare settlement and its implications for policy can be found in UK post-1997 policy documents. Nevertheless, the 'recognition of new social risks' argument has functionalist overtones. For it is also apparent that work–family balance policies have played a part in the changing agendas of modern welfare states and the preoccupations of policymakers at European Union (EU) and Member State levels with the challenges of globalisation, as they have made renewed effort to harness social policies to effective economic and employment policies. The attempt to raise the level of mothers' employment and calls for the 'modernisation' of social provision have featured largely in this.

The hopes for work–family balance policies are many, and they vary between policy actors. Governments have the widest variety of goals, which include in virtually all EU15 Member States a strong focus on increasing women's employment, and have also included the need to address low fertility, the welfare and development of children, and to modernise working practices. Employers hope to control absenteeism and turnover, to retain valued workers, and to promote job commitment and performance. Parents seek to reduce stress and 'pressure', and, more positively, to achieve a 'balance' that is satisfying. Parents tend to be concerned about the key elements of both paid and unpaid work and how they manage these, but differ considerably in their ideas as to what constitutes an optimal balance. Policymakers are more likely to focus on only one of these key elements – in the recent past, paid work – and to have goals that are as, or more closely related to economic and productivity issues than to the welfare of individual family members.

But while there is a long tradition in many Northern and Western EU member states of state intervention in the work–family policy field, the current policy goals that are dominant, particularly the promotion of mothers' employment, but also the raising of fertility rates, can be achieved without substantial state support, as the experience of the US shows. Work–family issues are a matter of debate in the US, but mainly in relation to practices at the level of the firm; there has been very little by way of state involvement compared to Europe. Indeed, the whole way of thinking about work and family responsibilities in the US has been rather different: it has long been accepted that all adults will be, and should be, in the labour market, with substantial anti-discrimination legislation to enable this, but very little by way of state support for care responsibilities. This has been justified by the view that decisions about the gendered division of work and care should remain private, family ones, and that work–family balance is a matter for the individual and the firm, not for collective expenditure by the community or the state. Campaigners have tended to focus on making a business case for 'family-friendly' practices at the level of the firm, something that has also characterised some Western European countries, particularly the UK, but also Germany. However legislation has played a much more significant part in Europe, and social expenditure on family policies has remained very low in the US. Furthermore, neo-liberal thinking would consider expenditure of this kind to be inimical to the economic goals of increasing competitiveness and growth. However, Finland, where social expenditure is relatively high and policies are well developed, tops the World Economic Forum Growth Competitiveness Index, with the US in second place, and Finland also has the most equal distribution of income, regardless of the measure (Eurofound, 2006a). It seems that in respect of economic growth and competitiveness, as with female labour market participation, there are different ways of achieving similar overarching policy goals. The way that is chosen will depend largely on the social, economic and cultural context and on politics.

Since the late 1990s, the EU member states that have been slower to develop work–family balance policies and have often justified their increased level of intervention in terms of the support they argue that it provides for economic and employment policies. Early-years education in particular has been lauded in this respect by the OECD and even in the UK by a leading management consultancy company (see above p. 155) because it enables mothers' employment and there is evidence that it enhances 'school readiness'. The language of social investment has to a considerable extent – in relation to work–family policies for young children, but not for elderly people – trumped 1980s neo-liberalism to the extent that a case for intervention has been successfully made. However, policy implementation via a mixed economy of welfare – particularly, but not exclusively, in the UK – shows the continued influence of neo-liberal economic ideas, which have particularly strong implications for the development of care services, a dimension of provision that has been especially important in Scandinavia. Nor can it necessarily be assumed that government commitment to pursuing work–family policies is now strongly embedded everywhere. Nevertheless, at the EU level, the reformulation of the European Model in terms of 'flexicurity' has sought, yet again, more firmly to join social to economic and employment policy.

This book has focused on the three areas where work–family policies have been developed most: childcare services, leaves to care for children and flexible working. The approach to these has been mainly in terms of how to take account of unpaid care work so that employment rates are also increased. In other words, policies have tended to be instrumental, with the main focus being employment rather than care. Policies have been developed to address working time and time to care, and to provide for the care of children in formal childcare settings, using both cash transfers to parents and to providers, as well as the direct provision of services. We have seen that while there is a significant commitment to similar overarching goals, which the European Commission has played a part in formulating, different countries have put together policy packages that emphasise different policy dimensions and have implemented similar policies differently. There is nothing new in particular social policies being promoted for somewhat different ends in different national contexts and/or by different policy actors, just as the same policy may result in different outcomes due to context, or to the details of its implementation. But policies touching the family have tended to be particularly heavily infused with values and normative ideas as to how families should look and behave. In addition, policies in the social care field generally have also been particularly susceptible to hijack: they are often about something else. Thus social care has often been about the needs of health-care systems, just as childcare may be more about promoting mothers' employment than the welfare of children.

Many policies necessarily have multiple goals, but in the work–family field simple instrumentalism – whereby work–family balance policies are really about achieving other policy goals – is problematic. Instrumentalism has been more characteristic of the recent wave of work–family policies than it was in the much earlier Scandinavian developments. If it is hoped that a policy will above all serve the cause of, say, employment policy, then it may not help parents to achieve their work–family balance goals and may well exacerbate some of the problems that they face. There may be legitimate societal reasons for aiming primarily to increase participation in the labour market on the part of all adults, but this may also exacerbate problems of parenting which have been moving up the policy agenda in many Western countries, unless due consideration is given to the problems of the quality of care, and of rewarding and sharing care work. It may also be suggested that it is more legitimate for the state's main focus of concern to be the promotion of children's welfare first and foremost, yet there is strong historical evidence that children are unlikely to do well if their carers do not. However, trade-offs in terms of both policy goals and welfare outcomes are unavoidable to some degree.

Indeed earlier chapters have raised the issue of the different interests of both individual family members, and policy actors. The focus for analysis has been on gender and gender equality: on gender because the divisions of, and relationship between, paid and unpaid work are fundamentally gendered issues; and on gender equality because the new set of assumptions regarding individualisation and the desirability of an adult worker model family makes its achievement more pressing. The rest of this chapter will reflect on whether there are any useful conclusions about the role of the state in the work–family policy field in this respect. After all, there are very different ideas on the part of policy actors and people – women in particular – as to what constitutes work–family balance, both between and within countries. There are both broad similarities and yet considerable differences between countries in terms of the kind of balance exhibited in the policy packages on offer and the nature of the policy instruments. The differences reflect the different contexts – this book has paid particular attention to labour market behaviour and to attitudes – as well as the nature of existing policies and thinking about work–family issues. Thus the scope for policy learning may well be limited, even though Western states have in large measure agreed overarching goals regarding the desirability of higher employment and fertility rates, and even though some countries appear to be much more successful in implementing work–family balance policies than others. Nevertheless, no Member State is without a policy agenda in the work and family field and, in regard to achieving gender equality, there is a case for promoting more holistic policy thinking about both the work and care sides of the equation.

People have very different attitudes about what constitutes an appropriate balance between paid and unpaid work for men and for women, which makes it additionally possible for some to argue that for the most part this policy problem lies outside the purview of the state and should be left to households, and either to collective bargaining between employers and employees, or to individuals to negotiate with their employers. In terms of behaviour, the way in which two-parent households divide work and care responsibilities certainly varies enormously. There are no neat patterns mapping onto the welfare regime typologies that have been developed since the late 1980s. In the UK, the Netherlands, Germany and Austria part-time work for women has been and in large measure remains the main way of 'reconciling' work and family responsibilities, while working hours for fathers tend to be long, although not in the Netherlands. Fertility is particularly low in Germany. In Southern Europe except for Portugal, mothers' employment rates are relatively low, but those women in the labour market are likely to be working full-time. Mothers' labour market behaviour is thus polarised between full-time paid work and no paid work. In these countries, fertility rates are also the lowest. In the Nordic countries and to some extent France and Belgium, mothers tend to have high employment rates and are likely to work long part-time or full-time, as are mothers in the US.

Policymakers must decide how far to work with the grain of peoples' attitudes and behaviour, and how far to seek to induce change. While governments in Western countries have accepted the overarching policy goal of promoting an adult worker model family, they have varied widely: in terms of the amount of legislative effort and public expenditure they have devoted to work–family policies; in the balance of policy instruments used; and in the calibration of these instruments. Still, it is very difficult to identify causal relationships between policies and changes in behaviour. The Nordic countries have a range of supports in the form of cash benefits and services from the state, as well as job protection for mothers on leave and entitlements to reduce working hours, and these are the countries with high, near-full-time employment rates for mothers and relatively high fertility. In the Southern European countries, a deep commitment to familialism has actually meant in practice that the family has been left to take responsibility for 'reconciliation'. In a context which, unlike Western Europe, has relatively little by way of part-time work to offer, both mothers' employment rates and fertility remain low. Different starting places for policy, and different labour market, cultural and social contexts, mean that very different policy emphases are likely to be needed to promote change. In addition, long-established types of policy are always likely to thwart radical change, as in the case of the greater commitment shown to the development of maternity leave than to parental leave in the UK. Policy learning is therefore most likely to be useful at the level of calibration – the detail of implementation – rather than at the level of the policy package as a whole. For example, the Nordic experience shows that fathers are unlikely to take parental leave unless it is an individual entitlement, well compensated and flexible. Prescriptions in terms of the nature of the whole policy package are unlikely to be useful. It is also clear that a focus on only one dimension of work–family balance policies is also unlikely to be successful: work–family balance requires consideration of time, money and services, and a range of policy responses. It is increasingly tempting for governments to try to address social needs via cash transfers (the Dutch life-course savings scheme being a good example), which also more easily serve a simple choice agenda. However, ensuring the provision of high-quality services is crucial for both children's welfare and the promotion of gender equality.

So, even if it is allowed that state intervention in the work and family field is desirable for family members and the wider society, it is likely to be difficult to impose a particular model of work–family balance. The wide variety of attitudes and patterns of behaviour that characterise many countries militate against such an approach. Thus Catherine Hakim (2000) has argued that women have very different fundamental orientations to work and family, and that policies should work with the grain of those orientations. So, more policy effort could logically be expended to enable the minority of home-oriented women to have more children, something that is unlikely to have an impact on the minority of career-oriented women. However, even in Hakim's categorisation, by far the largest group of women seem in many ways to 'want it all', seeking ways to adapt to having and demonstrating commitment to both a job and children. In all probability they would like to be able to do both without undue stress or sacrifice. Nevertheless, given that parents do have very different ideas about the 'right' balance of work and care for cultural, social and historical reasons, both within and between countries, then it is possible to argue that no single model for 'balancing' work and family responsibilities should or can be prescribed.

Where does this leave the pursuit of gender equality? This book has worked with a definition of gender equality that respects agency and seeks to enable real choice (see Chapter 1). It is important to distinguish the idea of real or genuine choice from the political rhetoric of choice, which is increasingly prevalent in member states. In regard to work–family policies this rhetoric tends to be either gender-neutral, as in the case of the UK's Labour government – which effectively ignores the fact that men's choices have a habit of constraining those of women – or, as in the Scandinavian countries, to be part of an explicit political argument about what kind of gendered divisions of paid and unpaid work are desirable. Right-of-centre thinking in particular seems willing only to promote 'freedom of choice' for mothers (but not necessarily fathers) to stay at home with small children (for example Hakim et al., 2008). Of course, real choice to engage in paid work and unpaid work cannot be cheap because it involves making alternative forms of provision available. But the policy touchstone of enabling a real choice between socially desirable alternatives is particularly appropriate for diverse and pluralist societies, such as the UK, where there is little possibility that different groups in the population – men and women, but also different ethnicities – will sign up to a single family model in such a charged arena as work and family responsibilities. The definition of gender equality adopted in this book acknowledges the importance of unpaid care work, but also eschews the idea that the 'choice' to do it necessarily involves (mainly female) sacrifice, usually in the shape of income, promotion prospects and pension entitlements. This is a matter of social justice for individuals in households (Moller Okin, 1989).

Enabling care work by a range of people in formal settings and in the home by rewarding it appropriately is also crucial for the welfare of society as a whole, and is likely to become more so with population ageing. The UK household satellite accounts for 2000 estimated the monetary value of informal child and adult care to be £231 billion, equal to more than one-quarter of gross domestic product (GDP) in that year (Himmelweit and Land, 2007). Enabling paid work is also important for societies which need to make full use of all available talent, something that has been more readily recognised by policymakers in respect of attracting women into the workforce, even though this has sometimes been promoted more by the use of sticks than carrots especially in respect of particular groups of women (above all lone mothers), as in the case of some dimensions of welfare reform in some parts of the US. At the individual level, the shift in policymakers' assumptions towards the desirability of an adult worker model family, and hence the idea that all adults, male and female, will be increasingly economically independent, makes it more urgent to ensure that women can stay in the labour market in a 'good-quality' job.

In most countries policymakers have tended to acknowledge gender as an issue mainly in relation to women's lower levels of participation in the labour market, and to concentrate more on securing their access to paid work than on improving their labour market position. At EU and Member State levels, many work–family balance policies have been explicitly aimed at making the 'reconciliation' of work and family responsibilities easier for women in order to get mothers into the labour market, even if only on a part-time basis. The development of childcare policies since the late 1990s has usually made explicit reference to the goal of increasing mothers' employment, which in the UK has been linked in turn to the need to address child poverty. The desire to promote children's early learning has also been prominent on the policy agenda in some countries, and this has been shown to require high-quality care. However, coverage rather than quality is the policy priority for improving mothers' access to employment, and in countries where there is also a prior commitment to a mixed economy of welfare (as in the UK and the Netherlands), quality is in any case harder to secure because highly qualified staff will push up the costs of independent providers. This in turn may affect coverage.

Policies designed to address the issue of time to care by providing childcare leaves and offering the possibility of reducing working time are usually used by mothers rather than fathers. Leaves longer than four to six months may have a detrimental impact on women's advancement in the workplace. Long leaves of over a year are likely to do so. In addition, cash benefits for those taking long leaves are usually paid at a low level of compensation, which fails to provide adequate recognition of, or compensation for, care work. Indeed, cash payments for care, which are sometimes promoted as furthering the 'choice' agenda for mothers, cannot be a part of a policy package that promotes 'real choice' unless there is also a realistic option to take up a good-quality childcare place. But it is possible to argue that mothers taking a substantial leave – as much as 12 months – is in the best interests of children. Fathers are not as likely as mothers to take up an entitlement to parental leave, for example, so given the widely acknowledged need of very young children for one-to-one care, it is arguably a pragmatic policy decision in the interests of children to focus work–family balance policies on women rather than men. In the case of working hours, employers are more likely to be sympathetic to requests from women for shorter hours, term-time working and the like, than they are to those from men. It is perceived as normal for women to care for children, who may also, of course, be seen as lacking commitment to the job.

Reconciliation policies for women thus meet the main policy goal of governments, providing a way of maintaining informal care and of promoting labour market re-entry. They are also easier to implement than policies that also address the behaviour of fathers in terms of questioning the standard notion of the male career path and the small amount of care work performed by fathers. In France, 'reconciliation for women' has had very little effect on fathers' behaviour, and there is evidence that the highly gendered division of unpaid work has resulted in considerable dissatisfaction, notwithstanding the highly developed work–family policy package. But attitudinal evidence suggests that in many countries such a reconciliation strategy is popular: for example, German mothers working more than 35 hours a week would overwhelmingly like to reduce their hours. There is always debate on how far social policies should reflect, or seek to influence, behaviour. In recent decades, Western governments have not hesitated to tighten conditionality in the work–welfare relationship, such that the expectation of employment on the part of all able-bodied adults is now firmly entrenched (and more is increasingly expected of disabled people too). However, the concern that 'the family' should continue to perform informal care work is also intense, which makes the promotion of some sort of paid or unpaid work balance on the part of women attractive. On the whole, the development of work–family policy packages have been more concerned to permit mothers to shoulder their dual and often conflicting responsibilities for both paid and unpaid work than to make real choices.

There are obvious problems with such a strategy for gender equality. First, given that no country has found a way of offering much by way of even average compensation for informal care work, or attractive rewards for formal care work, especially in childcare (England et al., 2002), to continue to expect this work of women much more than of men is bound to disadvantage them materially. Second, feeble expectations of fathers' participation in care work are likely to result in fathers continuing to do little. If a colleague in an academic department carries out a key administrative task – such as supervising examinations – badly, then it is tempting to give the task to someone else. This action will certainly benefit students and probably make the running of the department easier, but it will also increase the workload of a more conscientious colleague. There is then a case on grounds of fairness for seeking to share care responsibilities more equally between men and women, but compelling someone to care may have negative welfare outcomes for the person cared for that are of a more serious and immediate kind than those likely to result from compelling someone to do an administrative task. Third, while it may be easier to help women to reconcile work and family obligations, because of the substantial evidence in many countries that this is what women themselves want and because intervention on behalf of mothers has a long-established history in Europe, in the context of other policy trends towards individualisation this is likely to exacerbate gender inequalities. Neither assumptions regarding increasing individualisation in the labour market and greater economic autonomy, nor individualisation of the tax and benefit system, fit with existing gendered divisions of paid and unpaid work. It will not do to treat the 'ought' as an 'is' for policy purposes.

These issues make a policy decision to opt for promoting the kind of equal worker/carer model favoured by Nancy Fraser (1997) and Janet Gornick and Marcia Meyers (2003) look very attractive. This model actually informed policy in the Netherlands – in the shape of the 'combination scenario' (see Chapter 4, p. 131) – in the early 2000s. Even though the Netherlands has a one-and-a-half-earner model family, with women working short part-time hours, men also work shorter hours than in many member states and a higher proportion (19 per cent) take parental leave, even though this is still a low figure relative to women. But, the worker/ carer model family remains utopian. Its realisation would require radical legislation forcing a major change in men's behaviour, which would not only be opposed by many fathers, but also by many mothers in a large number of countries.

Gender equality has been an explicit policy goal only in the Scandinavian countries, particularly Sweden, but even here it has tended to focus mainly on 'reconciliation for women', as a means to securing greater equality in employment. Furthermore, policy has tended to promote a particular model of informal care by mothers for very young children, followed by extensive formal childcare provision. To provide a real choice of formal or (well-compensated) informal care means risking the possibility of empty childcare places, which is likely to be expensive. In Finland, where there is genuine choice even in respect of the care of children under three, as to whether to use a childcare place or a long homecare leave, women have tended to use the latter, albeit that they also tend to follow a long histori- cal tradition and eventually rejoin the labour market as full-time workers. However, in Sweden efforts have also been made, chiefly through the introduction of 'daddy leaves', to get men to do more informal care work. But in Denmark, where the effective model of work–family provision con- sists of high rates of long part-time and full-time work for women and the commodification of childcare in high-quality settings, 'daddy leave' was abolished because it was argued, controversially, that it constrained men's choices. In the labour market, the Scandinavian countries – and to a lesser extent Austria and Germany – have very high levels of sexual segregation (Dolado et al., 2004). All this contributes mightily to the view taken by many American feminists in particular that work–family balance policies do not succeed in promoting gender equality even when they set out to do so, and may be damaging to women's position in the labour market.

This book has sought to situate the development of the major dimen- sions of work–family balance policies in the EU15 and the UK in particu- lar. But the position of mothers in Scandinavia, where policies are most developed and where gender equality has been an explicit goal, raises important issues about both the nature of these policies and whether their scope is sufficient. It may well be much less stressful to juggle work and family responsibilities in the Nordic countries than in the US, for mothers especially, but is there a price to pay in terms of occupational segregation and a glass ceiling (Smith, 2003)? Genuine choice to engage in paid and unpaid work necessarily entails support for both forms of work. The US model has supported paid work by strong anti-discrimination legislation; the European model has tended to pay more attention to care work in order both to enable primarily mothers to exit the labour market or reduce their working hours in order to care, as well as providing care services to enable employment.

Arguably, both approaches are necessary and should be part of a more holistic approach to work–family balance policies, so that in the European context somewhat more emphasis is put on what happens in the workplace under the banner of work–family balance policies, which may involve more attention to anti-discrimination policies. Walsh's (2007) analysis of the 2004 British Workplace Employment Relations Survey showed that 'family-friendly' policies at the level of the firm were much more likely to exist where there were also formal equal opportunities policies. The focus of policy at both the EU and member state levels has focused primarily on securing mothers' access to jobs – on increasing the numbers of mothers in work – but more attention is needed to their conditions of work and to securing the kind of job quality that results above all in better pay (Ashiagbor, 2006). In addition, as we have seen, fathers are more likely to engage in care work the more hours their female partners work and the more those partners earn. If women were to occupy a much improved position in the labour market, then their leverage regarding care work at the household level might be expected to improve.

Equal pay was one of the few social commitments in the 1957 Treaty of Rome, even though it was understood primarily as part of market-making rather than social policy and social justice, but no member state has achieved it. Together with the steep 'family penalty' that women pay in many countries in terms of earnings, promotions and pensions foregone, as well as difficulties in even gaining access to many private sector jobs where employers may not want to deal with women who become mothers, this perpetuates gendered divisions of paid and unpaid work for a large majority of women, regardless of how they feel about them. But both the US and European approaches to work–family balance could usefully pay more attention to the persistent expectation of the standard, uninterrupted, often long-hour, male career path as the norm. There is a case for making a shorter working week – possibly a shorter working day – the norm for both sexes and for people with and without children (Hill et al., 2006; Bielenski et al., 2002), a form of universality that the advocates of work–life balance have advocated strongly. This would mean that those with no family responsibilities would also have a right to shorter working hours, but the prize in terms of addressing work cultures which reserve the best rewards for those putting in long hours of 'face time', and hence tackling a major impediment to gender equality at the workplace, may make this worthwhile. The need for measures to ensure that shorter working hours do not necessarily mean more precarious employment, and to secure pro rata pay and conditions of employment, are also urgent for some countries, especially the UK. As the European Commission's 2007 document on gender equality commented, flexicurity policies 'should avoid stressing the "flexibility" aspect for women and the "security" aspect for men' (CEC, 2007a: 7). In fact it has been possible for most Commission documents to interpret flexible working as necessary both for getting women into the labour market and also as a form of social protection that provides for reduced working hours and thus enables women to stay in the labour market, but without thinking through the implications of such work in relation to the parallel expectation of greater economic independence. Enabling transitions in and out of the labour market over a longer working life must be desirable, but if policy is developed in a gender-blind fashion, as in the case of the Dutch life-course savings scheme, then further gender inequality is likely to result.

At the end of the day, much depends on the kind of society policymakers want to see. As de Henau et al. (2006: 145) put it: 'The major element determining conception and design of policies remains the set of prevailing cultural values, social ideas and historical legacies'. Most Northern and Western European countries have a long-standing commitment to state intervention in the work–family policy arena. The implications for the pursuit of gender equality have not been wholly beneficial, but reaching a balance between paid and unpaid work is more possible for more people – albeit more women than men – and greater attention has also been paid to the welfare of children. Many American women working full-time for large firms with in-house work–family programmes who also have good access to relatively cheap, market-provided care may not face many problems in juggling responsibilities, but nor do they necessarily have much choice to care without severe penalties. The position of women at the bottom of the labour market heap is considerably more stressful.

The European approach makes work and care more possible, particularly for women. While it is very difficult to identify the precise ways in which policy affects behaviour, there is sufficient evidence of effects on particular groups, especially lone mothers – for example in the UK and the Netherlands – as well as negative evidence as to the lack of impact of the Southern European familialist approach, to suggest that policy matters. This is all the more important if we also accept that 'just institutions matter' (Rothstein, 1998), and that there is likely to be an iterative relationship between policy, behaviour and attitudes (Himmelweit, 2005). Legislation and exhortation are important in legitimising, as well as in attempting to change, particular kinds of behaviour. If gender equality is not made a prominent policy goal, then it is likely to be assumed that it does not matter. It is also problematic when reconciliation for women is assumed to constitute a policy that promotes gender equality. The main policy driver in the recent past has had as much to do with employment policies directed at mothers as with the welfare of family members. This instrumentality is dangerous: because the wide range of policies that are needed to enable both paid work and unpaid work is unlikely to be considered; because policy effort aimed at a particular way of combining paid and unpaid work is unlikely to find widespread favour when attitudes and behaviour are so diverse; and also because work–family policies may well not become institutionally embedded – there are some signs that this is the case in the UK. When member states are increasingly assuming that adults will be able to be more self-provisioning, and in societies where the volume of care needed particularly for elderly people is set to increase, gender equality in respect of paid and unpaid work is likely to become more important.

Bibliography

d'Addio, A.C. and d'Ercole, M.M. (2005), *Trends and Determinants of Fertility Rates in OECD Countries: The Role of Policies*, OECD Social, Employment and Migration working paper no. 27, Paris: OECD.

Adserà, A. (2004), 'Changing fertility rates in developed countries: the impact of labor market institutions', *Journal of Population Economics*, **17**: 17–43.

Ahn, N. and Mira, P. (2002), 'A note on the relationship between fertility and female employment rates in developed countries', *Journal of Population Economics*, **15** (4): 667–82.

Akerloff, G. and Kranton, R.E. (2000), 'Economics and identity', *Quarterly Journal of Economics*, **CXV** (3): 715–53.

Algava, E. and Bressé, S. (2005), 'Les Beneficiaries de l'Allocation Parentale d'Education: Trajectories d'Activité et Retour a l'Emploi', *Etudes et Resultats*, 399, Paris: DREES.

Aliaga, C. (2005), 'Gender gaps in the reconciliation between work and family life. Statistics in focus', 4/2005, Luxembourg: Eurostat.

Alwin, D. (2005), 'Attitudes, beliefs and childbearing', in A. Booth and A.C. Crouter (eds), *The New Population Problem. Why Families in Developed Countries are Shrinking and What It Means*, London: Lawrence Erlbaum.

Anttonen, A. and Sipilä, J. (1996), 'European social care services: is it possible to identify models?', *Journal of European Social Policy*, **6** (2): 87–100.

Anttonen, A., Baldock, J. and Sipilä, J. (2007), *The Young, the Old and the State: Social Care Systems in Five Industrialised Nations*, Cheltenham, UK and Northampton, MA, USA: Edward Elgar.

Anxo, D. and Boulin, J.-Y. (2006), 'The organisation of time over the life-course: European trends', *European Societies*, **8** (2): 319–41.

Anxo, D., Boulin, J.-Y., Fagan, C., Cebrián, I., Keuzenkamp, S., Klammer, U., Klenner, C., Moreno, G. and Toharía, L. (2006), *Working Time Options Over the Life Course: New Work Patterns and Company Strategies*, Dublin: Eurofound.

Anxo, D., Fagan, C., Smith, M., Letablier, M.-T. and Perraudin, C. (2007), *Part-time Work in European Companies*, Dublin: Eurofound.

Ashiagbor, D. (2006), 'Promoting precariousness? The response of EU employment policies to precarious work', in J. Fudge and R. Owens (eds), *Precarious Work, Women, and the New Economy: The Challenge to Legal Norms*, Oxford: Hart.

Atkinson, J. (2000), *Employment Options and Labour Market Participation*, Dublin: Eurofound.

Bacchi, C. (2004), 'Policy and discourse: challenging the construction of affirmative action as preferential treatment', *Journal of European Public Policy*, **11** (1): 128–46.

Bahle, T. (2003), 'The changing institutionalization of social services in England and Wales, France and Germany: is the welfare state on the retreat?', *Journal of European Social Policy*, **13** (1): 5–20.

Bailleau, G. (2007), 'L'accueil Collectif et an Crèche Familiale des Enfants de Moins de 6 ans en 2005', *Etudes et Résultats*, 548, Paris: DREES.

Balbo, L. (1987), 'Crazy quilts: rethinking the welfare state debate from a woman's point of view', in A. Showstack Sasson (ed.), *Women and The State*, London: Hutchinson.

Baldock, J. and Hadlow, J. (2004), 'Managing the family: productivity, scheduling and the male veto', *Social Policy and Administration*, **38** (6): 706–20.

Balls, E. (2005), 'Universal childcare: towards a progressive consensus', Daycare Trust 2nd Annual Childcare Lecture, London.

Balls, E. (2007), 'Childcare and child poverty: delivering solutions', speech at the Daycare Trust Conference, 13 June, London, Her Majesty's Treasury.

Barnes, M., Bryson, C. and Smith, R. (2005), *Working Atypical Hours: What Happens to Family Life?*, London: National Centre for Social Research.

Beck, U. (1992), *Risk Society: Towards a New Modernity*, London: Sage.

Beck, U. and Beck-Gernsheim, E. (1995), *The Normal Chaos of Love*, Oxford: Polity Press.

Beck, W., Van de Maesen, L., Thomese, F. and Walker, A. (eds) (2001), *Social Quality: A Vision for Europe*, the Hague: Kluwer Law International.

Becker, P.E. and Moen, P. (1999), 'Scaling back: dual-earner couples' work–family strategies', *Journal of Marriage and the Family*, **61** (4): 995–1007.

Bell, A. and Bryson, C. (2005), 'Work–life balance – still a "women's issue"?' in A. Park, J. Curtice, K. Thomson, C. Bromley, M. Phillips and M. Johnson (eds), *British Social Attitudes, 22nd Report*, London: Sage.

Belsky, J., Burchinal, M., McCartney, K., Vandell, D.L., Clarke-Stewart, K.A. and Owen, M. (2007), 'Are there long-term effects of child care?', *Child Development*, **78** (2): 681–701.

Bergmann, B. (2004), 'What policies toward lone mothers should we aim for?', *Feminist Economics*, **10** (2): 240–46.

Bergmann, B. (2009), 'Long leaves, child well-being, and gender equality', in J. Gornick, M. Meyers and E. Olin Wright (eds), *Earning and Caring: Creating the Conditions for Gender-Egalitarian Families*, New York: Verso.

Bernardi, L. (2003), 'Channels of social influence on reproduction', *Population Research and Policy Review*, **22**: 527–55.

Berthoud, R. (2007), *Work-Rich and Work-Poor: Three Decades of Change*, Bristol: The Policy Press.

Bertram, H., Krüger, H. and Spieß, Katherina, C. (eds) (2006), *Wem gehört die Familie der Zukunft?Expertisen zum 7. Familienbericht der Bundesregierung*, Opladen, Germany: Verlag Barbara Budrich.

Bettio, F. and Plantenga, J. (2004), 'Comparing care regimes in Europe', *Feminist Economics*, **10** (1): 85–113.

Bettio, F., Simonazzi, A. and Villa, P. (2006), 'Change in care regimes and female migration: the "care drain" in the Mediterranean', *Journal of European Social Policy*, **16** (3): 271–85.

Bettio, F. and Villa, P. (1998), 'A Mediterranean perspective on the break-down of the relationship between participation and fertility', *Cambridge Journal of Economics*, **22**: 137–71.

Bevan, S., Dench, S., Tamkin, P. and Cummings, J. (1999), *Family-Friendly Employment: The Business Case*, DfEE research report RR136, London.

Bianchi, S. (2000), 'Maternal employment and time with children: dramatic change or surprising continuity?', *Demography*, **37** (4): 401–14.

Bianchi, S.M. and Casper, L.M. (2004), 'The stalled revolution: gender and time allocation in the US', paper given to the International Conference on Work and Family, CRFR, University of Edinburgh, 30 June–2 July.

Bianchi, S.M., Robinson, J.P. and Milkie, M.A. (2006), *Changing Rhythms of American Family Life*, New York: Russell Sage Foundation.

Bielenski, H., Bosch, G. and Wagner, A. (2002), *Working Time Preferences in Sixteen European Countries*, Dublin: Eurofound.

Björklund, A. (2006), 'Does family policy affect fertility?', *Journal of Population Economics*, **19** (1): 3–24.

Blair-Loy, M. and Wharton, A.S. (2002), 'Employees' use of work–family policies and the workplace social context', *Social Forces*, **80** (3): 813–45.

Bleses, P. and Seeleib Kaiser, M. (2004), *The Dual Transformation of the German Welfare State*, Basingstoke: Palgrave Macmillan.

Bloom, N. and van Reenen, J. (2006), 'Management practices, work–life balance and productivity: a review of some recent evidence', *Oxford Review of Economic Policy*, **22** (4): 457–82.

Blossfeld, H.-P. (1995), *The New Role of Women: Family Formation in Modern Societies*, Boulder, CO: Westview Press.

BMFSFJ (Bundesministerium für Familie, Senioren, Frauen und Jugend). (2006) *Siebter Familienbericht*. Bonn: BMFSFJ. (English summary version: 'Seventh Family Report. Families between flexibility and dependability – perspectives for a life cycle-related family policy. Statement by the Federal Government. Results and scenarios of the report drafted by the committee of experts. Summary', accessed at www.bmfsfj.de).

Boeri, T., del Boca, D. and Pissarides, C. (eds) (2005), *Women at Work: An Economic Perspective*, Oxford: Oxford University Press.

Bond, S. and Sales, J. (2001), 'Household work in the UK: an analysis of the British Household Panel Survey 1994', *Work, Employment and Society*, **15** (2): 233–50.

Bonoli, G. (2005), 'The politics of the new social policies: providing coverage against new social risks in mature welfare states', *Policy and Politics*, **33** (3): 431–49.

Bonoli, G. (2008), 'The impact of social policy on fertility: evidence from Switzerland', *Journal of European Social Policy*, **18** (1): 64–77.

Borchorst, A. (2006), 'The public/private split re-articulated: abolishment of the Danish daddy leave', in A.-L. Ellingsaeter and A. Leira (eds), *Politicising Parenthood in Scandinavia*.

Bosch, G. and Wagner, A. (1998), *Employment and Working Time in Europe*, Dublin: Eurofound.

Bovenberg, A.L. (2005), 'Balancing work and family life during the life course', *De Economist*, **153**: 399–423.

Bovenberg, A.F. and Conneman, P.J. (2007), 'Naar één fiscale regeling voor infomensderving', *Weekblad voor Fiscaal Recht*, **136** (6726): 711–19.

Bradshaw, J. and Mayhew, E. (2006), 'Family benefit packages', in J. Bradshaw and A. Hatland (eds), *Social Policy, Employment and Family Change in Comparative Perspective*, Cheltenham, UK and Northampton, MA, USA: Edward Elgar.

Brandth, B. and Kvande, E. (2001), 'Flexible work and flexible fathers', *Work, Employment and Society*, **15** (2): 251–67.

Brannen, J. (2005), 'Time and the negotiation of work–family boundaries. Autonomy or illusion?', *Time and Society*, **14** (1): 113–31.

Breen, R. and Prince Cooke, L. (2005), 'The persistence of the gendered division of labour', *European Sociological Review*, **21** (1): 43–57.

Brewer, M., Crawford, C. and Deardon, L. (2005), 'Reforms to childcare policy', in R. Chote, C. Emmerson, D. Miles and Z. Oldfield (eds), *The IFS Green Budget*, London: IFS.

Brighouse, H. and Olin Wright, E. (2009), 'Strong gender egalitarianism', in J. Gornick, M. Meyers and E. Olin Wright (eds), *Earning and Caring: Creating the Conditions for Gender-Egalitarian Families*, New York: Verso.

Brody, E.M. (1981), '"Women in the middle" and family help to older people', *Gerontologist*, **21**: 471–80.

Bronchain, P. (2003), 'Managing diversity in health and social care', presentation, to the conference European Foundation for the Improvement of Living and Working Conditions, Dublin.

Brooks, C. and Manza, J. (1999), *Why Welfare States Persist: The Importance of Public Opinion in Democracies*, Chicago, IL: University of Chicago Press.

Bruning, G. and Plantenga, J. (1999), 'Parental leave and equal opportunities: experiences in eight European countries', *Journal of European Social Policy*, **9** (3): 195–209.

Brush, L. (2002), 'Changing the subject: gender and welfare regime studies', *Social Politics*, **9** (2): 161–86.

Bryson, C., Bell, A., La Valle, I., Barnes, M. and O'Shea, R. (2005), *Use of Childcare among Families from Minority Ethnic Backgrounds and among Families with Children with Special Educational Needs*, London: Sure Start.

Bryson, C., Kazimirski, A. and Southwood, H. (2006), *Childcare and Early Years Provision: A Study of Parents Use, Views and Experiences*, research report 723, London: DfES.

Bryson, V. (2007), *Gender and the Politics of Time*, Bristol: The Policy Press.

Burchell, B., Fagan, C., O'Brien, C. and Smith, M. (2007), *Working Conditions in the European Union: The Gender Perspective*, Dublin: Eurofound.

Burgess, A. (2007), *The Costs and Benefits of Active Fatherhood*, London: Fathers Direct.

Burri, S. (2005), 'Working time adjustment policies in the Netherlands', in A. Hegeswich (ed.), *Working Time for Working Families: Europe and the United States*, Washington, DC: Friedrich-Ebert-Stiftung.

Butt, S., Goddard, K. and La Valle, I. with Hill, M. (2007), *Childcare Nation? Progress on the Childcare Strategy and Priorities for the Future*, London: NatCen and the Daycare Trust.

Bygren, M. and Duvander, A.-Z. (2006), 'Parents' workplace situation and fathers' parental leave use', *Journal of Marriage and Family*, **68** (2): 363–72.

Calderwood, L., Kiernan, K., Joshi, H., Smith, K. and Ward, K. (2005), 'Parenthood and parenting', in S. Dex and H. Joshi (eds), *Children of the 2st Century from Birth to Nine Months*, Bristol: The Policy Press.

Callender, C., Millward, N., Lissenburgh, S. and Forth, J. (1997), *Maternity Rights and Benefits in Britain 1996*, Department of Social Security research report no. 67, London: DSS.

Cameron, C. and Moss, P. (2007), *Care Work in Europe: Current Understandings and Future Directions*, Abingdon: Routledge.

Campbell, J.L. (2002), 'Ideas, politics, and public policy', *Annual Review of Sociology*, **28**: 21–38.

Carnoy, M. (2000), *Sustaining the New Economy: Work, Family, and Community in the Information Age*, New York: Russell Sage Foundation.

Castles, F.G. (2003), 'The world turned upside down: below replacement fertility, changing preferences and family-friendly public policy in 21 OECD countries', *Journal of European Social Policy*, **13** (3): 209–27.

Confederation of British Industry (CBI) (2001), Response to 'Work and Parents: Competitiveness and Choice', London: CBI.

CBI (2005), 'Firms make family friendly policies a reality – but new employment legislation having negative impact on business', news release, 12 September, London: CBI.

CBS (Centraal Bureau voor de Statistiek) Statline (2007), *Deelname levenslopp-en spaarloonregeling*, Voorburg/Heerlen: CBS, accessed 30 November at http://statline.cbs.nl/statWeb.

Commission of the European Communities (CEC) (1993), *Growth, Competitiveness and Employment: The Challenges and Ways Forward into the 21st Century*, COM (93) 700 of 5/12/93.

CEC (1994), *European Social Policy – a Way Forward for the Union*, COM (94) 333 of 27/7/94.

CEC (1997), *Partnership for a New Organisation of Work*, COM (97) 128 final, 16/04/97.

CEC (1997a), *Modernising and Improving Social Protection*, COM (97) 102 of 12/03/97.

CEC (1998), *Reconciliation between Work and Family Life in Europe*, Luxembourg: OOPEC.

CEC (2000), communication on the *Social Policy Agenda*, COM (2000) 379 final of 28/6/00.

CEC (2001), communication on *Employment and Social Policies: A Framework for Investing in Quality*, COM (2001) 313 final of 20/6/01.

CEC (2002), *Increasing Labour Force Participation and Promoting Active Ageing*, COM (2002) 9 final, Brussels.

CEC (2003), communication concerning certain aspects of working time, COM (2003) 843, final.

CEC (2004), *Delivering Lisbon. Reforms for the Enlarged Union*, COM (2004) 29 final/2 of 20/2/04.

CEC (2005), communication on: *Confronting Demographic Change: A New Solidarity between the Generations*, COM (2005) 94 final of 16/3/05.

CEC (2006), *Employment in Europe 2006*, Brussels: DG Employment and Social Affairs.

CEC (2006a), *First-Stage Consultation of European Social Partners on Reconciliation of Professional, Private and Family Life*, SEC (2006) 1245.

CEC (2006b), *The Demographic Future of Europe – from Challenge to Opportunity*, 14114/06. COM (2006) 571 final of 12/10/06.

CEC (2006c), *Roadmap for Equality between Women and Men, 2006–2010*, COM/2006/92 final.

CEC (2007), *Towards Common Principles of Flexicurity: More and Better Jobs through Flexibility and Security*, COM (2007) 359 final of 27/6/07.

CEC (2007a), *Second Stage of Consultation of European Social Partners on Reconciliation of Professional, Private and Family Life*, EMPL/F/1/FZ/ mc D (2007) 10137.

CEC (2007b), *Equality between Women and Men*, report from the Commission to the Council, the European Parliament, the European Economic and Social Committee and the Committee of the Regions, Brussels: European Commission, COM (2007) 49 final of 7/2/07.

CEC (2007c), *Promoting Solidarity between the Generations*, communication from the Commission, COM (2007) 244 final of 10/5/07.

Centre d'Analyse Stratégique (2007), *Rapport sur le Service Public à la Petite Enfance*, report no. 8, Paris: La Documentation Française.

Council of the European Union (CEU) (1992), Recommendation 92/241/ EEC of 31 March 1992 on 'Childcare', OJ L 123, 8.5.1992.

CEU (1996), Directive 96/34/EC of 3 June 1996, on *The Framework Agreement on Parental Leave concluded by UNICE, CEEP, and the ETUC*, OJ L 145, 19.6.1996.

CEU (1998), Resolution of 15/12/97 on the 1998 Employment Guidelines, OJ C 30 of 28.1.1998.

CEU (2000), *Conclusions of the Presidency*, Lisbon European Council of 23 and 24 March 2000.

CEU (2003), Decision 2003/578/EC on guidelines for the employment policies of the Member States, OJ L197/13 of 5/8/03.

CEU (2006), *Conclusions of the Presidency*, Annex II 'European Pact for Gender Equality'. Brussels European Council of 23-24 March.

Chesnais, J.-C. (1996), 'Fertility, family, and social policy in contemporary Western Europe', *Population and Development Review*, **22** (4): 729–39.

Christie + Co. (2007), 'Childcarefocus. Child centric sector news from Christie + Co.' accessed at www.christiecorporate.com/ccc/news/publications/childcarefocus_07/childcarefocus_07.pdf, accessed 18 March 2008.

Clegg, D. (2007), 'Continental drift: on unemployment policy change in Bismarckian welfare states', *Social Policy and Administration*, **41** (6): 597–617.

Cleveland, G. and Krashinsky, M. (2003), *Financing ECEC Services in OECD Countries*, Paris: OECD.

Coleman, D. and Chandola, T. (1999), 'Britain's place in Europe's population', in S. McRae (ed.), *Families and Household in the 1990s*, Oxford: Oxford University Press.

Coltrane, S. (forthcoming), 'Fatherhood, gender and work–family policies'. in J. Gornick, M. Meyers and E. Olin Wright (eds), *Earning and Caring: Creating the Conditions for Gender-Egalitarian Families*, New York: Verso.

Commissie Herverdeling Onbetaalde Arbeid (1997), *Onbetaalde zorg gelijk verdeeld.toekomstscenario's voor de herverdeling van onbetaalde zorgarbeid*, Amsterdam: VUGA

Communities and Local Government (CLG) (2007), *Towards a Fairer Future: Implementing the Women and Work Commission Recommendations*, London: CLG.

Cooke, G. and Lawton, K. (2008), *For Love or Money: Pay, Progression and Professionalisation in the 'Early Years' Workforce*, London: ippr.

Correll, S.J., Benard, S. and Paik, I. (2007), 'Getting a job: is there a motherhood penalty?', *American Journal of Sociology*, **112** (5): 1297–1338.

Crompton, R. (2006), *Employment and the Family*, Cambridge: Cambridge University Press.

Crompton, R. and Brockman, M. (2006), 'Class, gender and work–life articulation', in D. Perrons, C. Fagan; L. McDowell; K. Ray and K. Ward (eds), *Gender Divisions and Working Time in the New Economy*, Cheltenham, UK and Northampton, MA, USA: Edward Elgar.

Crompton, R., Brockman, M. and Wiggins, R.D. (2003), 'A woman's place . . . employment and family life for men and women', in P. Curtice, K. Thomson, L. Jarvis and C. Bromley (eds), *British Social Attitudes Survey, 20th Report*, London: Sage.

Crompton, R. and Harris, F. (1998), 'Employment, careers and families: the significance of choice and constraint in women's lives', in R. Crompton (ed.), *Restructuring Gender Relations and Employment: The Decline of the Male Breadwinner*, Oxford: Oxford University Press.

Crompton, R., Lewis, S. and Lyonette, C. (2007), 'Introduction: the unravelling of the male breadwinner model – and some of its consequences', in R. Crompton, S. Lewis, and C. Lyonette (eds), *Women, Men, Work and Family in Europe*, London: Palgrave Macmillan.

Crompton, R. and Lyonette, C. (2006), 'Work–life "balance" in Europe', *Acta Sociologica*, **49** (4): 379–93.

Crompton, R. and Lyonette, C. (2006a), 'Some issues in cross-national comparative research methods: a comparison of attitudes to promotion, and women's employment, in Britain and Portugal', *Work, Employment and Society*, **20** (2): 389–400.

Crompton, R. and Lyonette, C. (2008), 'Who does the housework? The division of labour within the home', in A. Park, J. Curtice, K. Thomson, M. Phillips, M. Johnson and E. Clery (eds), *British Social Attitudes: the 24th Report*, London: Sage.

Crouch, C. and Farrell, H. (2004), 'Breaking the path of institutional development? Alternatives to the new determinism', *Rationality and Society*, **16** (1): 5–43.

Cully, M., Woodland, S., O'Reilly, A. and Dix, G. (1999), *Britain at Work: As Depicted by the 1998 Workplace Employee Relations Survey*, London: Routledge.

Daly, K.J. (1996), *Families and Time: Keeping Pace in a Hurried Culture*, London: Sage.

Daly, M. (2000), *The Gender Division of Welfare: The Impact of the British and German Welfare States*, Cambridge: Cambridge University Press.

Daly, M. (2002), 'Care as a good for social policy', *Journal of Social Policy*, **31** (2): 251–70.

Daly, M. (2002a), 'A fine balance: women's labor market participation in international comparison', in F.W. Scharpf and V.A. Schmidt (eds), *Welfare and Work in the Open Economy*, vol. 2, Oxford: Oxford University Press, pp. 467–510.

Daly, M. (2005), 'Changing family life in Europe: significance for state and society', *European Societies*, **7** (3): 379–98.

Daly, M. and Lewis, J. (2000), 'The concept of social care and the analysis of contemporary welfare states', *British Journal of Social Policy*, **51**(2), 281–98.

Davies, C. (1995), *Gender and the Professional Predicament in Nursing*, Buckingham: Open University Press.

Davies, H., Joshi, H. and Peromaci, R. (2000), 'Forgone income and motherhood: what do recent British data tell us?', *Population Studies*, **54** (3): 293–305.

Daycare Trust (2006), *Childcare Today: A Progress Report on the Government's 10-year Childcare Strategy,* London: Daycare Trust.

Deacon, A. (2007), 'Civic labour or doulia? Care, reciprocity and welfare', *Social Policy and Society*, **6** (4): 481–9.

De Henau, J., Meulders, D. and O'Dorchai, S. (2006), 'The childcare triad? Indicators assessing three fields of child policies for working mothers in the EU-15', *Journal of Comparative Policy Analysis*, **8** (2): 129–48.

de la Rica, S. and Iza, A. (2006), 'Career planning in Spain: do fixed-term contracts delay marriage and parenthood?', in S. Gustafsson and A. Kalwij (eds), *Education and the Postponement of Maternity: Economic Analyses for Industrialized Countries*, Dordrecht, the Netherlands: Kluwer Academic.

Del Boca, D. (2000), 'The effect of child care and part time opportunities on participation and fertility decisions in Italy', *Journal of Population Economics*, **15**: 549–73.

Delsen, L. and Smits, J. (2007), 'Ins and outs of the Dutch life course savings scheme', Organisation for Economic Cooperation and Development paper ELSEA/ELSA WP1 (2007) 3, Paris.

den Dulk, L. (2001), *Work–Family Arrangements in Organisations: A Cross-National Study on the Netherlands, the UK and Sweden*, Amsterdam: Rozenberg.

Department for Children, Schools and Families (DCSF) (2007), *The Children's Plan. Building Brighter Futures – Summary*, Cm 7280, London: DCSF.

Dermott, E. (2006), 'What's parenthood got to do with it? Men's hours of paid work', *British Journal of Sociology*, **57** (4): 619–34.

Deven, F. and Moss, P. (2002), 'Leave arrangements for parents: overview and future outlook', *Community, Work and Family*, **5** (3): 237–55.

Dex, S. (2003), *Families and Work in the Twenty-First Century*, York: Joseph Rowntree Foundation.

Dex, S. and Scheibl, F. (1999), 'Business performance and family-friendly policies', *Journal of General Management*, **24** (4): 22–37.

Dex, S. and Scheibl, F. (2001), 'Flexible and family-friendly working arrangements in UK-based SMEs: business cases', *British Journal of Industrial Relations*, **39** (3): 411–31.

Dex, S. and Smith, C. (2002), *The Nature and Pattern of Family-Friendly Employment Policies in Britain*, Bristol: The Policy Press.

Dex, S. and Ward, K. (2007), Parental Care and Employment in Early Childhood', working paper series no. 57, Manchester: Equal Opportunities Commission.

Dey, I. (2006), 'Wearing out the work ethic: population ageing, fertility and work–life balance', *Journal of Social Policy*, **35** (4): 671–88.

Department for Education and Employment (DfEE) (1998), *Meeting the Childcare Challenge: A Framework and Consultation Document*, Cm. 3959, Norwich: The Stationery Office.

DfEE (2000) *Work Life Balance: Changing Patterns in a Changing World*, Department for Education and Skills, discussion document, London.

Dolado, J.J., Felgueroso, F., and Jmeno, J.F. (2004), 'Where do women work? Analysing patterns in occupational segregation by gender', *Annales D'Economie et de Statistique*, **71** (2): 293–315.

Department of Trade and Industry (DTI) (1998), *Fairness at Work*, Cm. 3968, Norwich: The Stationery Office.

DTI (2000), *Work and Parents: Competitiveness and Choice*, Cm. 5005, Norwich: The Stationery Office.

DTI (2001), *Work and Parents: Competitiveness and Choice, A Framework for Parental Leave*, consultation document, London: DTI.

DTI (2001a), *About Time: Flexible Working*, report of the Work and Parents Taskforce, London: DTI.

DTI (2001b), *Work and Parents: Competitiveness and Choice, A Framework for Simplification*, London: DTI.

DTI (2004), *UK Response to Commission's 2003 Re-examination of Directive 93/104/EC*, London: DTI.

DTI (2005), *Work and Families: Choice and Flexibility*, discussion document, London: DTI.

DTI (2005a), *Work and Families: Choice and Flexibility, Regulatory Impact Assessment*, London: DTI.

DTI, Scotland Office and New Ways to Work (2001), *Essential Guide to Work–Life Balance*, London: Department of Trade and Industry.

Duncan, S. and Edwards, R. (1999), *Lone Mothers, Paid Work and Gendered Moral Rationalities*, London: Macmillan.

Department of Work and Pensions (DWP) (2007), *Ready for Work: Full Employment in our Generation*, London: DWP.

Ehrenreich, B. and Hochschild, A. (eds) (2003), *Global Woman: Nannies, Maids and Sex Workers in the New Economy*, London: Granta Books.

Ekberg, J. (2004), 'Sharing responsibility? Short and long-term effects of Sweden's daddy month reform', paper presented to the DTI, London, 27 May.

Ellingsaeter, A.-L. (2006), 'The Norwegian childcare regime and its paradoxes', in A.-L. Ellingsaeter and A. Leira (eds), *Politicising Parenthood in Scandinavia*, Bristol: The Policy Press.

Ellingsaeter, A.-L. and Leira, A. (eds) (2006), *Politicising Parenthood in Scandinavia: Gender Relations in Welfare States*, Bristol: The Policy Press.

Emmott, M. (2007), 'Government right to highlight decline in 9–5 working – but benefits should not be restricted to working parents', Chartered Institute of Personnel Development press release, 4 December. London.

England, P. (2005), 'Emerging theories of care work', *Annual Review of Sociology*, **31**: 381–99.

England, P., Budig, M. and Folbre, N. (2002), 'Wages of virtue: the relative pay of care work', *Social Problems*, **49** (4): 455–73.

Equal Opportunities Commission (EOC) (2005), *Part-time is No Crime- So Why the Penalty? Interim Report of the EOC's Investigation into Flexible and Part-time Working, and Questions for Consultation*, Manchester: EOC.

EOC (2005a), *Britain's Hidden Brain Drain*, Manchester: EOC.

EOC (2007), *Enter the Timelords: Transforming Work to Meet the Future*, Manchester: EOC.

Esping-Andersen, G. (1990), *The Three Worlds of Welfare Capitalism*, Cambridge: Polity Press.

Esping-Andersen, G. (1999), *Social Foundations of Post-industrial Economies*, Oxford: Oxford University Press.

Esping-Andersen, G., Gallie, D., Hemerijck, A. and Myles, J. (2002), *Why We Need a New Welfare State*, Oxford: Oxford University Press.

Estévez-Abe, M. (2005), 'Gender bias in skills and social policies: the varieties of capitalism perspective on sex segregation', *Social Politics*, **12** (2): 180–215.

Eurobarometer (2004), *Europeans' Attitudes to Parental Leave*, Brussels: DG Employment and Social Affairs.

European Foundation for the Improvement of Living and Working Conditions (Eurofound) (2005), *Combining Family and Full-time Work*, Dublin: Eurofound.

Eurofound (2006), 'Working time and work–life balance: a policy dilemma?' background paper for joint European Foundation/European Parliament Seminar, Brussels.

Eurofound (2006a), 'Competitive Europe – social Europe partners or rivals?', foundation forum 2006 background paper, Dublin.

Eurofound (2007), 'Varieties of flexicurity: reflections on key elements of flexibility and security', background paper for the European Parliament Committee on Employment and Social Affairs, Brussels.

European Expert Group on Flexicurity (2007), *Flexicurity Pathways*, Brussels: DG Employment.

Eurostat (2005), 'Reconciling work and family life in the EU25 in 2003', news release 49/2005, Luxembourg.

Eurostat (2006), *Comparable Time Use Statistics: Hetus Pocketbook*, Luxembourg: Office for Official Publications of the European Communities.

Evans, J.M. (2002), 'Work/family reconciliation, gender wage equity and occupational segregation: the role of firms and public policy', *Canadian Public Policy – Analyse de Politiques* **28** (1) (Supplement), S187–S216.

Evers, A., Lewis, J. and Riedel, B. (2005), 'Developing childcare provision in England and Germany: problems of governance', *Journal of European Social Policy*, **15** (3), 195–209.

Fagan, C. (2003), *Working Time Preferences and Work–Life Balance in the EU: Some Policy Considerations for Enhancing the Quality of Life*, Luxembourg: European Foundation for the Improvement of Living and Working Conditions and Office for Official Publications of the European Communities.

Fagan, C., Hegewisch, A. and Pillinger, J. (2006), *Out of Time: Why Britain Needs a New Approach to Working Time Flexibility*, London: Trades Union Congress.

Fagan, C. and Lallement, M. (2000), 'Working time, social integration and transitional labour markets', in J. O'Reilly, I. Cebriean and M. Lallement (eds), *Working-Time Changes: Social Integration through Transitional Labour Markets*, Cheltenham, UK and Northampton, MA, USA: Edward Elgar.

Fagnani, J. (1998), 'Helping mothers to combine paid and unpaid work – or fighting unemployment? The ambiguities of French family policy', *Community, Work and Family*, **1** (3), 297–312.

Fagnani, J. (2007), 'Fertility rates and mothers' employment behaviour in comparative perspective: similarities and differences in six European countries', in R. Crompton, S. Lewis and C. Lyonette (eds), *Women, Men and Family in Europe*, London: Palgrave Macmillan.

Fagnani, J. and Letablier, M.-T. (2004), 'Work and family life balance: the impact of the 35-hour laws in France', *Work, Employment and Society*, **18** (3), 551–72.

Fahey, T. and Speder, Z. (2004), *Fertility and Family Issues in an Enlarged Europe*, Dublin: European Foundation for the Improvement of Living and Working Conditions, and Luxembourg: Office for Official Publications of the European Communities.

Ferrera, M., Hemerijck, A. and Rhodes, M. (2000), *The Future of Social Europe Recasting Work and Welfare in the New Economy*, report for the Portuguese Presidency of the European Union.

Finch, J. (1983), *Married to the Job: Wives' Incorporation in Men's Work*, London: Allen & Unwin.

Finch, J. and Groves, D. (1983), *A Labour of Love: Women, Work and Caring*, London: Routledge & Kegan Paul.

Finch, J. and Mason, J. (1993), *Negotiating Family Responsibilities*, London: Tavistock/Routledge.

Finch, N. (2006), 'Gender equity and time use: how do mothers and fathers spend their time?', in J. Bradshaw and A. Hatland (eds), *Social*

Policy, Employment and Family Change in Comparative Perspective, Cheltenham, UK and Northampton, MA, USA: Edward Elgar.

Flaquer, L. (2000), 'Is there a Southern European model of family policy?', in A. Pfenning and T. Bahle (eds), *Families and Family Policies in Europe: Comparative Perspectives*, Frankfurt: Peter Lang.

Flaquer, L. and Navarro, L. (2005), 'Change in family structures and informal care work', paper given at the Hidden Work Regimes conference, University of Hamburg, 27-29 May.

Folbre, N. (1994), *Who Pays for the Kids? Gender and the Structures of Constraint*, London: Routledge.

Folbre, N. (2008), *Valuing Children: Rethinking the Economics of the Family*, Cambridge, MA: Harvard University Press.

Folbre, N. and Bittman, M. (eds) (2004), *Family Time*, London and New York: Routledge.

Forth, J., Bewley, H. and Bryson, A. (2006), *Small and Medium-sized Enterprises: Findings from the 2004 Workplace Employment Relations Survey*, London: Routledge.

Franco, A. and Winquist, K. (2002), *Women and Men Reconciling Work and Family Life: Statistics in Focus*, theme 3-9/2002, Luxembourg: Eurostat.

Fraser, N. (1997), *Justice Interruptus: Critical Reflections On The 'Post-Socialist' Condition*, London: Routledge.

Fredricksen-Goldsen, K.I. and Scharlach, A.E. (2001), *Families and Work: New Directions in the Twenty-First Century*, Oxford: Oxford University Press.

Furstenberg, F. (1988), 'Good dads – bad dads: two faces of fatherhood', in A.J. Cherlin (ed.), *The Changing American Family and Public Policy*, Washington, DC: Urban Institute Press.

Gallie, D. (2003), 'The quality of working life: is Scandinavia different?', *European Sociological Review*, **19** (1), 61–79.

Galtry, J. and Callister, P. (2005), 'Assessing the optimal length of parental leave for child and parental well-being: how can research inform policy?', *Journal of Family Issues*, **26** (2), 219–46.

Gambles, R., Lewis, S. and Rapoport, R. (2006), *The Myth of Work–Life Balance: The Challenge of our Time for Men, Women and Societies*, Chichester: John Wiley.

Gatrell, C. (2005), *Hard Labour: The Sociology of Parenthood*, Maidenhead: Open University Press.

Gauthier, A.H. (1996), *The State and the Family: A Comparative Analysis of Family Policies in Industrialised Countries*, Oxford: Clarendon.

Gauthier, A.H. (2002), 'Family policies in industrialized countries: is there convergence?', *Population-E*, **57** (3), 447–74.

Gautié, J. and Gazier, B. (2003), 'Equipping markets for people: transitional labour markets as the central part of a new social model', paper given at the SASE conference, Aix en Provence, 18 June.

Gavanas, A. (2002), 'The fatherhood responsibility movement: the centrality of marriage, work and male sexuality in reconstructions of masculinity and fatherhood', in B. Hobson (ed.), *Making Men into Fathers: Men, Masculinities and the Social Politics of Fatherhood*, Cambridge: Cambridge University Press.

Gershuny, J. (2000), *Changing Times: Work and Leisure in Post-Industrial Society*, Oxford: Oxford University Press.

Gershuny, J. and Sullivan, O. (2003), 'Time use, gender, and public policy regimes', *Social Politics* **10** (2): 205–28.

Gilbert, N. (2002), *The Transformation of the Welfare State: The Silent Surrender of Public Responsibility*, Oxford: Oxford University Press.

Glucksman, M. (1998), '"What a difference a day makes": a theoretical and historical exploration of temporality and gender', *Sociology*, **32** (2), 39–58.

Goldin, C. (2006), 'The quiet revolution that transformed women's employment, education, and family', *American Economic Review*, **96** (2), 1–21.

Goldstein, J., Lutz, W. and Testa, M.R. (2004), 'The emergence of sub-replacement family size ideals in Europe', *Population Research and Policy Review*, **22**, 479–96.

Gornick, J. and Heron, A. (2006), 'The regulation of working time as work–family reconciliation policy: comparing Europe, Japan and the United States', *Journal of Comparative Policy Analysis*, **8** (2), 149–66.

Gornick, J. and Meyers, M. (2003), *Families that Work: Policies for Reconciling Parenthood and Employment*, New York: Russell Sage.

Gornick, J. and Meyers, M. (2009), 'Institutions that support gender egalitarianism in parenthood and employment', in J. Gornick, M. Meyers and E. Olin Wright (eds), *Earning and Caring: Creating the Conditions for Gender-Egalitarian Families*, New York: Verso.

Gornick, J., Meyers, M. and Olin Wright, E. (eds) (2009), *Earning and Caring: Creating the Conditions for Gender-Egalitarian Families*, New York: Verso.

Gottfried, H. and O'Reilly, J. (2002), 'Reregulating breadwinner models in socially conservative welfare systems: comparing Germany and Japan', *Social Politics*, **9** (1), 29–59.

Graham, H. (1983), 'Caring: a labour of love', in J. Finch and D. Groves (eds), *A Labour of Love: Women, Work and Caring*, London: Routledge & Kegan Paul.

Gray, A. (2005), 'The changing availability of grandparents as carers and its implications for childcare policy in the UK', *Journal of Social Policy*, **34** (4), 557–77.

Gregg, P. and Waldfogel, J. (2005), 'Symposium on parental leave, early maternal employment and child outcomes: introduction', *The Economic Journal*, **115** (February), F1–F6.

Gregory, M. and Connolly, S. (2008), 'Feature: the price of reconciliation: part-time work, families and women's satisfaction', *The Economic Journal*, **118** (February), F1–F7.

Grimshaw, D. and Rubery, J. (2007), *Undervaluing Women's Work*, working paper series no. 53, Manchester: Equal Opportunities Commission.

Guest, D. (2001), 'Perspectives on the study of work–life balance', accessed 17 July 2006 at www.ucm.es/info/Psyap/enop/guest.htm.

Gustafsson, S. and Kalwij, A. (eds.) (2006), *Education and the Postponement of Maternity: Economic Analyses for Industrialized Countries*, Dordrecht, the Netherlands: Kluwer Academic.

Haas, B. (2005), 'Work–care balances – is it possible to identify typologies for cross-national comparisons?', *Current Sociology*, **53** (3), 487–508.

Haas, B., Steiber, N., Hartel, M. and Wallace, C. (2006), 'Household employment patterns in an enlarged European Union', *Work, Employment and Society*, **20** (4), 751–71.

Haas, L., Allard, K. and Hwang, P. (2002), 'The impact of organizational culture on men's use of parental leave in Sweden', *Community, Work and Family*, **5** (3), 319–42.

Hacker, J. (2006), *The Great Risk Shift: The Assault on American Jobs, Familiesm, Health Care, and Retirement*, Oxford: Oxford University Press.

Hakim, C. (2000), *Work–Lifestyle Choices in the Twenty-First Century: Preference Theory*, Oxford: Oxford University Press.

Hakim, C., Bradley, K., Price, E. and Mitchell, L. (2008), *Little Britons: Financing Childcare Choice*, London: Policy Exchange.

Halpern, D.F. (2006), 'Introduction: how organizations can alleviate the traffic jam at the intersection of work and family', *American Behavioral Scientist*, **49** (9), 1147–51.

Hansen, L. (2007), 'From flexicurity to flexicArity? Gendered perspectives on the Danish model', *Journal of Social Sciences*, **3** (2), 88–93.

Hantrais, L. (2004), *Family Policy Matters: Responding to Family Change in Europe*, Bristol: The Policy Press.

Hardarson, O. (2007), *The Flexibility of Working Time Arrangements for Women and Men*, Statistics in Focus 96/2007, Luxembourg: Eurostat.

Harkness, S. (2003), 'The household division of labour: changes in families' allocation of paid and unpaid work', in R. Dickens, P. Gregg and

J. Wadsworth (eds), *The Labour Market Under New Labour: The State of Working Britain*, Basingstoke: Palgrave Macmillan.

Harkness, S. and Waldfogel, J. (2003), 'The family gap in pay: evidence from seven industrialized countries', *Research in Labor Economics*, **22**, 369–414.

Harvey, M. (1999), 'Economies of time: a framework for analysing the restructuring of employment relations', in A. Felstead and N. Jewson (eds), *Global Trends in Flexible Labour*, London: Macmillan.

Hatten, W., Vinter, L. and Williams, R. (2002), *Dads on Dads: Needs and Expectations at Home and at Work*, Manchester: Equal Opportunities Commission.

Hayward, B., Fong, B. and Thornton, A. (2007), *The Third Work–Life Balance Employer Survey: Executive Summary*, Department of Business Enterprise and Regulatory Reform, Employment Relations research series no. 86, London.

House of Commons (HC) (1998), *Budget Statement*, 17 March London: Hansard.

HC (1999), Social Security Select Committee, 1998–1999 Session, *Ninth Report*, HC 543, London: Hansard.

HC (2001), Education and Employment Select Committee, *First Report*, HC 33, London: Hansard.

HC (2001a), Education and Employment Select Committee, *Early Years Follow-up*, HC 438, London: Hansard.

HC (2001b), Education and Employment Select Committee, *Work–Life Balance*, HC 461, London: Hansard.

HC (2002), *Budget Statement*, 17 April, London: Hansard.

HC (2003), Select Committee on Work and Pensions, *Childcare for Working Parents. Fifth Report of Session 2002–3*, HC 564-1, London: Hansard.

HC (2004), European Scrutiny Committee, *34th Report*, HC42 – XXXIV, London: Hansard.

HC (2005), Trade and Industry Select Committee, *16th Report*, HC300, London: Hansard.

HC (2006), Select Committee on Education and Skills, *Children's Services Minutes of Evidence*, HC 62-i, London: Hansard.

HC (2006a), Work and Families Bill, 3rd reading, 18 January, London: Hansard.

HC (2007), Committee of Public Accounts, *Sure Start Children's Centres, 38th Report*, HC 261, London: Hansard.

HC (2008), Select Committee on Business, Enterprise and Regulatory Reform, *Second Report*, HC 291 II, London: Hansard.

Hegewisch, A. (2005), 'Individual working time rights in Germany and the UK: how a little law can go a long way', in A. Hegewisch (ed.), *Working*

Time for Working Families: Europe and the United States, Washington, DC: Friedrich-Ebert-Stiftung.

Henwood, K. and Procter, J. (2003), 'The "Good Father": reading men's accounts of paternal involvement during the transition to first-time fatherhood', *British Journal of Social Psychology*, **42**: 337–55.

Hertz, R. (1999), 'Working to place family at the center of life: dual-earner and single-parent strategies', *Annals of the American Academy of Political Science*, **562** (March), 16–31.

Hewlett, S.A. (2007), *Off-Ramps and On-Ramps: Keeping Talented Women on the Road to Success*, Cambridge, MA: Harvard Business School Press.

High Level Group on the Future of Social Policy in an Enlarged European Union (2004), *Report*, Brussels: DG Employment and Social Affairs.

Hiilamo, H. and Kangas, O. (2006), 'Trap for women or freedom to choose? Political frames in the making of homecare allowance in Finland and Sweden', University of Turku Department of Social Policy working paper no. 18/2006, Turku.

Hildebrandt, E. (2006), 'Balance between work and life: new corporate impositions through flexible working time or opportunity for time sovereignty?', *European Societies*, **8** (2), 251–71.

Hill, E.J., Mead, N.T., Dean, L.R., Hafen, D.M., Gadd, R., Palmer, A.A. and Ferris, M.S. (2006), 'Researching the 60-hour dual-earner work-week: an alternative to the "opt-out revolution"', *American Behavioral Scientist*, **49** (9), 1184–1203.

Himmelweit, S. (1995), 'The discovery of "unpaid work": the social consequences of the expansion of "work"', *Feminist Economics*, **1** (2), 121–39.

Himmelweit, S. (2005), *The Determinants of Caring Behaviour*, full report of research activities and results, Swindon: ESRC.

Himmelweit, S. (2005a), 'Caring: the need for an economic strategy', *Public Policy Research*, **12** (5), 168–73.

Himmelweit, S. and Land, H. (2007), *Supporting Parents and Carers*, working paper series no. 63, Manchester: Equal Opportunities Commission.

Himmelweit, S. and Sigala, M. (2004), 'Choice and the relationship between identities and behaviour for mothers with pre-school children: some implications for policy from a UK study', *Journal of Social Policy*, **33** (3), 455–78.

Her Majesty's Revenue and Customs (HMRC) (2007), *Child and Working Tax Credit Statistics, December 2007*, London: National Statistics.

Her Majesty's Treasury (HMT) (1999), *Pre-Budget Report*, London: HMT.

HMT (2002), *Realising Europe's Potential: Economic Reform in Europe*, Cm. 5318, Norwich: The Stationery Office.

HMT (2005), *Lisbon Strategy for Jobs and Growth: UK National Reform Programme*, London: HMT.

HMT, DES (Department for Education and Skills), DWP, DTI (2004), *Choice for Parents, the Best Start for Children: A Ten Year Strategy for Childcare*, London: HMT.

HMT, DES, DWP, DTI (2005), *Choice for Parents, the Best Start for Children: A Ten Year Strategy for Childcare. Summary of Consultation Responses*, London: HMT.

HMT and DTI (2003), *Balancing Work and Family Life: Enhancing Choice and Support for Parents*, London: HMT.

Hobson, B. (2004), 'The individualised worker, the gender participatory and the gender equity models in Sweden', *Social Politics and Society*, **3** (1), 75–84.

Hobson, B., Duvander, A.-Z. and Hallden, K. (2006), 'Men and women's agency and capabilities to create a worklife balance in diverse and changing institutional contexts', in J. Lewis (ed.), *Children, Changing Families and Welfare States*, Cheltenham, UK and Northampton, MA, USA: Edward Elgar.

Hochschild, A. (1989), *The Second Shift: Working Parents and the Revolution at Home*, New York: Piatkus.

Hodson, D. and Maher, I. (2001), 'The open method as a new mode of governance: the case of soft economic policy co-ordination', *Journal of Common Market Studies*, **39** (4), 719–46.

Hogarth, T., Hasluck, C. and Pierre, G. (2001), *Work–Life Balance, 2000: Results from the Baseline Study*, research report RR249, London: DfEE.

Holmes, K., Ivins, C., Yaxley, D., Hanson, J. and Smeaton, D. (2007), *The Future of Work: Individuals and Workplace Transformation*, Manchester: Equal Opportunities Commission.

Holt, H. and Grainger, H. (2005), *Results of the Second Flexible Working Employee Survey*, employment relations research series no. 39, London: DTI.

Home Office (1998), *Supporting Families*, Norwich: The Stationery Office.

Hook, J.L. (2006), 'Care in context: men's unpaid work in 20 countries, 1965–2003', *American Sociological Review*, **71**, 639–60.

Hooker, H., Neathey, F., Casebourne, J. and Munro, M. (2007), *The Third Work–Life Balance Employee Survey: Main Findings*, employment relations research series no. 58, London: DTI.

Houston, D.M. and Waumsley, J.A. (2003), *Attitudes to Flexible Working and Family Life*, Bristol: The Policy Press.

Hoxhallari, L., Conolly, A. and Lyone, N. (2007), *Families with Children in Britain: Findings from the 2005 Families and Children Study* (*FACS*), research report no. 424, London: DWP.

Hudson, M., Lissenburgh, S. and Sahin-Dikmen, M. (2004), 'Maternity and paternity rights in Britain, 2002: survey of parents', Department for Work and Pensions in-house report no. 131, London.

Jacobs, J.A. and Gerson, K. (2004), *The Time Divide: Work, Family and Gender Inequality*, Cambridge, MA: Harvard University Press.

Jaumotte, F. (2003), *Female Labour Force Participation: Past Trends and Main Determinants in OECD Countries*, working paper no. 376, Paris: OECD.

Jenson, J. (2006), 'The LEGO paradigm and new social risks: consequences for children', in J. Lewis (ed.), *Children, Changing Families and Welfare States*, Cheltenham, UK and Northampton, MA, USA: Edward Elgar.

Jones, A., Visser, F., Coats, D., Bevan, S. and McVerry, A. (2007), *Transforming Work: Reviewing the Case for Change and New Ways of Working*, working paper series no. 60, Manchester: Equal Opportunities Commission.

Jones, F., Burke, R.J. and Westman, M. (2006), *Work–Life Balance: A Psychological Perspective*, New York: Psychology Press.

Joos, M. (2002), 'Tageseinrichtungen fur Kinder zwischen Dienstleistung und Bildungsanforderungen', *Zeitschrift für Soziologie der Erziehung und Sozialisation*, **22** (3), 231–48.

Joshi, H. (2002), 'Production, reproduction, and education: women, children, and work in a British perspective', *Population and Development Review*, **28** (3), 445–74.

Kangas, O. and Rostgaard, T. (2007), 'Preferences or institutions? Work family life opportunities in seven European countries', *Journal of European Social Policy*, **17** (3), 240–56.

Kazimirski, A., Smith, R., Butt, S., Ireland, E. and Lloyd, E. (2008), *Childcare and Early Years Survey 2007: Parents' Use, Views and Experiences*, London: DCSF.

Kazimirski, A., Smith, R., Mogensen, E. and Lemmetti, F. (2006), *Monitoring of the Reform of the Income Tax and National Insurance Rules for Employer-supported Childcare*, London: HMRC and NatCen.

Kent, K. (2007), 'New LFS questions on economic activity', *Economic and Labour Market Review*, **1** (12), 30–36.

Kenworthy, L. (2009), 'Who should care for under-threes?', in J. Gornick, M. Meyers and E. Olin Wright (eds), *Earning and Caring: Creating the Conditions for Gender-Egalitarian Families*, New York: Verso.

Kersley, B., Alpin, C., Forth, J., Bryson, A., Bewley, H., Dix, G. and Oxenbridge, S. (2006), *Inside the Workplace: Findings from the 2004 Workplace Employment Relations Survey*, London: Routledge.

Kiernan, K., Land, H. and Lewis, J. (1998), *Lone Motherhood in Twentieth Century Britain*, Oxford: Oxford University Press.

Kilkey, M. (2005), 'New Labour and reconciling work and family life: making it fathers' business?', *Social Policy and Society*, **5**(2), 167–75.

Kilpatrick, C. and Freedland, M. (2004), 'How is EU governance transformative?', in S. Sciarra, P. Davies and M. Freedland (eds), *Employment Policy and the Regulation of Part-time Work in the European Union*, Cambridge: Cambridge University Press.

Kinnaird, R., Nicholson, S. and Jordan, E. (2007), *2006 Childcare and Early Years Providers Surveys: Overview Report*, research report DCSF-RR009, London: DCSF.

Kittay, E.F. (1999), *Love's Labour: Essays on Women, Equality and Dependency*, New York: Routledge.

Kittay, E.F. and Feder, E.K. (eds), (2000), *The Subject of Care: Feminist Perspectives on Dependency*, New York: Rowman & Littlefield.

Klammer, U. and Letablier, M.-T. (2007), 'Family policies in Germany and France: the role of enterprises and social partners', *Social Policy and Administration*, **41** (6), 672–92.

Klein, T. and Eckhard, J. (2007), 'Educational differences: value of children and fertility outcomes in Germany', *Current Sociology*, **55** (4), 505–25.

Knegt, R. (2005), 'Life cycle arrangements and the concept of unemployment', *European Journal of Social Security*, **7** (4), 379–402.

Knijn, T. (2004), 'Challenges and risks of individualisation in the Netherlands', *Social Policy & Society*, **3** (1), 57–65.

Knijn, T. and Kremer, M. (1997), 'Gender and the caring dimension of welfare states: toward inclusive citizenship', *Social Politics*, **4** (3), 328–61.

Knijn, T., Martin, C. and Millar, J. (2007), 'Activation as a common framework for social policies towards lone parents: beyond continental specificity?', *Social Policy and Administration*, **41** (6), 638–52.

Knijn, T. and Ostner, I. (2008), 'The "meaning" of children in Dutch and German family policy', in A. Leira and C. Saraceno (eds), Childhood: Changing Contexts. *Comparative Social Research*, vol. 25, Bingsley: Emerald Group Publishing, pp. 79–110.

Kok, L., Groot, I., Mulder, J., Sadiraj, K. and Van Ham, M. (2005), *De Markt voor Kinderopvang in 2004*, Amsterdam: SEO Economisch Onderzoek.

Koopmans, I., Plantenga, J. and Vlasblom, J.D. (2005), 'Life courses, diversity and the reform of the unemployment insurance act', *European Journal of Social Security*, **7** (4), 363–77.

Korpi, W. (2000), 'Faces of inequality: gender, class, and patterns of inequalities in different types of welfare states', *Social Politics*, **7** (2), 127–91.

Kossek, E.E. and Lambert, S.J. (eds) (2005), *Work and Life Integration: Organizational, Cultural and Individual Perspectives*, Mawah, NJ: Lawrence Erlbaum Associates.

Kotlikoff, L.J. (2003), *Generational Policy*, Cambridge, MA: MIT Press.

Kremer, M. (2007), *How Welfare States Care. Culture, Gender and Parenting in Europe*, Amsterdam: Amsterdam University Press.

Kröger, T. and Sipilä, J. (eds) (2005), *Overstretched: European Families up Against the Demands of Work and Care*, Oxford: Blackwell.

Kyi, G. (2005), 'Population in Europe 2004, first results', in *Statistics in Focus: Population and Social Conditions*, 15/2005, Luxembourg: Eurostat.

La Valle, I.S., Arthur, C., Scott Millward, J. and Clayden, M. (2002), *The Influence of Atypical Working Hours on Family Life*, York: Joseph Rowntree Foundation.

Labour Party (1997), *New Labour Because Britain Deserves Better*, manifesto, London: Labour Party.

Laing & Buisson (2007), *Children's Nurseries: UK Market Report 2007*, London: Laing & Buisson.

Land, H. and Lewis, J. (1998), 'Gender, care and the changing role of the state in the UK', in J. Lewis (ed.), *Gender, Social Care and Welfare State Restructuring in Europe*, Aldershot: Ashgate.

Land, H. and Rose, H. (1985), 'Compulsory altruism for some or an altruistic society for all?', in P. Bean, J. Ferris and D. Whynes (eds), *In Defence of Welfare*, London: Tavistock.

Larsson, J. et al. (2006), 'Let the state pay a reduction of working hours for parents', *Dagens Nyheter*, 21 August, translation by J. Larsson.

Le Bihan, B. and Martin, C. (2005), 'Atypical working hours: consequences for childcare arrangements', in T. Kröger and J. Sipilä (eds), *Overstretched: European Families Up Against the Demands of Work and Care*, Oxford: Blackwell.

Le Grand, J. (2003), *Motivation, Agency and Public Policy: Of Knight and Knaves, Pawns and Queens*, Oxford: Oxford University Press.

Lehmann, P. and Wirtz, C. (2004), *Household Formation in the EU: Lone Parents*, Statistics in Focus theme, 3–5/2004, Luxembourg: Eurostat.

Leibfried, S. (2005), 'Social policy: left to the judges and the markets?', in H. Wallace and W. Wallace (eds), *Policy-Making in the European Union*, Oxford: Oxford University Press.

Leira, A. (1992), *Welfare States and Working Mothers*, Cambridge: Cambridge University Press.

Leira, A. (1998), 'Caring as social right: cash for child care and daddy leave', *Social Politics*, **5** (3), 362–79.

Leitner, S. (2003), 'Varieties of familialism', *European Societies*, **5** (4), 353–75.

Leitner, S. (2005), 'Rot-Grüne Familienpolitik: Kind und Karriere für alle?', *Blätter für deutsche und internationale Politik*, **50** (8), 958–64.

Leitner, S., Ostner, I. and Schmitt, C. (2008), 'Family policies in Germany', in I. Ostner and C. Schmitt (eds), *Family Policies in the Context of Family Change: The Nordic Countries in Comparative Perspective*, Zeitschrift für Familienforschung (special issue), Wiesbaden: VS Verlag Für Sozialwissenschaften.

Leprince, F. and Martin, C. (2003), *L'accueil des Jeunes Enfants en France: Etat des Lieux et Pistes d'Amélioration*, rapport pour le Haut Conseil de la Population et de la Famille, Paris: La Documentation Française.

Letablier, M.-T. (2007), 'Income security of women and changes in gender role models in France: empirical findings, current patterns and perspectives', presentation to the international expert conference on Self Responsibility, Private and Public Solidarity: Gender Role Models in Family Law and Social Protecton Law in Europe, 4-6 October.

Lewis, J. (1992), 'Gender and the development of welfare regimes', *Journal of European Social Policy*, **2** (3), 159–73.

Lewis, J. (2001), 'The decline of the male breadwinner model: the implications for work and care', *Social Politics*, **8** (2), 152–70.

Lewis, J. (2001a), *The End of Marriage? Individualism and Intimate Relations*, Cheltenham, UK and Northampton, MA, USA: Edward Elgar.

Lewis, J. (2002), 'Gender and welfare state change', *European Societies*, **4** (4), 331–57.

Lewis, J. (2003), 'Developing early years childcare in England, 1997–2002: the choices for (working) mothers', *Social Policy and Administration*, **37** (3), 219–39.

Lewis, J. (2005), 'Perceptions of risk in intimate relationships: the implications for social provision', *Journal of Social Policy*, **35** (1), 39–57.

Lewis, J. (2006), 'Employment and care: the policy problem, gender equality and the issue of choice', *Journal of Comparative Policy Analysis*, **8** (2), 103–14.

Lewis, J. (2006a), 'Work/family reconciliation, equal opportunities and social policies: the interpretation of policy trajectories at the EU level and the meaning of gender equality', *Journal of European Public Policy*, **13** (3), 420–37.

Lewis, J. (2007), 'Gender, ageing and "The New Social Settlement"': the importance of developing a holistic approach to care policies', *Current Sociology*, **55** (2), 271–86.

Lewis, J. and Aström, G. (1992), 'Equality, difference and state welfare: the case of labour market and family policies in Sweden', *Feminist Studies*, **18** (1), 13–25.

Lewis, J. and Campbell, M. (forthcoming), 'What's in a name? "Work and family" or "Work and life" balance policies in the UK since 1997 and the implications for the pursuit of gender equality', *Social Policy and Administration*, **42**(5), 524–37.

Lewis, J., Campbell, M. and Huerta, C. (2008), 'Patterns of paid and unpaid work in Western Europe: gender, commodification, preferences and the implications for policy', *Journal of European Social Policy*, **18** (1), 21–37.

Lewis, J. and Giullari, S. (2005), 'The adult worker model family, gender equality and care: the search for new policy principles and the possibilities and problems of a capabilities approach', *Economy and Society*, **34** (1), 76–104.

Lewis, J. and Glennerster, H. (1996), *Implementing the New Community Care*, Buckingham: Open University Press.

Lewis, S. (1997), '"Family friendly" employment policies: a route to changing organisational culture or playing about at the margins?', *Gender, Work and Organization*, **4** (1), 3–23.

Lindley, J. and Dale, A. (2004), 'Ethnic differences in women's demographic, family characteristics and economic activity profiles, 1993 and 2002', *Labour Market Trends*, April, 153–64.

Liska, A.E. (1984), 'A critical examination of the causal structure of the Fishbein/Ajzen Attitude–Behavior Model', *Social Psychology Quarterly*, **47** (1), 61–74.

Lister, R. (1997), *Citizenship: Feminist Perspectives*, Basingstoke: Macmillan.

Lister, R. (2003), 'Investing in the citizen-workers of the Future: transformations in citizenship and the state under New Labour', *Social Policy and Administration*, **37** (5), 427–43.

Lødemel, I. and Trickey, H. (eds) (2000), *An Offer You Can't Refuse: Workfare in International Perspective*, Bristol: The Policy Press.

Lovell, V., O'Neill, E. and Olsen, S. (2007), *Maternity Leave in the United States*, Washington, DC: Institute for Women's Policy Research.

Luck, D. and Hofäcker, D. (2003), *Rejection and Acceptance of the Male Breadwinner Model: Which Preferences do Women Have Under Which Circumstances?* GLOBALIFE working paper no. 60, Bamberg, Germany: Department of Sociology, Otto Friedrich University.

Lutz, W. (2006), 'Alternative paths for future European fertility: will the birth rate recover or continue to decline?', in W. Lutz, R. Richter and

C. Wilson (eds), *The New Generations of Europeans: Demography and Families in the Enlarged European Union*, London: Earthscan.

Lutz, W. (2007), 'The future of human reproduction: will birth rates recover or continue to fall?', *Ageing Horizons*, issue no. 7, 15–21.

Mahon, R. (2006), 'The OECD and the work–family reconciliation agenda: competing frames', in J. Lewis (ed.), *Children, Changing Families and Welfare States*, Cheltenham, UK and Northampton, MA, USA: Edward Elgar.

Maier, R. (2007), 'Life-course and social policy', paper presented to the RECWOWE Conference, Warsaw, 12-16 June.

Major, B. (1993), 'Gender, entitlement, and the distribution of family labor', *Journal of Social Issues*, **49** (3), 141–59.

Manning, A. and Petrongolo, B. (2005), *The Part-Time Pay Penalty*, London: DTI.

Manning, A. and Petrongolo, B. (2008), 'The part-time pay penalty for women in Britain', *The Economic Journal*, **118** (February), F28–51.

Martin, C., Math, A. and Renaudat, E. (1998), 'Caring for very young children and dependent elderly people in France: towards a commodification of social care?', in J. Lewis (ed.), *Gender, Social Care and Welfare State Restructuring in Europe*, Aldershot: Ashgate.

Maternity Alliance (2000), *What Women Want; Women's Views on Maternity Pay Compiled from Research Carried Out by the Maternity Alliance in October 2000*, London: Maternity Alliance.

Mathers, S., Sylva, K. and Joshi, H. (2007), *Quality of Childcare Settings in the Millennium Cohort Study*, London: HMSO.

Mattingly, M. and Sayer, L.C. (2006), 'Under pressure: gender differences in the relationship between free time and feeling rushed', *Journal of Marriage and Family*, **68** (1), 205–21.

Maximiliens, L. and Schneewind, K. (2006), *Family Life: Conflict and Synergy*, Brussels: European Commission.

Mazey, S. (2000), 'Introduction: integrating gender – intellectual and "real world" mainstreaming', *Journal of European Public Policy*, **7** (3), 333–45.

McDonald, P. (2000), 'Gender equity in theories of fertility transition', *Population and Development Review*, **26** (3), 427–39.

McDonald, P. (2002), 'Sustaining fertility through public policy: the range of options', *Population-E*, **57** (3), 417–46.

McRae, S. (2003), 'Choice and constraints in mothers' employment careers: McRae replies to Hakim', *British Journal of Sociology*, **54** (4), 585–92.

Méda, D. and Orain, R. (2002), 'Transformations du Travail et du Hors Travail. Le Jugement des Salariés', *Travail et Emploi*, **90**, 23–38.

Melhuish, E. (2004), *Child Benefits. The Importance of Investing in Quality Childcare*, Facing the Future policy papers no. 9, London: Daycare Trust.

Messenger, J.C. (ed.) (2004), *Working Time and Workers' Preferences in Industrialized Countries: Finding the Balance*, London: Routledge.

Meulders, D. and Gustafsson, S. (2004), 'The rationale of motherhood choices: influence of employment conditions and of public policies', final report EU grant SERD-2000-00039, accessed 28 March 2008 at www.ulb. ac.b/soco/mocho/reports/external/MOCHO_final_report_Oct_2004-pdf.

Moen, P. and Roehling, P. (2005), *The Career Mystique: Cracks in the American Dream*, Oxford: Rowman & Littlefield.

Moller Okin, S. (1989), *Justice, Gender and the Family*, New York: Basic Books.

Morel, N. (2007), 'From subsidiarity to "free choice": child- and elderly-care policy reforms in France, Belgium, Germany and the Netherlands', *Social Policy and Administration*, **41** (6), 618–37.

Morgan, D. (1996), *Family Connections*, Cambridge: Polity Press.

Morgan, K. (2006), 'Working mothers and the welfare state', in *Religion and the Politics of Work-Family Policies in Western Europe and the US*, Stanford, CA: Stanford University Press.

Morgan, K. and Zippel, K. (2003), 'Paid to care: the origins and effects of care leave policies in Western Europe', *Social Politics*, **10** (1), 45–85.

Moss, P. (2006), 'From a childcare to a pedagogical discourse: or putting care in its place', in J. Lewis (ed.), *Children, Changing Families and Welfare States*, Cheltenham, UK and Northampton, MA, USA: Edward Elgar.

Moss, P. and Deven, F. (2006), 'Leave policies and research: a cross-national overview', *Marriage and Family Review*, **39**, 255–85.

Moss, P. and Wall, K. (2007), *International Review of Leave Policies and Related Research*, employment relations research series no. 80, London: DTI.

Mutari, Ellen and Figart, Deborah (2001), 'Europe at a crossroads: harmonization, liberalization, and the gender of work time', *Social Politics*, **8**, 36–64.

Nadeem, S. and Metcalf, H. (2007), *Work–Life Policies in Great Britain: What Works, Where and How?*, employment relations research series no. 77, London: Department for Business, Enterprise and Regulatory Reform.

Naegele, G. (2003), *A New Organisation of Time over Working Life*, Dublin: Eurofound.

National Audit Office (NAO) (2004), *Early Years: Progress in Developing High Quality Childcare and Early Education Accessible to All*, HC 268, London: The Stationery Office.

NAO (2006), *Sure Start Children's Centres*, London: The Stationery Office.

NAO (2007), *Helping People from Workless Households into Work*, London: The Stationery Office.

National Statistics (2007), *Provision for Children Under Five Years of Age in England*, statistical first release 19/2007, London: Department for Education and Skills.

Naz, G. (2004), 'The impact of cash-benefit reform on parents' labour force participation', *Journal of Population Economics*, **17**, 369–83.

Neyer, G. (2006), *Family Policies and Fertility in Europe: Fertility Policies at the Intersection of Gender Policies, Employment Policies and Care Policies*, working paper WP 2006-010, Rostock, Germany: Max Planck Institute for Demographic Research.

National Institute of Child Health and Human Development (NICHD) Early Child Care Research Network (2005), *Childcare and Child Development*, New York: Guilford Press.

Nickell, S. (2006), 'Are Europeans lazy? Or Americans crazy?', paper delivered at the Annual Conference of Fondazione Rodolfo Benedetti, La Spezia, Italy, May.

Nowotny, H. (1994), *Time: The Modern and Postmodern Experience*, Cambridge: Polity.

Nussbaum, M. (1999), *Sex and Social Justice*, Oxford: Oxford University Press.

Nussbaum, M. (2000), *Woman and Human Development: The Capabilities Approach*, Cambridge: Cambridge University Press.

Nussbaum, M. (2003), 'Capabilities as fundamental entitlements: Sen and social justice', *Feminist Economics*, **9** (2–3), 33–59.

Nyberg, A. (2004), 'Parental leave, public childcare and the dual earner/dual carer-model in Sweden', meeting of the Peer Review Programme of the European Employment Strategy, Stockholm, 19-20 April.

O'Brien, M. and Shemilt, I. (2003), *Working Father: Earning and Caring*, Manchester: EOC.

O'Connor, J. (2005), 'Employment-anchored social policy, gender mainstreaming and the open method of policy coordination in the European Union', *European Societies*, **7** (1), 27–52.

OECD (Organisation for Economic Co-operation and Development) (2001), *Employment Outlook 2001*, Paris: OECD.

OECD (2001a), *Knowledge and Skills for Life: First Results from the OECD Programme for International Student Assessment (PISA) 2000*, Paris: OECD.

OECD (2004), *Employment Outlook*, Paris: OECD.

OECD (2005), *Babies and Bosses: Reconciling Work and Family Life*, vol. 4, Paris: OECD.

OECD (2007), *Babies and Bosses. Reconciling Work and Family Life: A Synthesis of Findings for OECD Countries*, Paris: OECD.

Ofsted (Office for Standards in Education) (2003), *Registered Childcare Providers and Places in England, Quarterly Statistics*, March, Manchester: Ofsted.

Ofsted (2007), *Early Years. Getting on Well: Enjoying, Achieving and Contributing*, London: Ofsted.

Ofsted (2007a), *Registered Childcare Providers and Places in England*, Quarterly Statistics, September, Manchester: Ofsted.

Olah, L. (2003), 'Gendering fertility: second births in Sweden and Hungary', *Population Research and Policy Review*, **22**, 171–200.

Oppenheim Mason, K. (2001), 'Gender and family systems in the fertility transition', *Population and Development Review*, **27**, supplement, 160–76.

Oppenheimer, V. (1994), 'Women's rising employment and the future of the family in industrialised societies', *Population and Development Review*, **20** (2), 293–342.

Oppenheimer, V. (2000), 'The continuing importance of men's economic position in marriage formation', in L.J. Waite (ed.), *The Ties that Bind*, New York: de Gruyter.

Orloff, A. (1993), 'Gender and the social rights of citizenship: state policies and gender relations in comparative research', *American Sociological Review*, **58** (3), 303–28.

Orloff, A.S. (2006), 'From maternalism to "employment for all": state policies to promote women's employment across the affluent democracies', in J. Levy (ed.), *The State after Statism*, Cambridge: Harvard University Press, pp. 230–68.

Orloff, A. (2009), 'Should feminists aim for gender symmetry? Why the dual-earner/dual care model may not be every feminist's Utopia', in J. Gornick, M. Meyers and E. Olin Wright (eds), *Earning and Caring: Creating the Conditions for Gender-Egalitarian Families*, New York: Verso.

Osborne, G. (2006), 'Women at work and childcare', speech at Conservative Party Central Office, 27 February.

Ostner, I. (2006), 'Paradigmenwechsel in der (west)deutschen Familienpolitik', in P.A. Berger and H. Kahlert (eds), *Der demographische Wandel. Chancen für die Neuordnung der Geschlechterverhältnisse*, Frankfurt am Main, Germany and New York: Campus Verlag, pp. 165–99.

Ostner, I. and Schmitt, C. (2007), 'Introduction', in I. Ostner and C. Schmitt (eds), *Family Policies in the Context of Family Change: The Nordic*

Countries in Comparative Perspective, Zeitschrift für Familienforschung (special issue), Wiesbaden: VS Verlag Für Sozialwissenschaften.

Palmer, T. (2004), results of the first flexible working employee survey, employment relations occasional paper, London: DTI.

Parent-Thirion, A., Fernández Macias, E., Hurley, J. and Vermeylen, G. (2007), *Fourth European Working Conditions Survey (EWCS)*, Dublin: Eurofound.

Paull, G. (2008), 'Children and women's hours of work', *The Economic Journal*, **118** (February), F8–F27.

Pécresse, V. (2007), *Mieux Articuler Vie Familiale et Vie Professionnelle*, rapport au Premier Ministre, Paris: La Documentation Française.

Pedersen, S. (1993), *Family, Dependence, and the Origins of the Welfare State: Britain and France, 1914–1945*, Cambridge: Cambridge University Press.

Penn, H. (2007), 'Childcare market management: how the United Kingdom government has reshaped its role in developing early childhood education and care', *Contemporary Issues in Early Childhood*, **8** (3), 192–207.

Penn, H. and Randall, V. (2005), 'Childcare policy and local partnerships under Labour', *Journal of Social Policy*, **34** (1), 79–97.

Périvier, H. (2003), 'La Garde des Jeunes Enfants: Affaires de Femmes ou Affaire d'Etat?', *Lettre de L'OFCE*, no. 228, Paris: Presses de Science-po.

Perrons, D. (1999), 'Flexible working patterns and equal opportunities in the European Union: conflict or compatibility?', *European Journal of Women's Studies*, **6** (4), 391–418.

Perrons, D. (2000), 'Care, paid work and leisure: rounding the triangle', *Feminist Economics*, **6** (1), 105–14.

Perrons, D., Fagan, C., McDowell, L., Ray, K. and Ward, K. (eds) (2007), *Gender Divisions and Working Time in the New Economy: Changing Patterns of Work, Care and Public Policy in Europe and North America*, Cheltenham, UK and Northampton, MA, USA: Edward Elgar.

Perry-Jenkins, M., Goldberg, A.E., Pierce, C. and Sayer, A.G. (2007), 'Shift work, role overload, and the transition to parenthood', *Journal of Marriage and Family*, **69** (1), 123–38.

Petrongolo, B. (2004), 'Gender segregation in employment contracts', *Journal of the European Economic Association*, **2** (2–3), 331–45.

Pfau-Effinger, B. (1998), 'Gender cultures and the gender arrangement: a theoretical framework for cross-national gender research', *Innovation*, **11** (2), 147–66.

Pfau-Effinger, B. (2004), 'Welfare state policies and the development of care arrangements', *European Societies*, **7** (2), 321–47.

Pfau-Effinger, B. (2006), 'Cultures of childhood and the relationship of care and employment in European welfare states', in J. Lewis (ed.), *Children, Changing Families and Welfare States*, Cheltenham, UK and Northampton, MA, USA: Edward Elgar.

Phillips, A. (2001), 'Feminism and liberalism revisited: has Martha Nussbaum got it right?', *Constellations*, **8** (2), 249–66.

Phoenix, A. (1991), *Young Mothers*, Cambridge: Polity Press.

Pierson, P. (1994), *Dismantling the Welfare State? Reagan, Thatcher and the Politics of Retrenchment*, Cambridge: Cambridge University Press.

Pierson, P. (2001), *The New Politics of the Welfare State*, Oxford: Oxford University Press.

Piketty, T. (2005), 'Impact de l'Allocation Parentale d'Education sure l'Activité Féminine et la Fécondité en France', in C. Lefèvre (ed.), *Histoires de Familles, Histoires Familiales*, Les Cahiers de l'INED, no. 156, 79–109.

Plantenga, J. and Remery, C. (2005), *Reconciliation of Work and Private Life: A Comparative Review of Thirty European Countries*, Brussels: European Communities.

Plantenga, J., Remery, C., Siegel, M. and Sementini, L. (2008), 'Childcare services in 25 European Union member states: the Barcelona targets revisited', in A. Leira and C. Saraceno (eds), *Comparative Social Research*, volume 25, Bingsley: Emerald Publishing Group, pp. 27–53.

Pleck, J.H. (1997), 'Paternal involvement: levels, sources, and consequences', in M. Lamb (ed.), *The Role of the Father in Child Development*, 3rd edn, New York: John Wiley & Sons.

Population Trends (2008), 'Annual update: births in England and Wales, 2007', no. 131.

Portegijs, W., Hermans, B. and Lalta, V. (2006), *Emanicipatiemonitor 2006*, Den Haag; Sociaal en Cultureel Planbureau.

PricewaterhouseCoopers (2003), *Universal Childcare Provision in the UK: Towards a Cost–Benefit Analysis*, London: PricewaterhouseCoopers.

PricewaterhouseCoopers (2006), *DfES Children's Services: The Childcare Market*, London: DfES.

Rake, K. (2000), 'Gender and New Labour's Social Policy', *Journal of Social Policy*, **30** (2), 209–32.

Randall, V. (2000), *The Politics of Child Daycare in Britain*, Oxford: Oxford University Press.

Rapoport, R., Bailyn, L, Fletcher, J.K. and Pruitt, B.H. (2002), *Beyond Work–Family Balance: Advancing Gender Equity and Workplace Performance*, San Francisco, CA: Jossey Bass.

Rees, T. (1998), *Mainstreaming Equality in the European Union: Education, Training and Labour Market Policies*, London: Routledge.

Reeves, R. (2002), *Dad's Army: The Case for Father-Friendly Workplaces*, London: The Work Foundation.

Reid, P. and White, D. (2007), *Out-of-School Care for Children Living in Disadvantaged Areas*, Dublin: Eurofound.

Riggall, A. and Sharp, C. (2008), *The Structure of Primary Education: England and Other Countries*, primary review research briefings 9/1, Cambridge: University of Cambridge Faculty of Education.

Rostgaard, T. (2002), 'Caring for children and older people in Europe: a comparison of European policies and practice', *Policy Studies*, **23** (1), 51–68.

Rothstein, B. (1998), *Just Institutions Matter*, Cambridge: Cambridge University Press.

Royal Commission on Long-Term Care (1999), *With Respect to Old Age*, Cmnd 4192-I, London: The Stationery Office.

Rubery, J., Grimshaw, D., Fagan, C., Figueredo, H. and Smith, M. (2003), 'Gender equality still on the European agenda – but for how long?', *Industrial Relations Journal*, **34** (5), 477–97.

Rubery, J., Smith, M. and Fagan, C. (1999), *Women's Employment in Europe*, London: Routledge.

Rubery, J., Ward, K., Grimshaw, D. and Beynon, H. (2005), 'Working time, industrial relations and the employment relationship', *Time and Society*, **14** (1), 89–111.

Ruhm, C.J. (1998), 'The economic consequences of parental leave mandates: lessons from Europe', *The Quarterly Journal of Economics*, **113** (1), 285–317.

Salmi, M. (2006), 'Parental choice and the passion for equality in Finland', in A.-L. Ellingsaeter and A. Leira, *Politicising Parenthood in Scandinavia: Gender Relations in Welfare States*, Bristol: Polity Press

Saraceno, C. (2002), 'Paradoxes and biases in the policy view of the gendered use of time: the Italian case', unpublished paper.

Saraceno, C., Olagnero, M. and Torrioni, P. (2005), *First European Quality of Life Survey: Families, Work and Social Networks*, Dublin: Eurofound.

Sayer, L.C. (2007), 'More work for mothers? Trends and gender differences in multitasking', in T. van der Lippe and P. Peters (eds), *Competing Claims in Work and Family Life*, Cheltenham, UK and Northampton, MA, USA: Edward Elgar.

Schmid, G. (1998), 'Transitional labour markets: a new European employment strategy', WZB discussion paper FS 1 98-206, Berlin.

Schmid, G. (2000), 'Transitional labour markets', in B. Marin, D. Meulders and D. Snower (eds), *Innovative Employment Initiatives*, Aldershot: Ashgate.

Schmidt, V.A. (2001), 'Discourse and the legitimation of economic and social policy change in Europe', in S. Weber (ed.), *Globalization and the European Political Economy*, New York: Columbia University Press.

Schmidt, V.A. (2002), 'Does discourse matter in the politics of welfare state adjustment?', *Comparative Political Studies*, **35** (2), 168–93.

Schone, P. (2004), 'Labour Supply Effects of a Cash-for-Care Subsidy', *Journal of Population Economics*, **17**, 703–27.

Schor, J. (1991), *The Overworked American*, New York: Basic Books.

Schwartz, B. (2004), *The Paradox of Choice: Why More is Less*, New York: HarperCollins.

Scruggs, L. (2006), 'Welfare-state decommodification in 18 OECD countries: a replication and revision', *Journal of European Social Policy*, **16** (1), 55–72.

Sen, A. (1999), *Development as Freedom*, New York: Knopf.

Sigle-Rushton, W. and Waldfogel, J. (2006), 'Motherhood and women's earnings in Anglo-American, Continental European, and Nordic countries', *Feminist Economics*, **13** (2), 55–91.

Simon, A. and Whiting, E. (2007), 'Using the FRS to examine employment trends of couples', *Economic and Labour Market Review*, **1** (11), 41–7.

Simoni and Trifilleti (2005), 'Caregiving in transition in Southern Europe: neither complete altruists nor free-riders', in T. Kröger and J. Sipilä (eds), *Overstretched: European Families up against the Demands of Work and Care*, Oxford: Blackwell.

Skevik, A. (2006), 'Working their way out of poverty? Lone mothers in policies and labour markets', in J. Bradshaw and A. Hatland (eds), *Social Policy, Employment and Family Change in Comparative Perspective*, Cheltenham, UK and Northampton, MA, USA: Edward Elgar.

Skinner, C. and Finch, N. (2006), 'Lone parents and informal childcare: a tax credit childcare subsidy?', *Social Policy and Administration*, **40** (7), 807–23.

Sleebos, J.E. (2003), *Low Fertility Rates in OECD Countries: Facts and Policy Responses*, social, employment and migration working papers no. 15, Paris: OECD.

Smeaton, D. (2006), *Dads and Their Babies: a Household Analysis*, working paper series no. 44, Manchester: Equal Opportunities Commission.

Smeaton, D. and Marsh, A. (2006), *Maternity and Paternity Rights and Benefits: Survey of Parents 2005*, employment relations research series no. 50, London: Department for Business Enterprise and Regulatory Reform.

Smith, N. (2003), 'A Blessing or a boomerang? The Danish welfare state and the labour market careers of women', paper presented at the

ESPAnet Conference, Changing European Societies: The Role for Social Policy, 13-15 November.

Smith, T., Smith, G., Coxon, K., Sigala, M., Sylva, K., Mathers, S., LaValle, I., Smith, R., Purdon, S., Dearden, L., Shaw, J. and Sibieta, L. (2007), *National Evaluation of the Neighbourhood Nurseries Initiative. Integrated Report*, London: Sure Start.

Southerton, D. and Tomlinson, M. (2005), '"Pressed for time" – the differential impacts of a "time squeeze"', *The Sociological Review*, **53** (2), 215–39.

Sparkes, J. and West, A. (1998), 'An evaluation of the English nursery voucher scheme 1996–1997', *Education Economics*, **6** (2), 171–301.

Spieß, C.K. and Bach, S. (2002), 'Familienförderung – Hintergründe, Instrumente und Bewertungen aus ökonomischer Sicht', *Vierteljahreshefte zur Wirschaftsforschung*, **71** (1), 7–10

Stevens, J., Brown, J. and Lee, C. (2004), *The Second Work–Life Balance Study: Results from the Employees' Survey*, employment relations research series no. 27, London: Department of Trade and Industry

Stier, H. and Lewin-Epstein, N. (2007), 'Policy effects on the division of housework', *Journal of Comparative Policy Analysis*, **9** (3), 235–59.

Strandh, M. and Nordenmark, M. (2006), 'The interference of paid work with household demands in different social policy contexts: perceived work–household conflict in Sweden, the UK, the Netherlands, Hungary, and the Czech Republic', *The British Journal of Sociology*, **57** (4), 597–617.

Streeck, W. and Thelen, K. (eds) (2005), *Beyond Continuity. Institutional Change in Advanced Political Economies*, Oxford: Oxford University Press.

Strohmeier, K.P. (2002), 'Family policy – how does it work?', in F.-X. Kaufman, A. Kuijsten, H.-J. Schulze and K.P. Strohmeier (eds), *Family Life and Family Policies in Europe*, vol. 2, Oxford: Oxford University Press.

Sullivan, O. (2006), *Changing Gender Relations, Changing Families. Tracing the Pace of Change Over Time*, Lanham, MD: Rowman & Littlefield.

Supiot, A. (2001), *Beyond Employment*, Oxford: Oxford University Press.

Sylva, K., Melhuish, E., Sammons, P., Sirja-Blatchford, I. and Taggart, B. (2004), *The Effective Provision of Pre-School Education Project: Final Report Results*, London: DfES.

Sylva, K., Melhuish, E., Sammons, P., Sirja-Blatchford, I. and Taggart, B. (2007), *Promoting Equality in the Early Years. Report to The Equalities Review*, London: DfES.

SZW (Ministerie van Sociale Zaken en Werkgelegenheid) (1997), *Kansen op combineren: Arbeid, zorg en economische zelfstandigheid*, [*Opportunities to Combine: Work, Care and Economic Independence*], Den Haag: SZW.

SZW (1999), *Op weg naar een nieuw evenwicht tussen arbeid en zorg* [*On the Way to a New Balance of Work and Care*], Den Haag: SZW.

SZW (2000), *Meerjarenplan emancipatiebeleid: Van vrouwenstrijd naar vanzelfsprekendheid* [*Long-term Gender Equality Programme: From Women's Struggle to Self-evidence*], Den Haag: SZW.

Taylor Gooby, P. (ed.) (2004), *New Risks, New Welfare: The Transformation of the European Welfare State*, Oxford: Oxford University Press.

Thomas, R.R. (1990), 'From affirmative action to affirming diversity', *Harvard Business Review*, March/April, 107–17.

Thompson, L. and Walker, A.J. (1989), 'Gender in families: women and men in marriage, work, and parenthood', *Journal of Marriage and the Family*, **51**, 845–71.

Thompson, M., Finter, L. and Young, V. (2005), *Dads and Their Babies: Leave Arrangements in the First Year*, working paper series no. 37, Manchester: Equal Opportunities Commission.

Timonen, V. (2003), *Restructuring the Welfare State: Globalisation and Welfare Reform in Finland and Sweden*, Cheltenham, UK and Northampton, MA, USA: Edward Elgar.

Torres, A., Brites, L., Haas, B. and Steiber, N. (2007), *First European Quality of Life Survey: Time Use and Work–Life Options over the Life Course*, Dublin: Eurofound.

Tronto, J. (1993), *Moral Boundaries: A Political Argument for and Ethic of Care*, London: Routledge.

Trzcinski, E. (2000), 'Family policy in Germany: a feminist dilemma?', *Feminist Economics*, **6** (1), 21–44.

Trades Union Congress (TUC) (2005), *Response to 'Work and Families: Choice and Flexibility'*, London: TUC.

TUC (2007), 'Long hours working on the increase', press release, 28 November, London.

UN Social Indicators (2005), 'Indicators on child-bearing', New York: UN, accessed 7 March, 2008 at http://unstats.un.org/unsd/demographic/products/solind/childbr.htm.

Uunk, W., Kalmijn, M. and Muffels, R. (2005), 'The impact of young children on women's labour supply', *Acta Sociologica*, **48** (1), 41–62.

Van Bastelaer, A. and Vaguer, C. (2004), *Working Times*, Statistics in Focus theme 3, 7/2004, Luxembourg: Eurostat.

Van Echtelt, P.E., Glebbeek, A.C. and Lindenberg, S.M. (2006), 'The new lumpiness of work: explaining the mismatch between actual and preferred working hours', *Work, Employment and Society*, **20** (3), 493–512.

Van Peer, C. (2002), 'Desired and achieved fertility', in E. Klijzing and M. Corijn (eds), *Dynamics of Fertility and Partnership in Europe: Insights and Lessons from Comparative Research*, vol. 2, New York and Geneva: United Nations.

Van Staveren, I. (1999), *Caring for Economics: An Aristotelian Perspective*, Delft, the Netherlands: Eburon.

van Wel, F. and Knijn, T. (2006), 'Transitional phase or a new balance? Working and caring by mothers with young children in the Netherlands', *Journal of Family Issues*, **27** (5), 633–51.

Visser, J. (2002), 'The first part-time economy in the world: a model to be followed?', *Journal of European Social Policy*, **12** (1), 23–42.

Vlasblom, J.D. and Schippers, J. (2006), 'Changing dynamics in female employment around childbirth: evidence from Germany, the Netherlands and the UK', *Work, Employment and Society*, **20** (2), 329–47.

Waerness, K. (1984), 'The rationality of caring', *Economic and Industrial Democracy*, **5**, 185–211.

Waldfogel, J. (2006), *What Children Need*, Cambridge, MA: Harvard University Press.

Wall, K. (2007), 'Main patterns in attitudes to the articulation between work and family life: a cross-national analysis', in R. Crompton, S. Lewis and C. Lyonette (eds), *Women, Men, Work and Family in Europe*, London: Palgrave Macmillan.

Walling, A. (2005), 'Families and work', *Labour Market Trends*, July, 275–83.

Walsh, I. (2008), *Flexible Working: A Review of how to Extend the Right to Request Flexible Working to Parents of Older Children*, London: Department for Business Enterprise and Regulatory Reform.

Walsh, J. (2007), 'Equality and diversity in British workplaces: the 2004 Workplace Employment Relations Survey', *Industrial Relations Journal*, **38** (4), 303–19.

Warin, J., Solomon, Y., Lewis, C. and Langford, W. (1999), *Fathers, Work and Family Life*, London: Family Policy Studies Centre.

Warren, T. (2003), 'Class- and gender-based working time? Time poverty and the division of domestic labour', *Sociology*, **37** (4), 733–52.

Warren, T. (2004), 'Work part-time: achieving a successful "work–life" balance?', *British Journal of Sociology*, **55** (1), 99–122.

WBG (Women's Budget Group) (2005), *Women's and Children's Poverty: Making the Links*, London: WBG.

WBG (2005a), *Response to Department for Trade and Industry's Consultation: Work and Families: Choice and Flexibility*, London: WBG.

Webster, J. (2001), *Reconciling Adaptability and Equal Opportunities in European Workplaces*, report, Brussels: DG-Employment.

West, A. (2006), 'The pre-school education market in England from 1997: quality, availability, affordability and equity', *Oxford Review of Education*, **32** (3), 283–301.

Wheelock, J., Oughton, E. and Barris, S. (2003), 'Getting by with a little help from your family: towards a policy-relevant model of the household', *Feminist Economics*, **9** (1), 19–45.

White, M., Hill, S., McGovern, P., Mills, C. and Smeaton, D. (2003), '"High-performance" management practices, working hours and work–life balance', *British Journal of Industrial Relations*, **41** (2), 175–95.

Whitehouse, G., Haynes, M., Macdonald, F. and Arts, D. (2007), *Reassessing the Family-Friendly Workplace: Trends and Influences in Britain, 1998–2004*, London: Department for Business, Enterprise and Regulatory Reform.

Wikander, U., A. Kessler Harris and J. Lewis (eds) (1995), *Protecting Women: Labor Legislation in Europe, the US and Australia, 1880–1900*, Urbana, IL: University of Illinois Press.

Windebank, J. (2001), 'Dual-earner couples in Britain and France: gender divisions of domestic labour and parenting work in different welfare states', *Work, Employment and Society*, **15** (2), 269–90.

Wise, S. (2003), *Work–Life Balance Literature and Research Review*, London: DTI.

Woodland, S., Simmonds, N., Thornby, M., Fitzgerald, R. and McGee, A. (2003), *The Second Work–Life Balance Study: Results from the Employers' Survey: Main Report*, employment relations research series no. 22, London: Department of Trade and Industry.

Yaxley, D., Winter, L. and Young, V. (2005), *Dads and their Babies: The Mothers' Perspective*, Manchester: EOC.

Index

'activation' policies 2, 7, 69
active ageing policies 7, 77, 90
adult worker model
  attitudes and behaviour 69
  and gender equality 17, 74, 116–17,
    197
  and individualisation 120, 136–7
  problems 9–10
  Scandinavia 74
  US 74, 75
  and welfare policy changes 9–10,
    76
  Western Europe 74–5
    France 120–21, 133, 134, 135,
      136–7
    Germany 119–20, 128, 133–4,
      136–7
    Netherlands 74–5, 120, 133, 135
    UK 74–5, 116, 120, 134, 135,
      136–7
  see also dual-earner family model
age of child 35, 36, 62, 84, 85–7, 90,
  144, 184
age of women 27–8, 32–4, 43–4, 60
ageing population 5, 12, 197
agency 18–19, 196
Aliaga, C. 49, 50, 51
altruism 17–18, 78
Anxo, D. 31, 41, 137
attitudes 59, 66–70
attitudes to work-family balance
  contradictory nature 6, 60
  division of labour 194–5
  female paid work 147, 148
  France 60, 62, 87, 88, 116, 121–2,
    136
  Germany 60, 62, 63, 64–5, 121, 122,
    128, 136
  life-course changes of women 65
  and male breadwinner/female carer
    family model 60–63, 147

Netherlands 62, 63–5, 121, 122, 136
  parental leave 97, 102, 172–3
  UK 60, 62, 63, 64–5, 66, 87, 88, 90,
    121, 122, 135–6, 147–9, 172–3,
    176, 179
  US 66
  work-care prioritisation in EU-15
    59–64, 65–6, 97, 102, 116, 128
atypical paid working hours
  EU-15 42, 87, 106, 107, 108, 109,
    110, 111
  men 87, 108, 110, 141, 146
  UK 37–40, 41, 108, 110, 111, 141,
    146, 156, 177–8
  women 110, 146
Austria
  attitudes and preferences in work-
    family balance 60, 62, 67, 88
  childcare and early years education
    84, 86, 88, 93
  domestic division of labour 54
  fertility rates 43, 44
  flexible working patterns 110, 111,
    112
  paid work 29, 30, 32, 34, 35, 36, 37,
    38, 40, 195
  paid work patterns 49, 50
  parental leave 97, 98, 100

Balls, E. 154, 161–2
Barcelona targets on formal childcare
  13, 95, 101, 127
behaviour 59, 64, 65–6, 67–70
Belgium
  attitudes and preferences in work-
    family balance 62, 67, 88
  childcare and early years education
    84, 86, 88, 90, 93, 94, 95
  domestic division of labour 55, 56
  fertility rates 43, 44
  flexible working patterns 111

paid work 28, 29, 32, 34, 35, 36, 37, 38, 41
paid work patterns 49, 50
parental leave 97, 100
welfare model 75
Bergmann, B. 101, 103, 117
Bettio, F. 90, 91, 97
Bittman, M. 5, 58, 79
breastfeeding 96, 102
Brighouse, H. 69, 103, 105
British Social Attitudes Survey 146–7, 179, 180, 181
Bryson, C. 156, 157, 162, 164, 166, 176, 179, 180, 181

Callister, P. 102, 103, 174
care and care work 3, 18, 19, 25, 77–81, 103, 190, 199
    see also childcare; elder care; formal childcare; informal childcare; parental leave
care gap 3, 25
care workers 79
careers
    men 18, 106, 117, 176, 189, 190, 198
    women 17, 27–8, 41, 45, 47, 60, 64, 68, 117, 147, 176, 190, 196
cash transfers 19, 48, 74–5, 76
    see also compensation; financial support; tax credits
CEC 7, 11, 12, 13, 14–15, 46, 53, 67, 77, 97, 102, 106, 107, 178, 186, 193, 202
CEU 11, 12, 13, 14–15
child development 91, 94, 102, 155, 167
child poverty alleviation 2–3, 75, 149, 151, 154, 161, 197
child welfare 9–10, 94, 96, 152, 167, 187, 194
childcare 12, 87–91
    see also formal childcare; informal childcare
childcare leaves *see* maternity leave; parental leave; paternity leave
childcare vouchers 82, 127, 150
childcare workers 91, 94, 95, 123–4, 134, 165
childminders 83, 95, 123, 124, 128, 134, 153, 157, 160, 164

children *see* age of child; child development; child poverty alleviation; child welfare; childcare; children at risk; early years education/learning; educational achievement of children; value of children
children at risk 91, 95, 128, 149, 153
Children's Centres 156, 160, 161, 162, 165
choice
    care work 81
    female paid work 41, 42, 68
    fertility rates 14, 67, 68
    flexible working patterns 106, 184
    formal childcare 124, 154–5, 161, 167
    informal childcare 17–18, 116
    and parental leave 96, 103
    real choice 18–20, 64, 69–70, 73, 103, 116, 127, 154, 167, 196–7, 200
    work-care prioritisation 124, 125, 126, 128, 129–30, 133, 134, 135–6, 153, 154
    and work-family balance policies 69–70, 75, 133, 196–7
citizen worker/carer model 18, 19, 72–3
cohabitation 4, 47
combination scenario 131, 136, 199
commodification 8, 77, 78, 79, 95, 101
compensation
    carework 18, 78–9, 80, 190
    flexible working patterns 114–15
    informal care 17–18, 78–9, 199
    parental leave 76, 96, 97–8, 99, 100–101, 104–5, 127, 129, 131–2, 135, 168–70, 171–2, 174, 196, 198
competitiveness 7, 9, 11, 14
conditions of employment 13, 40, 41–2, 46, 201–2
corporatist welfare 43, 72
couples with older children 54, 55–6
couples with young children 54, 55, 56
Crompton, R. 15, 20, 58, 59, 60, 63, 65, 106–7, 110, 121, 146–7, 148
culture 16–17, 42, 46, 78, 131

daddy leave 16, 74, 97, 104, 127, 189, 200
day care for children 87, 94–5, 126–7, 157, 160–67
Daycare Trust 115–16, 163
De Henau, J. 91, 95, 105, 202
Denmark
    attitudes and preferences in work-family balance 62, 87, 88, 90
    childcare and early years education 84, 85, 86, 88, 90, 91, 92, 93, 94, 95
    female care workers 77
    fertility rates 44, 46
    flexible working patterns 108, 109, 110, 111
    paid work 29, 30, 34, 35, 36, 37, 38, 40, 41, 42, 43
    paid work patterns 50, 51
    parental leave 96, 97, 98, 100, 104, 200
    welfare regimes 74
    work-family balance policies 7, 14, 83
Dex, S. 104, 171, 172, 173, 174, 179, 180
disadvantaged areas 154, 161, 162, 166
division of labour 3, 15, 18, 25, 194–5
    see also adult worker model; citizen worker/carer model; domestic division of labour; dual-earner family model; male breadwinner/female carer family model; one-and-a-half earner model; one-and-three-quarter earner model
divorce 4, 6, 47
domestic division of labour
    EU-15 51–9, 121, 125, 126, 170–71, 189–90, 198
    and fertility rates 47
    and gender inequality 16, 52, 53, 54–5, 58–9, 69–70, 91, 191, 199
    and parental leave 170–71
    US 53
    and work-family balance conflict 58–9
dual-earner family model 4, 5, 6, 47, 49, 50, 51, 52, 54, 55–6, 66, 92, 93, 121
    see also adult worker model

early years education/learning
    EU-15 84–7, 91–2, 95, 126
    and OECD 91, 192–3
    policies 9, 83
    UK, 86, 115, 128, 133, 134, 150, 151–2, 154, 155–9, 160, 164, 166, 187, 188, 192–3, 197
economic growth 7, 8, 9, 11, 14
economic independence 8–9, 17, 190, 197, 199
economic policies 10–12, 13, 14, 15, 152
educational achievement of children 3, 9, 84, 91, 151
educational achievement of early-years professionals and childcare workers 92, 94, 95, 165
educational achievement of women
    and female paid work 28, 32–4, 174
    and fertility rates 43, 44, 48, 60, 67
    and flexible working patterns 115
    and formal childcare preferences 91
    and maternity leave 102
    and pay 42
elder care 5, 7, 9, 53, 65, 75, 76, 78, 80, 184
emotions 78, 81
employers
    and flexible working patterns 106, 107, 110, 112, 113–14, 115, 179–80, 183, 184, 185–6
    and formal childcare 130, 131, 135
    and parental leave 98, 170, 171–2
    and work-family balance policies 70, 76, 115, 117, 192, 195
employment policies 10–12, 13, 14, 15, 125, 126, 133, 134, 136, 152, 194
enabling policies 69, 70
England, P. 78, 79, 81, 199
equal opportunities policies 13, 14, 19, 48, 126, 200–201
Esping-Anderson, G. 6, 7, 13–14, 43, 72
ethic of care 80, 103
EU-15
    attitudes and preferences in work-family balance 59–66, 87–91, 102, 116
    attitudes to fertility rates 66–70

female paid work *see* female paid
    work in EU-15
fertility rates 43–8
flexible working patterns 41, 42,
    105–15
formal childcare 83–95, 115, 116
gender employment gap 30–31
gender pay gap 41, 42
household level 48–59
informal childcare 83, 88, 90, 93
lone mothers 28, 31, 74–5
male paid work 30–31, 32, 37, 41,
    49, 51, 53, 55–6, 58
paid working hours 37–40, 37–41,
    41, 49, 51, 53, 55–6, 58, 107–8
parental leave 95–105, 116, 121,
    124
part-time work insecurity 40–42
work-family balance policies 191–3
Eurobarometer 54, 66–7, 105, 125
European Employment Strategy 11,
    13, 90
European Labour Force Survey 48–9,
    108
European Quality of Life Survey 35,
    37, 54
European Social Survey 37–40, 49–51,
    60–63, 87–91, 108, 109–10, 111
European Union
    economic policies 10–12, 13, 14, 15
    female paid work policies 11–12, 13,
        14, 25, 197, 201
    'flexicurity' 7, 12, 13, 14, 46, 72, 137,
        186, 193, 202
    gender equality policies 12, 13,
        14–15, 16, 40, 168
    labour market participation policies
        7, 8–9, 10–11, 14, 25, 194
    and parental leave 12, 14–15, 168
    social policies 7, 10–12, 193, 201
    work-family balance policies 2,
        10–15, 178, 186
European Working Conditions Survey
    37, 40, 52, 108, 109
Eurostat 36, 37, 48–9, 54, 55–7, 84–7

familialism 14, 96, 125, 195, 202
family change 3–6
family forms 4–6, 127–8
family policy 1–2, 150

family size, ideal 46–7, 60, 67
family welfare 150, 152, 187
fathers
    attitudes to work-family
        prioritisation 62
    flexible working hours in EU-15
        107–8, 109, 110, 111, 114–15,
        181, 184, 185
    informal childcare 12, 53–4, 55–65,
        171, 172, 189, 199
    paid work in EU-15 35, 142, 144
    paid working hours in EU-15
        37–40, 144, 145
    see also fathers with older children;
        fathers with young children;
        paternity leave
fathers with older children 144
fathers with young children 62, 90,
    144, 184
female care work 5, 78
female care workers 11, 77
female full-time work
    EU-15 27, 28, 29–32, 36, 37, 38,
        108, 124–5, 195
    and formal childcare costs 64
    and parental leave 63–4
    UK 142, 143, 144
    US 5, 195
female housework 5, 53, 54
female labour market exit 16–17, 35,
    74
female labour market participation
    policies
    European Union 11–12, 13, 14, 25,
        197, 201
    and formal childcare in EU-15 91
    France 123–5, 133, 136–7
    Germany 126–7, 133–4, 136–7, 195
    increase 7, 8–10
    lone mothers 8, 69, 73–5
    Netherlands 8, 127–8, 133, 136–7,
        195
    Northern Europe 16–17
    Scandinavia 16–17, 69, 74
    UK 69, 128, 129–30, 133, 134–6,
        151, 154, 155–6, 166, 167, 187,
        193, 197
    US 69, 197
    Western Europe 16–17, 74–5,
        119–20

and work-family balance policies 69,
    119
female paid work
    attitudes 147, 148
    and childcare preferences 87–90
    choice 68, 124, 125, 126
    and fertility rates 25, 43, 44, 48, 65,
        68
    and formal childcare 69, 91, 95
    and formal childcare costs 5–6,
        59
    see also female full-time work;
        female paid work in EU-15;
        female part-time work
female paid work in EU-15
    and age of child 35, 36
    and age of women 28, 32–4
    attitudes and preferences 59, 64
    and educational achievement 28,
        32–4, 174
    and fertility rates 43, 44, 48
    France 27, 29, 30, 34, 35, 36, 37, 38,
        42, 121, 124–5, 133
    full-time work 28, 29–32, 36, 37, 38,
        108, 124–5
    and gender inequality 42, 136–7
    Germany 27, 28, 29, 30, 32, 34, 35,
        36, 37, 38, 40, 41, 42, 108, 126,
        133–4
    increase 4, 26–8, 31–2
    insecurity of part-time work 40,
        41–2
    lone mothers 28, 31, 69, 73–5, 134
    and long leaves 102
    low pay 32, 42
    mothers 35–7, 38–9, 40, 195
    Netherlands 27, 28, 29, 30, 32, 34,
        35, 36, 37, 38, 41, 42, 108, 130,
        132, 195, 199
    non-mothers 35, 36
    Northern Europe 25
    paid working hours 37–40, 41, 55–6,
        74, 107
    part-time work 27, 28, 29–31, 32, 35,
        36, 37, 38, 40, 41–2, 108, 121,
        125, 130, 132
    Southern Europe 4, 25, 195
    UK 6, 27–8, 29, 30, 32, 34, 35, 36,
        37, 38, 40, 41, 42, 108, 121, 141,
        142, 144, 162, 173, 181

    US 27, 29, 30, 34–5, 38
    Western Europe 25
female part-time work
    attitudes 63–4
    choice 41, 42
    EU-15 27, 29–31, 32, 35, 36, 37, 38,
        40, 41–2, 108, 121, 124, 130,
        132, 195, 199
    European Union policies 13
    lone mothers 8, 145
    low pay 41, 145
    UK 6, 27, 29, 30, 32, 37, 41, 42, 108,
        121, 145, 146–7, 173–4, 176, 195
    in Western and Northern Europe 4
female poverty 18, 19, 74
fertility rates
    attitudes 6, 66–7
    choice 14, 67, 68
    and conditions of employment 46
    and division of work 25
    and educational achievement of
        women 43, 44, 48, 60, 67
    EU-15 43–8, 44, 46–7, 122, 126–7,
        136, 195
    and family change 5
    and female paid work 25, 43, 44, 48,
        65, 68
    and flexible labour markets 46, 48
    and flexible working patterns 45, 48
    and formal childcare 45, 47, 48, 94
    and insecure employment 45–6
    Northern Europe 25, 47
    and parental leave 45, 46, 47, 48
    policies 9, 11, 12, 14, 67–8, 69, 94,
        122, 126–7, 136
    preferences 5–6
    Southern Europe 5, 25, 43, 46, 47,
        195
    and three worlds of welfare
        capitalism 43, 72
    US 44, 48
    Western Europe 25, 43, 47
    and work-family balance policies 45,
        47–8
financial support
    families 150
    formal childcare 82, 87, 123–4, 127,
        128, 129–30, 131, 134, 150, 155,
        163, 164, 199
    informal childcare 124, 125, 126, 130

Finland
attitudes and preferences in work-
family balance 60, 62, 87, 88, 90
childcare and early years education
84, 85, 86, 88, 90, 91, 93, 116
domestic division of labour 54, 55,
56
fertility rates 44, 46
flexible working patterns 108,
109–10, 111
paid work 26, 27, 28, 30, 32, 34, 35,
36, 37, 38, 40, 41, 43
paid work patterns 49, 50, 51
parental leave 97, 98, 100, 101–2,
103, 116, 200
welfare model 73
work-family balance policies 83,
103, 116, 192
flexible labour markets 6, 7, 12, 14, 46,
48
flexible working patterns
choice 106, 184
compensation 114–15
and employers 106, 107, 110, 112,
113–14, 115, 179–80, 183, 184,
185–6
EU-15 41, 42, 105–15
and fertility rates 45, 48
France 108, 109, 110, 111, 115, 125
and gender equality 112, 114–15,
176, 198, 201–2
Germany 106, 108, 109, 110–12,
113–14, 126, 127
men 181
Netherlands 109, 110, 111, 112,
113–14, 130–31
types 106
UK 106, 107, 108, 109, 110, 111,
112, 113–14, 129, 130, 134, 150,
174–86, 187, 189
exhortation 178–83
legislation 183–6, 187, 188
universalist approach 112, 114,
201
'flexicurity' 7, 12, 13, 14, 46, 72, 137,
186, 193, 202
Folbre, N. 5, 58, 79
formal care 11, 18, 77, 79
formal childcare
choice 124, 154–5, 161, 167

costs *see* formal childcare costs
and employers 130, 131, 135
EU-15 83–95, 115, 116
European Union policy 11, 13
and female paid work 69
and fertility rates 45, 47, 48, 94
financial support 82, 87, 123–4, 127,
128, 129–30, 131, 134, 150, 155,
163, 164, 199
France 83, 84, 85, 86, 88, 91, 94,
123–4, 125, 134
Germany 76, 84, 86, 88, 92, 126–7,
133, 134
legislation 126–7, 156, 162
Netherlands 84, 86, 88, 130, 134
policy goals 91–2, 95, 115
private sector services 5, 76, 156,
157, 160, 161, 162, 166
public expenditure 92, 94, 95, 123–4,
134
public sector services 5, 76, 156, 161,
162
quality 45, 64, 94–5, 155, 157, 162–3,
164–5
UK 76, 84–7, 88, 90, 115, 128, 133,
134, 150, 153–6, 157, 160–67,
164, 187
US 84, 86, 88, 200–201
work-family balance policy goals
115
formal childcare costs
and female full-time work 64
and female paid work 5–6, 59
and fertility rates 45
UK 41, 92–5, 146, 155, 161, 162–4,
167, 174
US 5, 48, 93, 202
France
adult worker model 120–21, 133,
134, 135, 136–7
attitudes and preferences in work-
family balance 60, 62, 87, 88,
116, 121–2, 136
domestic division of labour 54, 55,
56, 58, 59, 121, 125, 198
employment creation policies 125,
133, 134, 136
female paid work policies 123–5,
133, 136–7
fertility rates 5, 43, 44, 47

flexible working patterns 108, 109, 110, 111, 115, 125
formal childcare and early years education 83, 84, 85, 86, 88, 91, 93, 94, 123–4, 125, 134
gender equality policies 122
informal childcare 83, 90, 124, 125
paid work
 female paid work 27, 29, 30, 34, 35, 36, 37, 38, 42, 121, 124–5, 133
 female part-time work 29, 30, 37, 38, 42, 124
 paid work patterns 49, 50, 51, 120–21
 paid working hours 37, 38, 40, 42, 58, 110, 115, 124–5, 134
 parental leave 96, 97, 98, 100, 102, 121, 124, 125, 126, 134
 welfare model 75
 work-family balance policy change 123–5
 work-family balance policy goals 125, 133, 136
full-time paid work 66
 see also female full-time work; male full-time work

gender employment gap 29–31
gender equality
 and adult worker model 17, 74, 116–17, 197
 care work 81, 199
 concept and issues 15–20
 and difference 18, 73, 74, 189–90
 European Union 12, 13, 14, 16
 and flexible working patterns 112, 114–15, 176, 198, 201–2
 and individualisation 9, 199
 and parental leave 96, 101–3, 104, 105, 170–71, 174, 198
 policy deficit 3, 69
 and sameness 18, 73, 74, 189
 US 73, 74, 189, 200–201
 and welfare regimes 72–3
 and work-family balance policies 83, 196–203
gender equality policies
 cultural differences 16–17

European Union 12, 13, 14–15, 16, 40–41, 168
Germany 122, 133–4, 136
and real choice 19–20, 69–70, 73
Scandinavia 200
UK 18, 151, 176, 188–90
gender inequality
 and adult worker model 9
 care work 81
 and division of labour 3, 15, 18
 and domestic division of labour 16, 52, 53, 54–5, 58–9, 69–70, 91, 191, 199
 female paid work 42, 136–7
 Scandinavia 200
gender pay equality 201
gender pay gap 41, 42, 102, 108, 116, 145, 201
genuine choice *see* real choice
Germany
 adult worker model 119–20, 128, 133–4, 136–7
 attitudes and preferences in work-family balance 60, 62, 63, 64–5, 67, 88, 116, 121, 128, 136
 domestic division of labour 52, 54, 55, 56, 126
 educational achievement 3
 employment creation policies 126
 fertility rates and policies 43, 44, 46–7, 122, 126–7, 136, 195
 flexible working patterns 106, 108, 109, 110–12, 113–14, 126, 127
 formal childcare and early years education 76, 84, 86, 88, 92, 93, 95, 126–7, 133, 134
 gender equality policies 122, 133–4, 136
 informal childcare 88, 90, 126
 maternalist tradition 17, 73
 paid work
  female paid work 27, 28, 29, 30, 32, 34, 35, 36, 37, 38, 40, 41, 42, 108, 126, 133–4
  female paid work policies 126–7, 133–4, 136
  female part-time work 27, 29, 30, 32, 35, 37, 38, 40, 41, 42, 108, 195

paid work patterns 49, 50, 51, 120
paid working hours 37, 38, 40, 41,
    42, 126, 198
parental leave 96, 97, 98–101, 110,
    125–6, 127, 135
welfare model 75, 76
work-family balance policy change
    125–8
work-family balance policy goals
    126–7, 128, 133–4, 136
Gershuny, J. 3, 5, 52, 53, 58, 69
grandparents 77, 84, 88, 90, 124, 129,
    165
Greece
    attitudes and preferences in work-
        family balance 60, 62, 88
    childcare and early years education
        84, 86, 88, 90, 93
    fertility rates 44
    flexible working patterns 108, 109,
        110, 111
    paid work 26, 28, 29, 30, 32, 34, 35,
        36, 37, 38, 40
    paid work patterns 49, 50, 51
    parental leave 96, 97, 100

Hakim, C. 59, 64, 65, 68, 116, 147, 189,
    196
Himmelweit, S. 65–6, 69, 79, 81, 110,
    117, 120, 155, 177, 190, 197, 202
Hodge, Margaret 153, 177
home-oriented women 64, 68, 147, 196
household level in EU-15 48–59
housework 5, 53–4
human capital 9, 27, 103
human need 19, 80, 81

identity 65, 80, 81
individualisation 8–9, 17, 47, 120, 126,
    127–8, 130, 131, 133, 136–7, 190,
    199
informal care 5, 18, 77–9, 199
informal childcare
    choice 17–18, 116, 124, 125, 126
    compensation 17–18
    EU-15 83, 88, 90, 93
    fathers 12, 53–4, 55–6, 171, 172, 189
    financial support 124, 125, 126, 130
    France 83, 90, 124, 125
    Germany 88, 90, 126

importance 84, 199
    mothers 12, 53, 54, 55–6, 80, 173
    Netherlands 88, 90, 130, 131
    opportunity costs 17–18, 47, 110
    preferences 17, 59–60
    sharing 12, 16
    UK 88, 90, 128, 146, 153–4, 165,
        171, 172, 173, 185, 189–90, 197
    values 16, 68
insecure employment 6, 7, 40, 41–2,
    45–6
instrumentalism 18–19, 193–4, 202–3
International Social Survey
    Programme (ISSP) 54, 59, 63, 64,
    147
Ireland
    attitudes and preferences in work-
        family balance 60, 62, 67, 88
    childcare and early years education
        84, 86, 88, 92, 93
    fertility rates 44
    flexible working patterns 111
    paid work 28, 29, 30, 34, 36, 37–40,
        108
    paid work patterns 50, 51
    parental leave 97, 100
Italy
    attitudes and preferences in work-
        family balance 63, 65
    childcare and early years education
        84, 85, 86, 88, 94
    domestic division of labour 54, 55
    elder care 5, 65
    female paid work 65, 68
    fertility rates 44, 47, 65, 88
    flexible working patterns 110, 112
    paid work 26, 28, 29, 30, 32, 34, 35,
        36, 37, 65, 68
    paid work patterns 49, 50, 51
    parental leave 97, 100
    welfare model 75

job security 97–8, 101–2, 103, 169,
    173–4, 201–2

Kremer, M. 16, 72, 80, 84, 120, 153–4

Labour Force Survey 142–5, 149
labour market participation policies 2,
    7, 8–9, 10–11, 14, 25, 69, 76, 194

see also female labour market
   participation policies
legislation
   flexible working patterns 183–6, 187,
      188
   formal childcare 126–7, 156, 162
   paid working hours 58, 110, 115,
      125, 134
   parental leave 76, 129, 131, 171, 173,
      174
leisure time 15, 52, 55–6
Lewis, J. 4, 5, 6, 8, 9, 10, 39, 49–51, 69,
      72, 74, 77, 81, 106, 111, 121, 125,
      137, 153, 154, 155, 162, 165, 166
liberal welfare 43, 72
life-course perspective 65, 190
Life Course Saving Scheme (LCSS)
      131–2, 135, 137, 196, 202
Lisbon targets on female paid work 11,
      13, 28, 126, 141
lone mothers
   EU-15 28, 31, 74–5
   family change 4
   labour market participation policies
      8, 69, 73–5, 134, 142, 154, 166
   Netherlands 74–5, 202
   UK 28, 43–4, 69, 74–5, 134, 142,
      144, 145, 151, 154, 155, 166, 173
   US 73–4, 197
long parental leaves 98, 101–3, 121,
      124, 134, 168, 176, 189, 198
low pay 32, 41, 42, 79, 132, 145, 165,
      169, 170
Luxembourg
   childcare and early years education
      84, 86, 88, 93
   fertility rates 44
   flexible working patterns 108
   paid work 29, 30, 32, 34, 35, 36, 42
   paid work patterns 49
   parental leave 97, 100
Lyonette, C. 58, 59, 65, 106–7, 146–7,
      148

male breadwinner/female carer family
   model
   attitudes to 60–63, 147
   erosion 4, 8, 49, 119–20, 128, 191
   EU-15 48–9, 50, 51, 107
   and formal childcare costs 92, 93

Germany 49, 120
   and male wage increases 27
   Netherlands 49, 120, 200
   policy logic 72
   preferences 66
   problems 14
   and social protection 6
   UK 49, 120, 145, 147–9, 173
   Western Europe 48–9, 119–20
male care work 5
male full-time work 4, 30, 37
male housework 53–4
male paid work
   attitudes to right to employment
      60–63
   EU-15 30–31, 32, 35, 37–40, 49, 51,
      53, 55–6, 58, 107–8
   UK 142, 144, 145–6
   US 30–31
male part-time work 30, 41
male unpaid work 5, 53–4, 146
marriage 4, 27–8, 47
Marsh, A. 169, 170, 173, 174
maternalist tradition 17, 73, 120
maternity leave
   EU-15 35, 96, 97, 98, 99–103
   and gender equality 198
   UK 121, 128, 129, 134, 167, 168,
      169–70, 171, 172–3, 174, 176,
      188, 189
means-tested social assistance 8, 72,
      75
men
   attitudes to female paid work 147,
      148
   attitudes to fertility rates 67
   careers 18, 106, 117, 176, 189, 190,
      198
   flexible working patterns 181
   paid working hours in EU-15
      37–40, 41, 49, 51, 53, 55–6, 58,
      107–8, 131
      atypical 87, 108, 110, 141
      UK 141, 144, 145–6
   pay in EU-15 42
   see also fathers; male paid work;
      male unpaid work; paternity
      leave
modernised social policies 11, 12, 14,
      136, 191

Moss, P. 77, 95, 96, 97, 98, 100–101, 110, 129, 155, 171
mothers 12, 28, 53, 54, 55–6, 60–63, 80, 102, 121, 173
  see also lone mothers; mothers' paid work; mothers with older children; mothers with young children; non-mothers
mothers' paid work
  attitudes 59–60, 62, 63–4, 121
  EU-15 35–7, 38–9, 40, 42, 115, 134, 135, 195, 210
  flexible working hours 107, 108, 109–10, 111, 114–15, 181, 184, 185, 186
  and formal childcare costs 92
  pay 42, 169, 170
  UK 142, 143, 144, 151, 154, 155–6, 162, 166, 167, 173–4, 181, 184, 185, 186, 187, 193
  US 36
mothers with older children 54, 142, 144
mothers with young children
  attitudes to work-family prioritisation 60, 62, 63, 97
  childcare preferences 87–91
  flexible working patterns 184, 186
  informal childcare 54
  paid work 142, 144
  part-time work 27
  working hours 37, 38–9, 40, 142–4

Neighbourhood Nurseries 160, 161, 162, 166
Netherlands
  adult worker model 74–5, 120, 129, 133, 135, 136–7
  attitudes and preferences in work-family balance 62, 63–5, 88, 116, 121, 122
  combination scenario 131, 136, 199
  female labour market participation policies 8, 127–8, 133, 136–7
  fertility rates 43, 44, 46
  flexible working patterns 109, 110, 111, 112, 113–14, 130–31
  formal childcare and early years education 84, 86, 88, 93, 95, 130, 135

gender equality policies 122
informal childcare 88, 90, 130, 131
Life Course Saving Scheme (LCSS) 131–2, 135, 137, 196, 202
lone mothers 74–5, 202
paid work 27, 28, 29, 30, 32, 34, 35, 36, 37, 38, 40, 41, 42, 108, 130, 131, 132
  female paid work 27, 28, 29, 30, 32, 34, 35, 36, 37, 38, 41, 42, 108, 130, 132, 195, 199
  female part-time work 27, 29, 30, 32, 35, 37, 41, 108, 130, 132, 195, 199
paid work patterns 49, 50, 51, 121, 130, 132, 133, 136, 199–200
paid working hours 37, 38, 40, 41, 108, 133, 199–200
parental leave 97, 99, 100, 105, 126, 131–2, 199–200
welfare model 74–5
work-family balance policy goals 130, 131, 133, 134, 136
non-mothers 35, 36, 42, 43
Northern Europe 4–5, 16–17, 25, 47
Norway 60, 66, 73, 97, 102, 105, 116, 131
Nussbaum, M. 19, 64, 80, 81

obligation 78, 80
OECD 2, 10, 30, 32, 34, 35, 37, 49, 68, 84, 85–7, 91, 92, 94, 95, 98, 100–101, 102, 110, 117, 119, 154, 192–3
Olin Wright, E. 69, 103, 105
one-and-a-half earner model 4, 49–50, 51, 63–4, 66, 129, 131, 133, 136, 146, 199
one-and-three-quarter earner model 4, 50, 75
opportunity costs 17–18, 47, 81, 110
Orloff, A. 17, 72, 76, 120

paid work
  household level patterns in EU-15 48–51, 66
  US 27, 28, 29, 30, 32, 34, 35, 36, 40, 42, 43, 48
paid work patterns
  EU-15 48–51, 119

France 49, 50, 51, 120–21
Germany 49, 50, 51, 120
Netherlands 49, 50, 51, 121, 130,
    132, 133, 136, 199–200
UK 49, 50, 120, 145, 147–9, 173
paid working hours
    EU-15 37–40, 41, 55–6, 74, 107,
        124–5, 133, 142, 144, 145
    female paid work in US 38
    France 37, 38, 40, 42, 124–5
    Germany 37, 38, 40, 41, 42, 126,
        198
    legislation 58, 110, 115, 125, 134
    men in EU-15 37–40, 41, 49, 51, 53,
        55–6, 58, 107–8, 131, 144, 145–6
    Netherlands 37, 38, 40, 41, 108, 133,
        199–200
    preferences 66
    and real choice 19–20
    UK 18, 37–40, 38, 110, 142–5, 156,
        174
parental leave
    attitudes 97, 102, 172–3
    compensation 76, 96, 97–8, 99,
        100–101, 104–5, 127, 129,
        131–2, 135, 168–70, 171–2, 174,
        196, 198
    and domestic division of labour
        170–71
    and employers 98, 170, 171–2
    EU-15 35, 95–105, 110, 116, 189
        Finland 97, 98, 99, 100, 102, 103,
            116, 200
        France 96, 97, 98, 100, 102, 121,
            124, 125, 126, 134
        Germany 96, 97, 98–101, 110,
            125–6, 127, 135
        Netherlands 97, 99, 100, 105, 126,
            131–2, 199–200
        UK 97, 98, 99, 100, 105, 116, 126,
            128–9, 134, 167–74, 176, 187,
            188, 189
    European Union policies 12, 14–15,
        168
    and female full-time work 63–4
    and female paid work policies 69
    and fertility rates 45, 46, 47, 48
    and formal childcare 84
    and gender equality 96, 101–3, 104,
        105, 170–71, 174, 198

and job security 97–8, 101–2, 103,
    169, 173–4
    legislation 76, 129, 131, 171, 173,
        174
    and real choice 19–20
    Scandinavia 16, 74, 97, 102, 104,
        189, 195–6
    time 97–8, 99–103, 104, 126, 127,
        129, 131, 167, 168, 169, 198
    US 96, 98
    Western and Northern Europe 16
part-time work 6, 13, 30, 31, 40–42, 47,
    49, 66, 132
    see also female part-time work; male
        part-time work; paid working
        hours
Part-Time Work Directives 13, 40, 110,
    177
paternity leave
    and domestic division of labour 53
    EU-15 96, 97, 98, 100–101, 103–5,
        128, 129, 131
    and European Union 12, 14–15
    and gender equality 198
    Scandinavia 16, 74
    UK 168, 169, 170–71, 189
path dependence 21–2, 76
pay 10, 27, 42
    see also gender pay gap; low pay
Plantenga, J. 12, 90, 97, 98, 100–101,
    110, 125–6, 131
Portugal
    attitudes and preferences in work-
        family balance 60, 62, 63, 65, 88
    childcare and early years education
        86, 88, 90–91, 93
    domestic division of labour 54
    fertility rates 44
    flexible working patterns 110, 111
    paid work 27, 30, 32, 34, 35, 36, 37,
        38, 43
    paid work patterns 49, 50, 51
    parental leave 97, 100
preferences 59, 66–70
preferences in work-family balance
    and child welfare 10
    childcare 17, 59–60, 87–91
    in EU-15 64–6, 116
    and fertility rates 5–6
    France 60, 62, 87, 88, 116, 121

Germany 60, 62, 63, 64–5, 121
Netherlands 88, 116, 121, 122
UK 66, 87, 88, 90, 121
and work-family balance policies
    64–6
private sector services 5, 27, 76, 156,
    157, 160, 161, 162, 166
public expenditure
    formal childcare and early years
        education 86–7, 92, 94, 95,
        123–4, 134
    growth 1–2
    UK 1, 150, 153–4, 155, 156, 161,
        163, 165, 167, 187
public sector services 5, 27, 76, 156,
    161, 162

Rapoport, R. 15, 48, 115, 186
real choice 18–20, 64, 69–70, 73, 103,
    116, 127, 154, 167, 196–7, 200
risks 4, 6, 8, 136, 191
    see also opportunity costs

Scandinavia
    adult worker model 74
    attitudes and preferences in work-
        family balance 60, 67
    childcare and early years education
        84, 85, 88–90, 92, 94
    elder care and active ageing policies
        7
    female labour participation and exit
        policies 16–17, 69, 74
    fertility rates 43, 195
    gender equality and inequality 200
    paid work 26, 27, 28, 31–2, 35, 42,
        43
    paid work patterns 49, 51
    parental leave 16, 74, 97, 102, 104,
        189, 195–6
    welfare model 43, 72, 73, 74, 75
    work-family balance policies 68, 83,
        193
secure employment 13, 40, 41, 46, 132
self-realisation 46, 122
short-term contracts 42, 46, 96, 106
Smeaton, D. 169, 170, 172, 173, 174
social democratic welfare 43, 72
social investment 3, 91–2, 94, 155,
    193

social norms 69, 70, 193
social policies 7, 10–12, 152, 193, 201
social protection 6, 11, 13–14
social quality 13, 69
Southern Europe
    attitudes and preferences in work-
        family balance 63, 67
    domestic division of labour 52
    employment insecurity 6
    female paid work 4, 25, 195
    fertility rates 5, 25, 43, 46, 47, 195
    informal care 5
    paid work 32, 35, 37, 41–2, 102
    paid work patterns 49, 51
Spain
    attitudes and preferences in work-
        family balance 60, 62, 88
    childcare and early years education
        84, 86, 88, 90, 91, 93, 95
    domestic division of labour 54, 55
    fertility rates 44
    flexible working patterns 108, 111
    paid work 26, 27, 28, 29, 30, 32, 34,
        36, 37–40, 42, 108
    paid work patterns 49, 50, 51
    parental leave 96, 97, 100
statutory flexible working 110, 112,
    113–14, 129, 130, 134, 150–51,
    175, 177, 183–6, 187, 188, 189
statutory leave rights 96, 97, 98–101,
    170
Sure Start programme 154, 156, 161
Sweden
    attitudes and preferences in work-
        family balance 62, 87, 88
    childcare and early years education
        84, 85, 86, 88, 90, 91, 93, 200
    domestic division of labour 51, 54,
        55, 56, 59
    female care workers 77
    fertility rates 44, 45–6
    flexible working patterns 109–10,
        111, 115
    paid work 26, 29, 30, 32, 34, 35, 36,
        37, 38, 40, 41, 43
    paid work patterns 49, 50, 51
    parental leave 96, 97, 98, 99, 100,
        103, 104–5
    welfare regimes 74
    work-family balance policies 83

tax credits 72, 87, 94, 115, 123, 163
Ten Year Strategy for Childcare (UK)
    154, 156, 161–3
three worlds of welfare capitalism 43, 72
time
    and division of labour 4–5
    and domestic division of labour 52,
        53
    and informal care 79
    and opportunity costs of childcare
        responsibilities 47
    parental leave 97–8, 99–103, 126,
        127, 129, 131, 167, 168, 169, 198
    pressures 5, 52, 53, 54, 191
    and real choice 19–20
Tronto, Joan 80, 81

UK
    adult worker model 74–5, 116, 120,
        134, 135, 136–7
    attitudes and preferences in work-
        family balance 60, 62, 63, 64–5,
        66, 87, 88, 90, 121, 122, 135–6,
        147–9, 172–3, 176, 179
    child poverty alleviation 2–3, 149,
        151, 154, 161, 197
    domestic division of labour 52, 54,
        55, 56, 170–71, 189–90
    educational achievement of children
        3, 151
    female labour participation policies
        69, 128, 129–30, 133, 134–6,
        151, 154, 155–6, 166, 167, 187,
        193, 197
    fertility rates 5, 43–4
    flexible working patterns 106, 107,
        108, 109, 110, 111, 112, 113–14,
        129, 130, 134, 150, 174–86
        exhortation 178–83
        legislation 183–6, 187, 188
    formal childcare and early years
        education 76, 84–7, 88, 90, 128,
        133, 134, 150, 151–2, 153–67
    daycare 87, 157, 160–67
    early years education/learning 86,
        115, 128, 133, 134, 150,
        151–2, 154, 155–9, 160, 164,
        166, 187, 188, 192–3, 197
    financial support 82, 87, 128, 134,
        150, 155, 163, 164

formal childcare costs 41, 92–5, 146,
    155, 161, 162–4, 167, 174
formal childcare quality 94, 95, 155,
    157, 162–3, 164–5
gender equality policies 18, 122, 151,
    176, 188–90
gender inequality 116
informal childcare 88, 90, 128, 146,
    153–4, 165, 171, 172, 173, 185,
    189–90, 197
labour market participation policies
    for lone mothers 8, 74–5
lone mothers 28, 43–4, 69, 74–5, 134,
    142, 143, 144, 151, 154, 155,
    166, 173, 202
means-tested social assistance 72, 75
paid work 6, 27–8, 29, 30, 32, 34, 35,
    36, 37–40, 41, 42, 108, 121, 141,
    142, 144–5, 146, 162
    female full-time work 142, 143,
        144
    female part-time work 6, 27, 29,
        31, 32, 37, 41, 42, 108, 121,
        145, 146–7, 173, 176, 195
    female work 6, 27–8, 29, 30, 32,
        34, 35, 36, 37, 38, 40, 41, 42,
        77, 108, 121, 141, 142, 144,
        162, 173–4, 181
    male work 142, 144–6
paid work patterns 49, 50, 120, 145,
    147–9, 173
paid working hours 18, 37–40, 110,
    142–5, 156, 174
    atypical 37–40, 41, 108, 110, 111,
        141, 146, 156, 177–8
    parental leave 97, 98, 99, 100, 105,
        116, 126, 128–9, 134, 167–74,
        176, 187, 188, 189
    part-time work 6, 41
    public expenditure 1, 150, 153–4,
        155, 156, 161, 163, 165, 167, 187
    tax credits 72, 87, 94, 115, 163, 164
    unemployment 145–6
    unpaid work 18, 146–7
    welfare model 72, 74–5, 76
    work-family balance policy goals
        2–3, 128, 129–30, 133, 134,
        135–6, 149–53, 155–6, 167–8,
        174–7, 187–90
unemployment 45–6, 47, 145–6

universalist approach, in flexible
     working patterns 112, 114, 201
unpaid care leave 76, 98, 104, 105, 131,
     168, 169, 170
unpaid work 3, 15, 16, 52
     see also domestic division of labour;
          housework; informal childcare;
          male unpaid work
unpaid working hours 18
US
     adult worker model 74, 75
     attitudes and preferences in work-
          family balance 66
     domestic division of labour 53
     female full-time work 5, 195
     female paid work policies 69, 197
     fertility rates 44, 48
     formal childcare and early years
          education 5, 48, 84, 86, 88, 93,
          94, 95, 200–201, 202
     gender equality 73, 74, 189, 200–201
     lone mothers 73–4, 197
     paid work 27, 28, 29, 30, 32, 34, 35,
          36, 40, 42, 43, 48
     parental leave 96, 98
     welfare model 73–4, 75, 76
     work-family balance policies 115,
          192

value of children 46
values 16, 68, 193
voluntary formal childcare 156, 160,
     161, 162

Wall, K. 63, 96, 100–101, 110, 147
Ward, K. 104, 171, 172, 173, 174
welfare regimes 43, 72–7, 195
welfare state changes 6–10, 76, 77–8
Western Europe 2, 4–5, 16–17, 25, 27,
     43, 47, 48–9, 72, 74–5
women
     attitudes to female paid work 147,
          148
     attitudes to fertility rates 66–7
     atypical paid working hours 110
     and care 78, 80
     careers 17, 27–8, 41, 45, 47, 60, 68,
          117, 176, 190, 196
     economic independence 8–9, 17, 190,
          197

and formal childcare costs 93–4
     informal childcare 12, 53, 55–6, 80,
          173
     life-course changes in attitudes to
          work-family balance 65
     multitasking and coordinating
          unpaid work 52, 53
     opportunity costs of informal
          childcare 17–18, 47
     see also age of women; female care
          work; female housework;
          female labour market
          participation policies; female
          paid work; lone mothers;
          maternity leave; mothers
work-care prioritisation
     attitudes 59–64, 65–6, 97, 102, 116,
          128
     choice 124, 125, 126, 128, 129–30,
          133, 134, 135–6, 153, 154
work-family balance 2, 15, 20–21, 175
work-family balance conflict 58–9, 69
work-family balance policies
     and choice 69–70, 75, 133, 196–7
     and domestic division of labour 58
     and employers 70, 76, 115, 117, 192,
          195
     EU-15 191–3
     European Union 2, 10–15, 178,
          186
     and female paid work policies 69,
          119
     and fertility policies 68, 69, 94
     and fertility rates 45, 47–8
     formal childcare *see* formal childcare
     and gender equality 83, 196–203
     implications of attitudes, preferences
          and behaviour in work-family
          balance 67–70
     and labour participation policies
          7–8
     policy choice issues 82–3
     policy logics 72–7
     and preferences in work-family
          balance 64–6
     problem-solving role 2–3
     and real choice 103, 116, 127, 154,
          167, 196–7, 200
     types 2
     US 115, 192

work-family balance policy goals
  of formal childcare 91–2, 95, 115
  France 125, 133, 136
  Germany 126–7, 128, 133–4,
    136
  Netherlands 130, 131, 133, 134,
    136
  of parental leave 96
  UK 2–3, 128, 129–30, 133, 134,
    135–6, 148–53, 155–6, 167–8,
    174–7, 187–90
work-family prioritisation attitudes
  60–63, 102, 121

work-life balance, terminology 2, 15,
    150, 175–6
Work-Life Balance Surveys (WLBS)
    179, 180, 181, 182, 185, 186
work-life reconciliation, terminology 2
work-oriented women 64, 68, 147,
    196
working hours *see* paid working hours;
    unpaid working hours
Workplace Employment Relations
    Survey (WERS) 179–80, 181
World Health Organization (WHO)
    96, 102